MUIRHEAD LIBRARY OF PHILOSOPHY

An admirable statement of the aims of the Library of Philosophy was provided by the first editor, the late Professor J. H. Muirhead, in his description of the original programme printed in Erdmann's *History of Philosophy* under the date 1890. This was slightly modified in subsequent volumes to take the form of the following statement :

'The Muirhead Library of Philosophy was designed as a contribution to the History of Modern Philosophy under the heads : first of Different Schools of Thought – Sensationalist, Realist, Idealist, Intuitivist; secondly of different Subjects – Psychology, Ethics, Aesthetics, Political Philosophy, Theology. While much had been done in England in tracing the course of evolution in nature, history, economics, morals and religion little had been done in tracing the development of thought on these subjects. Yet "the evolution of opinion is part of the whole evolution".

'By the co-operation of different writers in carrying out this plan it was hoped that a thoroughness and completeness of treatment, otherwise unattainable, might be secured. It was believed also that from writers mainly British and American fuller consideration of English Philosophy than it had hitherto received might be looked for. In the earlier series of books containing, among others, Bosanquet's *History of Aesthetic*, Pfleiderer's *Rational Theology since Kant*, Albee's *History of English Utilitarianism*, Bonar's *Philosophy and Political Economy*, Brett's *History of Psychology*, Ritchie's *Natural Rights*, these objects were to a large extent effected.

'In the meantime original work of a high order was being produced both in England and America by such writers as Bradley, Stout, Bertrand Russell, Baldwin, Urban, Montague, and others, and a new interest in foreign works, German, French and Italian, which had either become classical or were attracting public attention, had developed. The scope of the Library thus became extended into something more international, and it is entering on the fifth decade of its existence in the hope that it may contribute to that mutual understanding between countries which is so pressing a need of the present time.'

The need which Professor Muirhead stressed is no less pressing today, and few will deny that philosophy has much to do with enabling us to meet it, although no one, least of all Muirhead himself, would regard that as the sole, or even the main, object of philosophy. As Professor Muirhead continues to lend the distinction of his name to the Library of Philosophy it seemed not inappropriate to allow him to recall us to these aims in his own words. The emphasis on the history of thought also seemed to me very timely; and the number of important works promised for the Library in the very near future augur well for the continued fulfilment, in this and other ways, of the expectations of the original editor.

H. D. LEWIS

MUIRHEAD LIBRARY OF PHILOSOPHY

General Editor : H. D. Lewis

Professor of History and Philosophy of Religion at the University of London

The Absolute and the Atonement by Dom Illtyd Trethowan
Absolute Value by Dom Illtyd Trethowan
Action by Sir Malcolm Knox
The Analysis of Mind by Bertrand Russell
Ascent to the Absolute by J. N. Findlay
Belief by H. H. Price
Brett's History of Psychology edited by R. S. Peters
Broad's Critical Essays in Moral Philosophy edited by David R. Cheney
Clarity is Not Enough by H. D. Lewis
Coleridge as Philosopher by J. H. Muirhead
The Commonplace Book of G. E. Moore edited by C. Lewy
Contemporary American Philosophy edited by G. P. Adams and W. P. Montague
Contemporary British Philosophy first and second series edited by J. H. Muirhead
Contemporary British Philosophy third series edited by H. D. Lewis
Contemporary Indian Philosophy edited by Radhakrishnan and J. H. Muirhead 2nd edition
Contemporary Philosophy in Australia edited by Robert Brown and C. D. Rollins
The Discipline of the Cave by J. N. Findlay
Doctrine and Argument in Indian Philosophy by Ninian Smart
The Elusive Mind by H. D. Lewis
Essays in Analysis by Alice Ambrose
Ethics by Nicolai Hartmann translated by Stanton Coit 3 vols
Ethics and Christianity by Keith Ward
The Foundation of Metaphysics in Science by Errol E. Harris
Freedom and History by H. D. Lewis
G. E. Moore: Essays in Retrospect edited by Alice Ambrose and Morris Lazerowitz
The Good Will: A Study in the Coherence Theory of Goodness by H. J. Paton
Hegel: A Re-examination by J. N. Findlay
Hegel's Science of Logic translated by W. H. Johnston and L. G. Struthers 2 vols

A History of Aesthetic by B. Bosanquet 2nd edition
A History of English Utilitarianism by E. Albee
Human Knowledge by Bertrand Russell
A Hundred Years of British Philosophy by Rudolph Metz translated by J. H. Harvey, T. E. Jessop, Henry Sturt
Hypothesis and Perception by Errol E. Harris
Ideas: A General Introduction to Pure Phenomenology by Edmund Husserl translated by W. R. Boyce Gibson
Identity and Reality by Emile Meyerson
Imagination by E. J. Furlong
In Contact with the Physical World by John Pennycuick
In Defence of Free Will by C. A. Campbell
Indian Philosophy by Radhakrishnan 2 vols revised 2nd edition
Introduction to Mathematical Philosophy by Bertrand Russell 2nd edition
Kant's First Critique by H. W. Cassirer
Kant's Metaphysic of Experience by H. J. Paton
Know Thyself by Bernadino Varisco translated by Guglielmo Salvadori
Language and Reality by Wilbur Marshall Urban
A Layman's Quest by Sir Malcolm Knox
Lectures on Philosophy by G. E. Moore edited by C. Lewy
Ludwig Wittgenstein: Philosophy and Language edited by Alice Ambrose and Morris Lazerowitz
Matter and Memory by Henri Bergson translated by N. M. Paul and W. S. Palmer
Meaning in the Arts by Arnold Louis Reid
Memory by Brian Smith
Mental Images by Alastair Hannay
The Modern Predicament by H. J. Paton
Natural Rights by D. G. Ritchie 3rd edition
Nature, Mind and Modern Science by E. Harris
The Nature of Thought by Brand Blanshard
Non-Linguistic Philosophy by A. C. Ewing
On Selfhood and Godhood by C. A. Campbell
Our Experience of God by H. D. Lewis
Our Knowledge of Right and Wrong by Jonathan Harrison
Perception by Don Locke
The Person God Is by Peter A. Bertocci
The Phenomenology of Mind by G. W. F. Hegel translated by Sir James Baillie revised 2nd edition
Philosophy in America by Max Black
Philosophical Papers by G. E. Moore
Philosophy and Illusion by Morris Lazerowitz
Philosophy and Political Economy by James Bonar

Philosophy and Religion by Axel Hagerstrom
Philosophy of Space and Time by Michael Whiteman
Philosophy of Whitehead by W. Mays
The Platonic Tradition in Anglo-Saxon Philosophy by J. H. Muirhead
The Principal Upanisads by Radhakrishnan
The Problems of Perception by R. J. Hirst
Reason and Analysis by Brand Blanshard
Reason and Goodness by Brand Blanshard
Reason and Scepticism by Michael A. Slote
The Science of Logic by G. W. F. Hegel
Some Main Problems of Philosophy by G. E. Moore
Studies in the Metaphysics of Bradley by Sushil Kumar Saxena
The Subject of Consciousness by C. O. Evans
The Theological Frontier of Ethics by W. G. Maclagan
Time and Free Will by Henri Bergson translated by F. G. Pogson
Values and Intentions by J. N. Findlay
The Ways of Knowing: or the Methods of Philosophy by W. P. Montague

MUIRHEAD LIBRARY OF PHILOSOPHY

EDITED BY H. D. LEWIS

ENIGMAS OF AGENCY
STUDIES IN THE PHILOSOPHY OF HUMAN ACTION

ENIGMAS OF AGENCY

STUDIES IN THE PHILOSOPHY OF HUMAN ACTION

BY

IRVING THALBERG

University of Illinois at Chicago Circle

LONDON: GEORGE ALLEN & UNWIN LTD
NEW YORK: HUMANITIES PRESS INC

First published in 1972

© George Allen & Unwin Ltd, 1972

ISBN 0 04 100034 x

Printed in Great Britain
in 11 point Baskerville type
by Clarke, Doble & Brendon Ltd
Plymouth

CONTENTS

	Introductory Remarks	15
I	Do We Cause Our Own Actions?	35
II	How Can We Distinguish Between Doing and Undergoing?	48
III	Are There Non-Causal Explanations of Action? (originally co-authored by Arnold B. Levison)	73
IV	Some Puzzles about Effort (originally co-authored by Suzanne McCormick)	87
V	Can One Intend the Impossible?	105
VI	How Is Ability Related to Performance?	115
VII	Can Our Wills Be Free?	143
VIII	Can I Foreknow Decisions I Have Not Yet Made?	157
IX	Can We hold People Strictly Liable for Their Deeds?	171
X	How Do I Know What I Am Doing?	186
XI	The Socratic Paradox and Remorse	201
	Selected Bibliography	221
	Index	227

INTRODUCTORY REMARKS

PROBLEMS ABOUT HUMAN ACTION IN RECENT PHILOSOPHY

I hope these preliminary comments will anticipate several questions that might otherwise trouble a non-specialist reader of these studies of mine on action. The essays themselves demand no particular expertise; and the riddles which are treated in them are set out in sufficient detail to be understood by laymen. But still the general reader might be unsure about this collection as a whole, and want some background. He might ask :

Just what are the leading issues about human agency that stir up philosophers nowadays? How did these issues develop in various current philosophical traditions? How do individual papers in the collection help to solve, or exacerbate, these contemporary problems? What are the common themes among the papers? In cases where I have deliberately neglected some burning controversy that is germane to my essays, why have I done so? Is it because I think someone has already propounded the right view? Or have I some reason for judging the issue to be insoluble at this time, perhaps because the scientific information we need is not yet available?

The problems
Since my purpose is only to furnish stage-setting which will make the essays clearer, I shall not offer exhaustive replies to the foregoing questions. To begin with the reader's first question, I would catalogue seven overlapping groups of current problems about action. We might call them problem areas. By reference to the central notion in each one, these problem areas concern, respectively :

(1) causal explanation of what people do;

(2) the nature of actions, as contrasted with bodily processes, things that happen to a person, and events of the inanimate world;

(3) the awareness which people have regarding their current behaviour;

(4) the *control* agents have over what they do, the power they have to act or not, as they choose;

(5) choice itself, and kindred phenomena such as desires and reasons for acting, which were traditionally regarded as functions of the will;

(6) the concept of freedom, as it applies to the actions and perhaps also to the will of an individual;

(7) the connection between what people believe or know they *ought* to do and their eventual conduct.

The history of these problems

Issues in areas (1), (3), (5) and (6) developed principally from objections, during the last forty years, against the views we encounter in classical rationalists such as Descartes, and empiricists such as Hume. These objections concern rationalistic and empiricist accounts of the mind, its operations, and the connection between these mental events and a person's overt behaviour. Problem areas (2), (5) and (7) were already explored by Plato and Aristotle. And for all seven problem areas, the advance of natural science and psychology, above all psychoanalysis, has led philosophers to question the apparently primitive and unrealistic notions we have of a human agent. Scientific progress makes us ask: Do we really know why people act as they do? Is human and perhaps animal behaviour so unique in nature? Do we have a clear idea of the mastery we suppose people to have over their deeds, the efficacy of their will, their freedom, and the influence of their moral convictions upon what they do? Perhaps all our notions about human behaviour are childish myths. At any rate, most of the doctrines we find on this subject in philosophers of the past sound either obscure or incredible, or both. John Hospers [59, 60][1] and Paul Edwards [in 58] have raised these questions with great force.

My approach

My approach to these problem areas depends upon the conceptual terrain in each case. That is, I have no magical formula

[1] All numbers in brackets refer to the Bibliography on pages 221–226.

for solving every enigma about action. I prefer struggling with each knot as it turns up. So here are samples of more specific puzzles that are found in each of the six problem areas I mentioned, together with hints of my reasoning in each case.

Issues about causality

With regard to (1), causal explanation of what people do, recent writers have aired a number of doubts: Are the things we do amenable to causal explanation at all? Perhaps only non-human events, bodily processes, and things that happen to us have causes. Are we to say that a person causes his own actions? Could a man's desires, beliefs, and similar reasons he has for acting be causes of his behaviour? And whether or not causal explanation is generally admissible in the sphere of action, is it the only kind of explanation worth giving?

Essay I is an attack on the view that a person causes his own actions. The old-fashioned analysis along causal lines – Hume's, for example, in [61] and [62] – is that we bring about our overt behaviour by doing something else first *in foro interno*. We engage in an act of willing; that is, we go through a process of deciding or perhaps simply hankering, which somehow results in our bodily motion. This view is easy to criticize, and my own brief onslaught upon it, at the beginning of Essay I, is derivative from such writers as Wittgenstein [122, 123, 124] and Ryle [103]. But a more up-to-date causal account, usually called the theory of agent causality, deserves and gets careful scrutiny in this paper.

Agent causality

Champions of this account hold that a person's voluntary action is only caused by the person. In other words, he does not run through prefatory high-jinks, such as acts of will, as a means of producing his overt behaviour. Nothing has to happen in him, either; for example, there does not have to be a surge of desire or wanting in him to cause his voluntary action. He causes it, but not by doing anything else, and not by having anything take place in him. The point is that this peculiar causal relation between agent and deed is proposed by agent-causationists as a criterion for saying that a particular event, in which a human being figures prominently, is a voluntary act. The criterion reads:

17

if a person is the cause of a particular event, in the sense of 'cause' just outlined, then the event is his voluntary action; otherwise it must be either a bodily movement of his or – what is taken to be equivalent, in the analysis of agent-causationists – something that happens to him. Both major contentions of agent-causationists are refuted in Essay I. I demonstrate, I hope, that their notion of a man bringing about his own action is incoherent, and that their criterion for separating his voluntary actions from things that happen to him is invalid.

Distinguishing what we do from what happens to us

A number of issues from problem-area (2), about the nature of action, come up in Essay I. It demonstrates, for example, that no concept of causality will serve as a distinguishing mark of action, or help us formulate the contrast between doing and undergoing. What then is an identifying feature of action, and how is action opposed to undergoing? As far as I can discover, philosophers have been fairly complacent about problems in this area. Apparently they have assumed that they understood what it is to do something, even if they could not say; and they have taken it for granted that the familiar categories of doing and undergoing are exhaustive, as well as mutually exclusive.

In Essay II, I challenge this complacency. I illustrate how difficult it is to single out actions; and I prove that human beings figure in other types of events besides things they do and undergo. In this study I find myself unable to discern a mark of action in the events themselves which are human actions; but I propose a quasi-linguistic criterion for distinguishing *verbs* of action from verbs and verb phrases of undergoing. I also offer a separate, non-linguistic mark of undergoing. Roughly, and omitting important qualifications, my criterion for verbs of action is that they are verbs which may be modified by terms for control and loss of control, without the sentence in which they appear becoming either self-contradictory or unintelligible. When verbs and verb phrases of *undergoing* consort with control and loss-of-control terms in a sentence, the combination is unintelligble. Thus a clear-cut verb of action, 'push', in the sentence 'John pushed George', may be modified by such control expressions as 'deliberately' and 'on purpose', and by loss-of-control terms like

18

'accidentally' and 'unintentionally'. On the other hand, it is nonsense to mix the undergoing term, 'being pushed', with these expressions. In fact, English syntax appears to prohibit us from saying of George, in his role of victim, that he was deliberate, had a purpose, or received the shove accidentally or unintentionally. Only in so far as he acted – for instance, either deliberately or unintentionally placing himself in John's way, so that John would bump him – could we describe George in the jargon of control and its absence. This criterion for verbs of action is not purely linguistic, because it appeals to the non-grammatical notion of control. The independent and non-linguistic criterion of undergoing which I propose is that the man who undergoes something must be acted upon. That is, when a person undergoes something, either: (i) another agent does something to him, in the sense of 'do' I have just defined; or (ii) some natural force acts upon him, in a different sense of 'act' (since we do not say that natural forces like tidal waves do things willingly or unintentionally); or else (iii) the agent acts upon himself in such a way that something happens to him.

Besides proposing these criteria of doing and undergoing, I demonstrate in Essay II that at least three different collections of verbs appear to fall outside our categories of doing and undergoing. 'Bleed', 'choke', and 'fumble' are examples, respectively, from each unclassifiable group. Do such verbs stand for intermediate events? This seems to be a new puzzle I have found in area (2). Another new but less significant point I make in this essay concerns bodily movements. Almost all contemporary philosophers who discuss physiological episodes such as bleeding, perspiring and trembling, take such events to be things that happen to a person. By my non-linguistic criterion of undergoing, mentioned above, it turns out that these episodes are not things that happen to a person, because the person who trembles, perspires or bleeds *may or may not* be acted upon. If you are pushed, someone *must* push you; but if you perspire, it is a contingent matter that anything acts upon you to make you perspire.

These findings give us some help in problem area (2), regarding the nature of actions, and the contrast between actions, bodily processes and things that happen to a person. Problem area (4),

19

concerning control, is also illuminated. In addition, some advance in area (1), having to do with causality, comes out as a by-product. For it turns out that having something happen to you is not to be analysed in causal terms. That is, besides the conclusion I reach in Essay I, that undergoing is different from *not* causing the event, I reach the further conclusion that there is no causal relation between a person or natural force acting upon you, and your having something happen to you. The relation is logical.

The next essay bears more directly, however, upon this area of causality and causal explanation.

No incompatibility between causal and other explanations of behaviour

Essay III, which my colleague Arnold B. Levison wrote with me, deals to some extent with questions from problem area (4), regarding the notion of control; and it has a fair amount to say about awareness (3) and reasons for acting (5). Our main contention is that the philosophical debaters in area (1) have mistakenly assumed that if you can explain what caused a human action, then anything else you might want to say about the performance is superfluous. Levison and I reject this incompatibility assumption. In Essay III we set forth in some detail the respects in which people's deeds are amenable to causal explanation, and the respects in which causal explanation is inappropriate. Then we outline one complementary non-causal form of explanation which we think was never clearly differentiated before from its more imposing causal congener. We call this other species 'essential explanation'. We find that it covers most of the things that philosophical opponents of causal explanation for human behaviour, such as Peters [94], Winch [121], Melden [82] and R. Taylor [114], thought vital for an understanding of actions. But while we try to do justice to their partiality towards non-causal patterns of explanation, we refute their belief that such patterns of explanation precludes causal accounts. Our thesis is that each species of account has its own job to do. Hence, causal accounts may not stand in for essential ones. Nevertheless, both kinds of account may be given for any human action.

20

'Reason' explanations

An agent's reasons for acting occupy a unique position in our scheme. Reasons are of the first importance when you give an essential account of someone's deed, for they identify the event he participated in as his action, and they also identify it as the specific sort of action it was. Suppose there is a dagger in Archibald's grip; subsequently Archibald's arm moves in such a way that the dagger pierces Mike's chest. Was this episode a convulsive movement? a random gesture? an accident? If you establish that it was Archibald's purpose to get even with Mike for an insult he believed Mike to have uttered, and that Archibald intended to settle the score at that moment by knifing him, then you can rank the episode as an action of Archibald's, instead of a random movement or something similar; furthermore, you may describe it as the specific action of stabbing, or of taking revenge – all by reference to Archibald's reasons: his purposes and beliefs. Despite the significance we thereby give to the agent's reasons in this sort of 'essential' account of his performance, Levison and I agree with Davidson [34] that an agent's reasons might still be among the causes of his performance. Unlike Davidson, however, we do not think that we *must* rank reasons as causes, in order to make sense of the 'because' in the phrase, 'The assailant stabbed his victim because he wanted to get even with him for an insult'. Our view is that this question should be postponed until neurophysiology or some other science has demonstrated how a person's desire and belief work to bring about his action; for causal relations are matters of fact, discoverable only through observation and experiment. For more on this point, see Thomas's criticism [116] of Kaufman [64].

These problems about causal explanation connect in an interesting way with problems of control, area (4) on my list, as well as choice, area (5). The most straightforward connection is this. If it were true that our attitudes and beliefs were causes of some things we do, then that would help account for the control over our behaviour with which we credit ourselves in these circumstances. But instead of pursuing that line of inquiry any further, I turn, in the next essays, to a direct analysis of control concepts, beginning with the concept of effort.

Varieties of control

In Essay IV, which was co-authored by Suzanne McCormick, the fundamental notion of trying serves as a beachhead for an attack upon broader issues about a man's control of his behaviour. The concept of trying is crucial for an analysis of what people do, because many of their actions are attempts to reach some goal. Their desires and decisions are revealed in their endeavours. Besides, a distinctive feature of human actions alone, the fact that they may be successful or defective in various ways, is clearly displayed in the arena of endeavour. Finally, in this essay several previously unnoticed philosophical puzzles about trying crop up, and solutions to them are offered.

A paradox about intention

Issues from groups (4) and (5) continue to absorb my attention in the next two essays. Essay V is focused on a single aspect of the fundamental notion of intending. So much has been written about intention in general, and Miss Anscombe's book [1] seems to me on the whole so incisive and reasonable, that I only examine one problem: What is the connection between a man's aims, and his beliefs about what he *can* do? In order to illuminate the ties between one's practical judgements and one's goals, I defend the paradoxical view that a person might intend the impossible. I have to restrict the paradox, of course, and I must also explain why it actually sounds absurd to say that someone intends to accomplish some task which he believes he cannot accomplish. Part of my argument is based upon individual cases, and part of it is founded upon an analysis of trying which follows from the view developed in Essay IV.

Power

Like the concept of intention, the concept of a human power, of what it is to be able to perform some action, has received much attention from first-rate philosophers – in this case over centuries. To be sure, prolonged debate has produced interesting muddles, but unfortunately very little of importance remains unsaid. Therefore in Essay VI, I have a shot at exegesis and defence of J. L. Austin's ground-breaking 1956 paper on this subject, 'Ifs and Cans' [11]. I think I manage thereby to make some analytical

22

advance, and to correct some otherwise tempting misinterpretations of Austin's subtle reasoning.

In the next two essays, I turn away from a direct examination of human powers and human choice, and focus on a neighbouring problem area, (5). The issues we find piled up here belong to the 'free will' problem. All of them are riddled with confusions, of course, but the existing literature also contains nearly every reasonable view one is likely to think of. So again I ignore the profound and overworked questions, for example, 'Is determinism compatible with, or even presupposed by, freedom?', and I select a couple of manageable and relatively fresh quandaries.

Can the will itself be free?

Essay VII is an attempt to analyse the complaint that is regularly lodged against the view of freedom we find in classical determinists, namely Hobbes [57], Locke [74], Hume [61, 62], J. S. Mill [84], and in our century Russell [102], Schlick [107] and Nowell-Smith [88]. Speaking roughly, as usual, their deterministic position is that you are free to do something where you are not hindered – by prison bars, for instance; and that you do something freely where what you do accords with, and perhaps results from, your desires, rather than springing from external compulsion. The main grumble against this view, which occupies me in Essay VII, is that surely there must be 'something more' to human liberty. Critics ask : How can it really be up to me whether I accept a bribe unless I am also free, in some deeper sense, to *decide* whether or not I will take it? And how can I be free to decide if my decision is bound to be influenced by my desires? Again, suppose I pocket the bribe because I like money and decide to take it, rather than as the result of blackmail or other external pressures. How can classical determinists say I acted freely unless they can show that my volitional capers – my desiring and deciding – were also free?

Hobbes, Locke and Hume were right to poke fun at such complaints; these questions are very odd. But these philosophers should have tried to make clearer sense of such expressions of discontent towards their analysis. And Hobbes, Hume, Russell and Schlick certainly should not have denied, as they sometimes did, that there is such a thing as freedom of will, over and above freedom of action. Nor should J. S. Mill have tried to prove that there actually is such a thing, without first establishing exactly what the questioner thinks has been left out by determinists, exactly what it would be like to have liberty of will. These clarifications are my goals in Essay VII.

The approach I take is modelled on another paper of J. L. Austin, 'A Plea for Excuses' [10]. In this brilliant and influential work, Austin undercuts much of the philosophical wrangle about free *action* by inquiring: ' "Free" as contrasted with what?' If you say that someone gave you his watch freely, what are you ruling out? Are you contrasting his manner with the manner of someone handing over a watch at gunpoint? On impulse? Under hypnosis? In Essay VII, I search for some intelligible kind of freedom on the volitional level, and by means of similar Austinian procedures. My investigation confirms to a large extent the suspicions of Hobbes and other evangelists of determinism, that their critics, who want something beyond freedom of action, labour under many confusions. But I try to prove this by analysis of what the opponents of determinism demand, instead of mere ridicule. In addition, my detailed survey of the contrasts we might have in mind if we attempt to speak more coherently about freedom of will, over and above freedom of action, encourages me to propose a limited sense for freedom concepts on the volitional level. Most important, I conclude that when circumstances give an agent liberty of action, they always ensure whatever liberty there might be for his will. Consequently, if there is 'something more' than mere freedom to act, and freedom in action, we need not leave it out of our deterministic account of freedom. To say this only answers one objection to determinism, of course, and hardly immunizes the view against other criticisms, or purifies it of the internal inconsistencies which may trouble it.

Predicting what one will decide

My second contribution in the area of the 'free will' problem, Essay VIII, isolates another narrow but manageable question: 'Is it possible to predict what a free agent will decide to do?' This question also has bearing upon issues (4) and (5). Saint Augustine [6] first dealt with this question in a theological context. He proved that even if God knows beforehand what you will decide to do, God's prescience neither robs you of freedom at the time God begins to know of your forthcoming decision; nor at the moment you decide; nor at the time you carry out your decision. To foresee a man's decision or his act is not the same as compelling, or even causing, him to reach that decision, or causing him to perform the action on which he has settled.

Augustine's reply to the general problem, whether foreknowledge and freedom are compatible, seems to me nearly irreproachable. However, Hampshire and Hart discovered a new angle of the problem in their 1958 article, 'Decision, Intention and Certainty' [47]. They asked about the agent himself, instead of a prescient God. And they were not so concerned whether the agent would be free if he knew beforehand what he would decide; instead they asked whether there would be any future decision left for him to predict. In becoming certain what he is going to decide, is he not reaching that decision in advance? Essay VIII is an attempt, first of all, to unravel a number of strands in the dispute, which most commentators on the Hampshire-Hart doctrine have tangled together. Secondly, I try to explain what a 'decision in advance' might be. And finally, I offer some new reasons for accepting a limited version of the Hampshire-Hart thesis. My reformulation is, roughly, that if we interpret 'decide' strictly, an undecided agent cannot have all the grounds that observers could have to forecast with confidence what he is going to decide.

In Essay VIII, I circumnavigate two controversies that are allied with the issue of self-prediction. One controversy develops from the supposition that an independent observer has sufficient evidence to forecast what the agent will decide to do. This onlooker's forecast would be knowledge, except for the fact that if the agent himself discovers what the observer expects him to do, he may perversely decide to act differently. Does the forecaster still know what the agent will decide? How can he have knowledge if he is not able to let the agent know what he knows? Further complications arise if we suppose that the forecaster makes allowances for the agent's counter-suggestibility, by tacking a second-level clause on his prediction, which specifies that the agent will act differently than originally forecast if he gets wind of the original prognosis. I do not plunge into these diffi-

culties about foreknowledge and decisions because I think they
have been satisfactorily discussed and resolved by MacKay [75,
76], C. J. F. Williams [119, 120] and Goldman [45, Chapter VI].

The other controversy I pass over in Essay VIII is an ingenious
extension of the Hampshire-Hart thesis by Carl Ginet, in his
article, 'Can the Will be Caused?' [43]. In brief, Ginet adds two
more steps to the Hampshire-Hart doctrine that you cannot know
ahead of time what you will decide to do. His additions go :

(i) If an event is caused, then it is possible for *anyone* to know
ahead of time that it is going to occur, by discovering that conditions hold which will bring it about;

(ii) Since, by the Hampshire-Hart thesis, *an agent* cannot know
beforehand what his decision will be, Ginet concludes that
decisions 'are outside the causal order'.

These contentions of Ginet, as well as other arguments in his
paper, have touched off intense discussion; but I found, when I
composed Essay VIII in 1963, that I had nothing to add but a
few carping demands for clarification. For example, I wondered
what Ginet meant when he said that decisions were 'not caused'.
I wanted to ask : 'Not caused by what? Not by the agent's
reasons, his attitudes and beliefs? Not influenced in any way by
anything, even the condition of the agent's nervous system?' How
could Ginet's argument rule out all these innumerable candidates
for the role of a cause? I do not pursue these points at all in
Essay VIII, however, because previous commentators have
already brought other conclusive objections against Ginet's argument as it stands. See Kaufman [64], Lehrer [70], Roxbee Cox
[101] and Stocker [110], for details.

A shift to moral perspectives
Thus far my selection from the problem areas I marked out
must seem excessively narrow. I have talked about causality;
differences between actions and other types of event; control,
choice and freedom; but what has become of the social and moral
dimensions of agency? Essay IX explores the social dimension of
responsibility, through Professor H. L. A. Hart's imaginative
work [54] on how courts hold lawbreakers liable for what they
have done if, and only if, they had minimal awareness and control over their behaviour at the time they acted illegally. Since a

great deal has been said on this general subject, by Hart and his predecessors, I have chosen to concentrate on a secondary but persistent theme in Hart's writings about responsibility and states of mind. He constantly makes comparisons within law between offences which must be, in a variety of specifiable ways, intentional and 'conscious', and another group of offences for which it seems that the agent may be convicted even though he was, in Hart's phrase, 'unconscious' when he acted illegally. The latter category of offences are traditionally called strict (or absolute) liability offences. Hart follows the majority of progressive social thinkers in arguing against this manner of holding people responsible for what they do.

I do not evaluate Hart's objections to strict liability practices by law courts, because I believe that the whole contrast is bogus. I try to prove that the offender's mental state is taken into account in the best-known strict liability cases, which Hart himself discusses. Then I go on to generalize, in line with the reasoning of Essays II, III, IV and VII, that our legal as well as our everyday concept of action makes some form of awareness and intention integral elements of agency. Evidently my results are useful in problem area (3), concerning awareness, and (4), which has to do with control.

Essay X goes deeper into the enigma of an agent's peculiar awareness of his current and future voluntary behaviour. This study ought to resolve some issues which were postponed in Essays II, III, IV, V, VIII and IX. For instance, I put forth a systematic account of what it is to succeed or to fail in what you do and try to do; and I elucidate the respects in which you can know without evidence that you succeed or fail. Briefly, my view is that we have ordinary perceptual knowledge of our surroundings and how we affect them when we act. The residue of non-observational awareness we have I link with social conventions, our current aims and our control over our bodies. As with all forms of empirical knowledge, I consider this type fallible. Moreover, although you may not be going on evidence, or need any, when you report that you are blinking your eyes, your report can express knowledge only because it is confirmed by other people's observation and evidence.

The final study turns back to reasons we have for what we

do. Moral and social dimensions come in again because among our grounds for some course of action is our judgement that it is the best course, or our belief that we ought to pursue it. As with many of the problem areas I have explored so far, again here it seems to me that most of the insights in this field have been elaborated by writers of genius, from the earliest times in Greece and the Orient. If I went into any of the 'perennial issues' concerning our beliefs about what we ought to do, and their justification, all I could do would be to expose muddles here and there. So once again the perspective I take is limited. The enigma I grapple with is appropriate for this series of essays, however, because it is found at a conceptual intersection. Here many problematic notions I have been dealing with – desire, choice, control – run together. The crux of ethical theory in which these notions reappear is familiarly known as the Socratic paradox; and it is part of the broader view, defended by Plato [96] and attributed by him to Socrates, that virtue is wisdom. The paradox which interests me in Essay XI more or less follows from the broader doctrine : it is that if you really know what is the best course of action for yourself, then you necessarily want to pursue it, and you will necessarily attempt to pursue it when you find out that you have the opportunity. Aristotle [4] believed that this doctrine flew in the face of experience. For who has not occasionally acted contrary to his better judgement? Still, Aristotle himself appears to settle finally upon the Socratic conclusion that a person who behaves this way either does not really know that a certain course of action would be best for him, or else the person is not acting willingly when he goes against his better judgement.

Unfortunately the arguments for this doctrine in Plato and Aristotle are none too clear. More straightforward arguments for a Socratic view have turned up in present-day ethical theories, such as Hare's [50, 51] and Nowell-Smith's [88]. But the solutions of Hare and Nowell-Smith demand that we postulate a split within the agent between potentially subversive interests such as his desires for profit and pleasure, on one side, and his joyless convictions, on the other, about his duties and obligations. The idea is that a man acts against his moral judgement regarding what is best because one of these non-moral drives has overcome him. I think that Plato and Aristotle were more nearly right, and also offered us a more challenging problem, precisely because they did not set up this tug of war between what I *should* do and what I should *like* to do. In 'Acting Against One's Better Judgment', which is readily available elsewhere (115), I take what I suppose is Plato's and Aristotle's approach to the Socratic paradox. The most important advances I make in 'Acting Against One's Better Judgment' are as follows. I construct an unimpeachable case of a rational, uncoerced agent deliberately pursuing a course of action which he believes is both contrary to his interest and morally questionable. More important, I explain why such cases are bound to strike us as paradoxical; that is, why we are still inclined to doubt that the agent was both aware and in control of his behaviour. We always wonder if he was insincere or deceiving himself when he produced reasons which he failed to act upon. Perhaps we look for unacknowledged neurotic compulsions. But this is only half the story. I argue that any moderately thorough analysis of what it is to have grounds for acting in a certain way must leave room for these paradoxical deliberate failures. Thus Socrates seems to have noticed a vital tension in our concept of what a person acts. Incidentally, these results have some bearing upon the contemporary debate between philosophers who believe that reasons are causes of action, and those who follow Melden [82] and hold that reasons entail action, when nothing interferes. If you side with Melden, how can you avoid the Socratic paradox? If you see desires as causal factors, you must disagree with Socrates.

Remorse and Moral Failure

Essay XI covers much of this same conceptual territory, but from the rather moralistic standpoint of Hare and Nowell-Smith. For the sake of argument, I impose their dichotomy, between moral and non-moral reasons to act, upon Plato and Aristotle. Then I see whether Aristotle, thus reinterpreted, as well as Hare and Nowell-Smith, can avoid the full rigour of a Socratic position. At times each of these philosophers seems ready to concede that people on occasion knowingly and willingly act contrary to their judgement of what is morally best. What then proves that the agents believed they ought to act otherwise? The most plausible solution for Aristotle, even though he does not suggest it, is the one adopted by Hare and Nowell-Smith : to say that the agent's feelings of remorse over what he did prove that he believed he ought to have acted differently.

Will this solution escape the Socratic paradox that nobody chooses to act against his moral convictions? I demonstrate that it will not, by taking the discussion a step further. That is, I analyse what it means to ascribe remorse to someone. The upshot is that if you appeal to remorse as your criterion for saying that a man has deliberately failed to act as he knew or believed he ought, your explanation is nothing but an elastic version of the Socratic paradox that it was designed to elude. Instead of holding, with Socrates and Plato, that a man always lives up to his moral convictions, unless he is ignorant or prevented, defenders of the remorse-provision must say that sooner or later the agent will act as he believes (or knows) he ought. For how could it be true that I am remorseful about failing, last month, to send part of my wages to my grandparents, if again this month, and next month, and so on, I make no efforts to do so? Perhaps I am afflicted with guilt feelings, but my attitude cannot be remorse, since I do not mend my ways. Once again we see how difficult it is to escape the Socratic doctrine. Moreover, we realize how this doctrine furthers our understanding of what it is to be a rational agent.

Influences and themes in these papers

The eleven essays assembled here display many puzzling facets of human agency and its social setting. Is there any 'big picture' I have been trying to execute? Can I utter a key formula which entails every thesis I have defended, and every principle of reasoning about action I have used? I doubt it. I have not been deducing my doctrines from any transcendental super-truth. I do not have a 'theory of agency'. After a decade of fairly constant work on problems in these areas, I have not conjured up any set of axioms that will regiment the various concepts I have been investigating. Of course, I do not see chaos either. Alongside the specific results I get in the studies, what I mainly see are tendencies, various polemical temptations, which should be all too evident; and pervasive influences.

Among philosophers whom I have only read, the most influential upon me have been Austin, Ryle, Hart and Wittgenstein. Since I first met Donald Davidson in 1956, his lectures, discussions and writings have had the most profound bearing upon my work. I have also been stimulated by Miss Anscombe's essays, her lectures in the philosophy of mind at University of Chicago, and by conversations at the time I was working on an early draft of Essay II in the autumn of 1965. Essays III and IV benefited, respectively, from my collaboration with Arnold Levison and Suzanne McCormick. Levison's comments on some of the other papers, in earlier versions, were most helpful. A seminar of David Pears at Stanford in 1963 stimulated me to write Essay VIII. Although I argue against some of Roderick Chisholm's views in Essays I, VI and (by implication) VII, I have always found his way of doing philosophy a paradigm of lucidity and thoroughness. He has offered many useful suggestions as my thinking about action evolved.

Among the tendencies I notice in these studies, I would list the following: In Essays III, VI, VIII and XI, I am disposed to look for a reasonable interpretation of doctrines which strike one upon first acquaintance as both outrageous and compelling. In Essays III, VII, VIII and IX I have a kindred inclination of demonstrating that philosophical views or notions which appear incompatible really are not. Essays I, II, III and IV manifest a fairly deep-seated mistrust of the notion of causality as a tool of analysis, particularly as a device for analysing the relations between the various elements of action – desire, purpose, belief, decision and control. In Essays II, III, IV, V, VI, VIII, X, and XI, I am tempted to exploit the concepts of convention or pragmatic function, or both, in discussing links between these elements of action.

Besides the pervasive influences I mentioned above, finally, I want to acknowledge specific debts. Essay I benefited from three sets of critical comments: one by Daniel Bennett, at a meeting of the American Philosophical Association on May 3, 1967; one short criticism from Robert Binkeley in spring 1968, and one long criticism Norman Care sent to me in April 1969. Essay II improved as a result of three readings: at the University of Michigan, January 28, 1966; at Stanford University, October 30, 1967; and at the University of Pennsylvania, November 17, 1967.

The original of Essay XI was criticized by Robert Rosthal in *Mind* during 1967 [100], which induced me to strengthen it here. There were useful criticisms of earlier verions of Essays VI, VII and VIII in Harald Ofstad [90]. Very recently Dr Lars Hertzberg sent me comments on the whole collection, and I have taken account of some of them in my last-minute revisions. I am also grateful to innumerable colleagues and students, at places where I have taught, for discussion of the various enigmas I deal with. The Graduate College, University of Illinois, was kind enough to provide a Faculty Fellowship during the summer of 1966, when planned the details of this collection and worked on drafts of Essays I and II.

Earlier versions of all these essays have appeared in philosophical publications. I want to thank the respective editors for the encouragement they gave me by printing those articles; for their help in suggesting revisions; and for allowing me to reprint portions of the originals here. Specifically, I thank the editors of the following journals for permission to draw upon the articles listed below:

Analysis for 'Do We Cause Our Own Actions?' (27.6, June 1967, pp. 196–201, used in Essay I); 'Abilities and *Ifs*' (22.6, pp. 121–6, used in Essay VI); and 'Foreknowledge and Decisions in Advance' (24.3, January 1964, pp. 49–54, used in Essay VIII).

Australasian Journal of Philosophy for 'Intending the Impossible' (40.1, May 1962, pp. 49–56, used in Essay V).

Dialogue for 'Trying', by Suzanne McCormick and myself (6.1, June 1967, pp. 29–46, used in Essay IV).

Ethics for 'Hart on Strict Liability and Excusing Conditions' (81.2, January 1971, pp. 150–60, used in Essay IX).

Idealistic Studies for 'Free Will and Chisholm's Varieties of Causation' (1.2, May 1971, pp. 144–54, used in Essay VI).

Journal of Philosophy for 'Freedom of Action and Freedom of Will' (61.14, July 16, 1964, pp. 405–15, used in Essay VII).

Mind for 'Essential and Causal Explanations of Action', by Arnold Levison and myself (78.309, January 1969, pp. 91–101, used in Essay III); 'Remorse' (92.288, October 1963, pp. 545–55, used in Essay XI); and my answer to Robert Rosthal, 'Rosthal's Notion of Remorse and Irrevocability' (77.306, April 1968, pp. 288–9, used in Essay XI).

Theoria for 'Verbs, Deeds and What Happens to Us' (33.3, 1967, pp. 259–77, used in Essay II).

Essay X was originally an invited contribution to *International Logic Review*, whose editor made innumerable unauthorized deletions and stylistic changes, and printed an unrecognizable version in December 1970, without sending me galley proofs.

I am grateful to K. T. Fann for allowing me to use the nearly final version of Essay VI, which appeared in his anthology, *Symposium on Austin* (London, Routledge & Kegan Paul, 1969, pp. 182–204) under the title, 'Austin on Abilities'. Last but not least, I am very indebted for excellent typing to Mrs Janice Kelly, former head secretary of the Philosophy Department, University of Illinois at Chicago Circle, and to Mrs Dorothy Green, present head secretary.

I

DO WE CAUSE OUR OWN ACTIONS?

In recent philosophical literature we find widespread acceptance of the distinction between things people do and things that happen to them. Some notion of causality is often introduced to explain this contrast between the two kinds of events. Our deeds are said to be the events we ourselves produce; and events to which we make no causal contribution are said to be things that befall us. These two analytical contentions are mutually independent. Why are they important? They seem to provide an economical account of what it is to act and what it is to undergo something.

Some writers have no interest in elucidating the contrast between doing and undergoing, but a causal interpretation of agency seems plausible to them on its own. Thus Anthony Kenny declares: 'The form of description "A is bringing it about that p" is the fundamental one for the description of voluntary human action' ([65], p. 195; see also pp. 176–9 and 236–7). On Kenny's view, washing the dishes is bringing it about that the dishes are clean. A similar analysis is propounded by Daniel Bennett. He declares: 'Someone does something, i.e. he acts, only if he causes (determines, makes) some object or objects to have some property or properties' ([16], p. 85). Roderick M. Chisholm offers the same causal re-description of what we do, and extends his analysis so that the category of events we cause includes many events that are not our deeds. For Chisholm, the causal expression

' "make happen" is to be taken in such a way that we may say, of a man who raises his arm, not only that he makes it happen that his arm goes up, but also that he makes it happen, just before, that certain other physiological events occur inside his body, and that he makes it happen, just subsequently, that air particles move in various ways' ([24], p. 613).

Even a steadfast opponent of causal analyses of action, A. I. Melden, repeatedly falls back upon the very causal idioms he

35

intended to avoid. Melden rejects the theory that we lift our arm by doing something else first that produces the rising of our arm. Yet his own account has an equally causal ring. He asserts that 'one is able to *make* the proposition "I am raising my arm" true' ([82], p. 37; also pp. 38–41, 130). With regard to physiological changes that occur within a person's body while he acts, Melden usually ranks them as mere 'happenings', of which the person is a 'helpless victim' (a phrase which recurs frequently in Melden's running contrast between actions and 'bodily movements' ([82], pp. 24, 128–33, 208, 212–15).

As for taking bodily processes to be things that happen to us, Richard Taylor's position is even more emphatic. And Taylor explicitly offers a causal account of people's deeds. Comparing one's gestures with the beating of one's heart, Taylor asserts:

'When I am moving my limbs, I am acting, . . . when parts of my body are moving in a manner with which I have nothing to do – as in the case of my heart beating in response to internal impulses . . . – I am passive, having something done *to* me' [114], pp. 159–60).

On Taylor's view, to describe an event as an action is to 'state that some agent has caused it'. Thus he says, 'In acting, I make something happen, I cause it, or bring it about'. Nevertheless, warns Taylor,

'the word "cause" in such contexts has not the ordinary meaning of a certain relationship between events, but has rather the older meaning of the efficacy or power of an agent to produce certain results' ([114], pp. 109–12).

Chisholm suggests a pair of Latin terms for the general notions that Taylor is contrasting: 'ordinary' event-event causality Chisholm dubs 'transeunt', while the 'older' notion, which comprises agent causality, he baptizes with the title of 'immanent' causality ([26], pp. 17–23). On the strength of the previous passage I quoted from Chisholm, I would say that he takes immanent causality to be broader than agent causality. When Chisholm says that a man 'makes it happen, just before [he raises his arm], that certain other physiological events occur inside his body', I assume that Chisholm means that the man 'immanently' causes, but not that he agent-causes, the cerebral processes that figure in his action of raising his arm. However, Chisholm obscures things with the remark that 'whenever a man does something A, then (by "immanent causation") he makes a certain cerebral event happen, and this cerebral event (by "transeunt causation") makes A happen' ([26], p. 20).

Instead of worrying about this and related complications in Chisholm's general notion of immanent causality, I shall focus on the more specific concept of agent causation that we find in the writings of Chisholm and others. For his part, Richard Taylor believes that this 'older' meaning of the verb 'cause' will resist analysis. Still, he intends to deploy this unanalysable notion of 'cause' in his own analysis of what it is to act.

Initial Problems

For convenience I follow Richard Taylor and call his and similar doctrines theories of 'agent causality', since they all contain the idea of a peculiar causal relationship between an agent and something else when he acts. Ironically enough, *what* the agent is related to by agent-causality is unclear. A lot depends upon whether a theory of agent causality is given in answer to the question, (1) 'What does an action consist in?'; or the question, (2) 'What is the relation between a deed and the agent who performs it?' If you are replying to (1), you cannot say, 'My action of chewing bubblegum consists in my agent-causing my action of chewing'. An infinite regress would ensue. We simply go on to ask for the analysis of the action of chewing that you agent-caused. Therefore this type of reply must be directed towards question (2). But if you say 'the connection between myself and and my act of chewing is that I agent-cause it', you leave the concept of what it is to act unanalysed.

What would be an analysis of action, in reply to (1)? Something like: 'My action of chewing bubblegum consists in my agent-causing the *event* of my jaws opening and closing upon the bubblegum'. This proposal would have the additional merit that it goes nicely with the complementary analysis of undergoing which is sometimes offered by agent-causationists, namely: 'A golfer's being struck by a stray ball consists in his *not* causing the event of the ball striking him'.

37

Against all these views my objection will be quite blunt. There seem to be no situations in which we do use, or could intelligibly use, the recommended causal idioms to describe people's behaviour. As far as I can discover, what Richard Taylor calls the 'older meaning' of the verb 'cause' does not exist. Furthermore, I shall object that it is simply false to equate things that happen to us with events that we do not agent-cause or otherwise cause.

No doubt theories of agent causality are philosophical advances upon the traditional causal view they supersede, which requires that our action should be the upshot of a separable antecedent episode. On the traditional theory, this prefatory occurrence is either some further performance of ours, such as an act of willing; or else it is merely a process in our mind or nervous system. Whether it is mental or physical, an act or not, this preliminary episode has the job of bringing about our overt behaviour.

Against this traditional theory, agent causationists and others have entered three decisive objections: (i) If our actions require antecedent performances to bring them about, and if the exertions of our will count as actions, then we must also do something to bring about an exertion of our will, and so on *ad infinitum*. (ii) If we reply that antecedent performances are unnecessary to bring about our acts of will, then why not allow the same for overt deeds, thereby dispensing with the causal theory? Finally, (iii) if the causes of our actions are not things we do, but simply occur in us, how can their efforts be attributed to us as our deeds? This alternative seems to transform an agent into a mere instrument.

Reviving the 'older' notion of agent causality liberates us from these inexplicable preliminaries to action. On the rejuvenated theory, when you engage in an elementary performance such as turning your head, you cause the rotation of your head, but without doing anything first to bring it about.

Attempting to apply the theory
What does this negative stipulation mean? If indeed agent causality is so unlike its 'ordinary' counterpart (which Chisholm dubs 'transeunt' causality), then the differences must be spelled out. How does agent causality diverge from event-event causality?

38

We need details. And if agent causality is *sui generis*, then we should be able to encounter a few cases in daily life where a person who acts is described in conformity with this 'older' notion of cause. Are there such uses of the verb 'cause' and its cohorts? I shall look for possible examples. Suppose you hear that someone you know caused a brawl at the tavern. You might naturally inquire: 'How did he bring it about?' What help would it be if your informant replied, 'He simply caused (produced, etc.) the scuffle, but not by doing anything that resulted in the scuffle'? You only grasp what was meant by 'He caused it' when you have an idea what the person did to initiate the fracas. Did he punch the bartender, thereby touching off a mêlée?

What he did when he caused the brawl may have involved little or no hustle and bustle. That is, perhaps your acquaintance was sitting quietly at the bar, but when a drunken bully attempted to throw him out, other patrons rushed to his defence, and a free-for-all ensued. Given this story, you could insist that our protagonist 'did nothing' to cause the fight. Certainly he did not do anything in order to set off a fight. He did not intend to make a fight occur. He did not instigate one. And evidently the bully was to blame for the disturbance. But if you pursue this line of reasoning any further, and maintain quite literally that our protagonist did nothing that helped bring about the fight, how can you say that he caused it? If you compromise, and admit that his presence in the tavern, among other circumstances, produced the disorder, you imply that after all he did something which contributed causally to it. What did he do that contributed? He went there, to begin with. He remained there when the bully menaced him. Perhaps his refusal to pay any attention to the oaf had a further effect on him. Admittedly it is unclear what we are after when we ask if your friend 'did anything', and whether his action helped cause the uproar. Still, I conclude that you must give some specification of what he did that contributed causally, or else you have to give up your claim that he brought about the scuffle.

When we discuss complex incidents like a bar-room brawl, which comprises the activity of many people, or a forest fire, which includes natural processes resulting from an agent's performance, at least it makes sense to say that an agent caused such events. The only hitch, as far as theories of agent causality go, is that we seem to be concerned with the ordinary concept of a 'transeunt' causal relation between the incident and something the agent did.

So now consider the simpler kind of events that the notion of agent causality was devised to explain, namely, basic performances like walking. Is it even intelligible to report that a person caused himself to walk, that he brought about his own locomotion? By yelling at an intruder, a housewife might cause him to dash away. How would she cause herself to walk? A proponent of agent causality will no doubt reply, for reasons I sketched earlier, that he intends to exclude this very 'How?' question by his analysis. 'How?' suggests that the housewife does something else as a means of bringing about her ambulation; and this conflicts with the agent-causality thesis, that doing is a relation between agent and event, not between a pair of events. Furthermore, if the agent-causality analysis of 'The lady walks' were 'She causes herself to walk', the analysis would be circular, since the phrase 'herself to walk' evidently records the same event as the action-statement we are trying to analyse, namely the statement that she walks. This circularity would be glaring if we used Kenny's terminology, which was mentioned earlier. Our analysis of 'She is walking' would read : 'She brings it about that she is walking'! We would prefix every action report with a phrase to the effect that the agent brought about what was reported. The danger of a regress is too obvious to bother with mentioning it.

Opening defence

The agent causationist will probably want to sidestep these perils by denying that he analyses 'She walks' as 'She causes herself to walk'. Instead he will probably substitute 'She causes her legs to move'. Of course her legs do not move off without her, so this means that she causes her body to move. On this form of agent causality theory, the housewife's action of walking is identical with, and hence reducible to, her agent-causing certain motions of her body. If her legs and the rest of her begin to move about, but she has not made a causal contribution to the movement, then of course no action would have occurred. But the important point is that the agent causationist would deny that her leg and body movement alone is identical with her action; as I have said, he would maintain that she agent-causes the movement and not the action of which the movement is a part.

In what sense a part? First of all, the agent causationist must deny that the housewife's action of walking and the movement of her body are themselves causally connected, in the ordinary 'transeunt' sense or any other. That is because a description of her act of walking and a description of her bodily movement, though far from synonymous, happen to single out the very same occurrence. The movement and the action begin and end at the same time, and she occupies the same regions of space, while she is walking, as her body occupies while it is in ambulatory motion. Since cause and effect cannot be events that are coterminous with each other in time and space, it follows that the housewife's action and the motion of her body are not causally related.

How are they then related? The agent causationist has already denied that there is any other event, or action by the housewife, causing the housewife's leg motion; for that would reduce his theory to the traditional event-event picture. So when we report that she agent-caused the motion of her body, this 'causing' is totally unlike the kind we spoke of in the example of someone causing a bar-room brawl. When the housewife is said to agent-cause the ambulatory motion of her body, our notion of 'causing' sounds empirically vacuous. What is there to observe beyond the motion of her body? It sounds as if the housewife's action of walking is the same event as the corresponding movement of her body, despite the admittedly vast difference in meaning between these two descriptions of that event.

This result creates new headaches for the agent causationist. He maintains that the housewife causes the motion of her body. Earlier, to avoid giving a circular analysis of action, namely that her act of walking consists in her agent-causing her act of walking, the agent causationist denied that she caused her action. But if we continue assuming that it is events that are agent-caused (and 'transeuntly' caused), then we realize that the agent causationist is both asserting and denying that the housewife agent-causes the very same event.

Further modifications

In the face of this contradiction, an unrepentant champion of agent causality has at least two alternatives. One option is for him to retract his statement that we agent-cause events. He might say that while ordinary 'transeunt' causation relates an event to an event, agent causation should be modelled upon the relations between a person and what he is thinking of. When I think of Arthur Ashe winning the 1968 U.S. Amateur Tennis Championship, it does not follow that I think of Tom Okker losing; even though Ashe's triumph was against Okker, which makes Ashe's victory the same event as Okker's defeat. One reason I might not think of Okker losing is that I may have no idea who Ashe's opponent was in the final round.

Evidently we think of events. My example seems to be a case of someone calling to mind an important event in sports during 1968. But the point that agent causationists can turn to their advantage is that it is at least questionable whether the statement 'I am thinking of Ashe's victory' entails 'I am thinking of Okker's defeat'. By analogy, it would now seem dubious whether the statement 'The housewife agent-caused the ambulatory motion of her body' entails 'She agent-caused her act of walking', even though both direct-object clauses record the same event.

But unfortunately for the agent-causationist, his analogy between thinking and agent-causing has another cutting edge. In fact, the analogy will destroy his defence. To begin with, my thinking, as well as similar mental occurrences such as believing, expecting, hoping, longing and dreading, is an event on its own, distinct from whatever it is that I think about. Thinking might be a mental performance, as well as an occurrence. I do not mean that one's thinking is a distinct, perhaps non-physical, *kind* of event, or that it occurs somehow within the secret confines of one's immaterial mind. No Cartesian mumbo-jumbo is intended. All I mean is that the analogy between thinking and agent-causation suggests, contrary to official theory, that agent-causing is a distinct event, over and above our bodily movements that occur when we act.

Another injury that results from modelling agent causation on thought is due to the well-known fact that it is possible to think of what does not occur or exist. A surgeon thinks, with confidence and with solid evidence to back him, that his patient will recover. But his patient declines. What the surgeon expects, the recovery of his patient, does not take place. By analogy, it looks as though you might agent-cause a motion of your body, and yet the motion could fail to occur. Notice how radically this would make agent causality diverge from ordinary 'transeunt' causality. It is logically impossible that a neglected camp fire should 'transeuntly' bring about a conflagration in the woods, but that the forest fire is prevented. If anything is 'transeuntly' caused, it takes place.

My final objection to the proposed analogy between thought and agent causation is fairly vague but still important. Because of peculiarities just mentioned, and others, many philosophers hold that our mental activities like thinking are not directed toward events at all. They hold that what I think of, when I muse about Ashe's victory, is not the event of Ashe winning the Amateur Championship. My thought would be directed toward the possible state of affairs, the possibility that he won, or the proposition that he won. Now my complaint does not concern this view of thinking and its objects. My grumble is that *if* we model agent causation on thought, and suppose that the housewife does not agent-cause the actual motion of her body, which we observe, but only directs her 'efforts' toward a possibility, or a proposition; *then* our analysis loses all connection with the very event it was designed to fit. Speaking less metaphorically, agent causationists were supposed to tell us what an observable act, such as the housewife's ambulation, consists of. Their contention, that deeds consist of bodily movements which are agent-caused, subsequently appeared to entail a contradiction. Accordingly, their contention was altered to read: actions are possible states of affairs comprising bodily movements, or possibilities of bodily motion, or propositions concerning bodily motion, all of which are agent-caused. The occurrences we wanted to account for are no longer mentioned in the analysis.

Here the agent causationist will probably retort that I have omitted a crucial part of his new doctrine. I should have said that on his modified analysis, the housewife's action of walking consists in her agent-causing the possible state of affairs *to obtain*; or that she agent-causes the possibility of her bodily movement *to be actualized*; or (using Melden's language in the passage I quoted) that she agent-causes the proposition, that her body is in ambulatory motion, *to be true*. Against this account, my criticism is that if these new idioms mean anything at all, they mean that the housewife agent-causes the event of her motion. And we already saw the difficulties of that view. In fact, those troubles were the rationale for this whole attempt to model our analysis of agent causation upon the standard account of thinking and its objects.

Does the agent causationist have to give up? Not yet. I said that besides the analogy with thinking, there is another possible escape route for him. He can plunge headlong into *a priori* neurophysiology, and alter his analysis to specify that the housewife, instead of agent-causing gross movements of her limbs, really only agent-causes certain antecedent patterns of electrical activity in her brain. This cerebral event 'transeuntly' brings about her subsequent ambulatory motions. This attempt to shelter a battered philosophical theory behind a wall of 'scientific' conjecture seems unpromising. At the very least, we can challenge the intelligibility of this view by raising 'How?' questions, which sufficed to undermine the view we started with, that the housewife agent-caused motions of her limbs.

One last attempt to illustrate the concept of agent causation

I have been challenging agent causationists to explain what they mean, to give an instance of someone bringing about his actions, or movements of his body, in the prescribed way. Before I conclude that their analysis is empty, or leads to contradictions, I must be sure that I have considered every example that might favour their account. So here is a more exotic case than our overworked instance of a housewife walking. Perhaps it will suffice.

We now have a lonely Arctic explorer who is about to succumb to hunger, fatigue and icy winds. We describe his behaviour by saying, 'He made himself continue walking', and 'He forced his legs to move'. In fact, these reports would be more accurate reports of his tenacity than saying simply, 'He continued walking' and 'He moved his legs'. Although the auxiliary verbs 'made' and 'forced' are not empirically vacuous in this example, do they indicate the causal connection that we have been pursuing? Do 'made' and 'forced' mean 'caused' in anything like the official 'agency' sense? Not by my understanding of the illustration. I think that we use these expressions to describe the wanderer's self-discipline in the face of extreme discomfort and privation. We mean that despite his fatigue, his numbness from the cold, and his longing to give up, he kept a grip on himself and struggled onward. How shall I prove that these obstacles and contrary impulses our wanderer must overcome are all that give meaning to the idioms, 'He made himself continue' and 'He forced his legs to move'? Transpose him into a situation where these features are missing. For instance, imagine that the explorer is rescued and flown home. He regains his health. One mild day he wakes up eager for exercise, and sets off on a stroll through the park. What would it mean to say now, 'He is making himself walk' and 'He is forcing his legs to move'? If 'making' and 'forcing' indicated a causal relationship when he was lost in the Arctic, they should be allowable here, since the same relationship must be present in both cases. Yet these expressions are wildly incongruous in the obstacle-free illustration. Therefore they must stand for the explorer's determination and endurance in my original story.

Refuting the complementary analysis of undergoing

I cannot think of any other promising examples that might exhibit the notion of agent causality. This is not a conclusive reason to reject it, since I may have overlooked contexts where it will fit what people do. But the complementary thesis, that things which happen to a person are events the person does *not* cause – in any way, and in any sense of 'cause' – lies open to decisive refutation. For we often have a lot to do, causally speaking, with events that befall us. A grim but uncontroversial case first, then a cheerier one, will show the compatibility of having something happen to you and helping to bring it about. If a skier is swept downhill by an avalanche, this is clearly something that happened to him. Yet he might have made a causal contribution to the incident. Perhaps he touched off the avalanche, intentionally or by accident, when he deliberately traversed a hazardous slope. Perhaps he wanted to see what an avalanche looks like, and mistakenly thought he could ski to the side of it. At any rate, the avalanche would not have carried him downhill if he had climbed around the slope, instead of crossing it.

The same is true of more agreeable things that happen to people, such as being elected to high public office. Being elected (that is, receiving more votes than other candidates) is not something a candidate does. But among the causes of a man's electoral triumph you would normally list his campaigning activities : speaking frankly on controversial issues, smearing his rivals, promising patronage jobs to his helpers. Once again we see that a person may contribute causally to things that happen to him.

Causal notions did not serve to mark off one's deeds, namely, as those events one brings about. Perhaps we can still use causal criteria to distinguish what happens to one. We concede that a person may make a causal contribution to what happens to him, but we tentatively characterize this class of events as those events which result from one or more of the following : actions of other people; one's own actions; and natural processes of inanimate objects or forces. On this analytical hypothesis, being elected is the result of more people voting for one than for one's opponents; and being swept downhill by an avalanche is the effect of both the victim's own foolish behaviour and the sudden rush of loose snow down the mountainside.

Even this limited causal account of what happens to us will not work. It is correct enough to say, 'Mike was elected because more people voted for him than for the other candidates.' But the 'because', in this sentence, is not causal. It sets forth a social convention or 'constitutive' rule. You explain what it is to be elected when you say that a candidate for whom the largest number of people vote is the winner. That is our rule for running elections.

Now I have already argued that the skier's actions may be a cause of what happens to him when he is caught in the avalanche. As a result of his imprudence, he was carried off by it. The remaining cases, of being acted upon by a natural force or another person, diverge from this pattern. It is odd to say, 'Because the loose snow cascaded down upon him and carried him downhill, he was caught in the avalanche.' It is equally strange to report, 'The loose snow fell upon him and swept him downhill; as a

46

result of this, he was caught in an avalanche.' We do not seem to be dealing with a causal relationship, but with an explication of what we mean by 'being caught in an avalanche'. The same holds when one person is acted upon by another. Details and qualifications of this non-causal analysis of undergoing will appear in Essay II, Section 1.

For present purposes, it seems safe to conclude that causal notions are unserviceable to us when we analyse what it is to act and to have something happen to one. Causality presumably has a central place in determining whether a man is responsible for some event, such as injury to another or property damage. Furthermore, it seems to be true that we appeal to causality in deciding whether to say that the result of one action by a person is also to count as his action. For example, I knock over a glass of wine. The wine spills on to a precious carpet. The carpet is stained. A potential buyer of it changes his mind. The causal relations in this case give us grounds for saying, not only that I knocked over the glass, but also that I spilled the wine upon the carpet, that I stained the carpet, and made it lose its value. Incidentally, we do not say that I made the buyer change his mind.

I shall not elaborate on this, since Donald Davidson, taking a lead from G. E. M. Anscombe ([1], pp. 33–45) and Joel Feinberg [41], develops these points very persuasively in his paper 'Agency' [38]. I merely note that this line of thinking in no way contradicts the objections I have made against giving a causal analysis of what it is to act.

II

HOW CAN WE DISTINGUISH
BETWEEN DOING AND UNDERGOING?

I have just belaboured causal theories of acting and having something happen to oneself. Now I want to make a fresh and more
positive approach to these traditional categories. I shall begin
with a few clear examples that we might select from the incidents
of a person's life. If a man walks or steals, he does something.
If he is carried or robbed, something happens to him. If what
befalls him is momentous – if he submits to surgery or a lie-
detector test, for instance – then we say that he undergoes something. For expository convenience, however, I shall equate undergoing and having something happen to one. The philosophical
question with which I shall approach the concepts of doing and
undergoing is this: although we have no trouble multiplying
instances of both types of occurrence, do we understand what
qualifies them for these categories? In other words, what makes
our examples cases of doing or undergoing? My point of
departure will be the verbs and verb phrases we use to report
events in which a human being figures prominently. Thus I shall
not be concerned with the 'actions' of inanimate objects and
forces, such as the action of hydrochloric acid upon copper, or
the behaviour of animals. I shall assume that the sense in which
inanimate things act is different from the sense in which people
act. One reason I assume this is that it sounds unintelligible to
assert that the hydrochloric acid deliberately stained the copper,
or that it did so by accident; whereas these adverbs combine
intelligibly with the statement that a jeweller stained the copper.
As for animals, I take it that their behaviour is partly analogous
to human deeds.

In asking what indicates that a particular verb or verb phrase
describes an episode of action or undergoing, I want to challenge
the long-standing assumption that all such expressions will slip
neatly into one or the other compartment. Are the categories of

doing and undergoing exhaustive? I shall be especially interested in three different families of verbs that appear to elude both categories.

The linguistic approach I am taking may sound philosophically trifling. Why study verbs, rather than look at events themselves for earmarks of doing and undergoing? For instance, are not needs set apart by the activity and motion of the doer, while passivity marks the person who is undergoing? No, because various forms of inactivity rank as deeds. If an energetic business-man relaxes from his normal routine, and sits motionless in his easy chair all the afternoon, has he not done something? At any rate, we would not dismiss his inactivity as something that befell him. On the other side, people to whom things are happening are not always passive. The victim of a robbery might struggle vigorously with the hold-up man. Incidentally, this last case shows that even if it were true that doing and undergoing are exhaustive categories, they are not mutually exclusive, since the man being robbed is simultaneously acting, namely, resisting his assailant. One event in which two agents figure here exemplifies both doing and undergoing. I am aware, of course, that it could be decom-posed into sub-events. At any rate, I have another reason for neglecting events and studying verbs instead. The occurrences themselves present us with too many features, including physio-logical ones, which have no bearing upon the status of the occur-rences as action or undergoing. A policeman's clubbing of a hippie may be noisy, and it may take a certain amount of time for the hippie to receive the blows; but these auditory and tem-poral characteristics of the incident are not germane to its being a deed and an undergoing. The verbs 'to club' and 'to receive' call our attention to relevant features of the episode, which make it an instance of doing and undergoing.

I have just attacked the view that deeds are marked by activity, and undergoing by passivity. If we shift now from the events themselves to language, will the contrast between active and passive sentence constructions take us any further than the notions of activity and passivity? Hardly. The verb 'undergo' itself, in the sentence 'John underwent an appendectomy', is in the active voice; yet this sentence would not be used to record an action of

John's. 'He suffered', 'He bore the pain heroically' and 'He finally received an anaesthetic' contain equally dubious verbs in the active voice. Passive constructions are more trustworthy, but they are not infallible signs of undergoing : a sentence like 'The sailors of the Kon-Tiki were swept by ocean currents from South America to Polynesia', may serve to report how some adventurers crossed the Pacific on their raft – an amazing feat !

We seem to be floundering in our attempt to clarify what we mean by doing and undergoing. So I shall sketch provisional criteria for both concepts.

1. *Preliminary criteria*

Although my criteria will make doing logically prior, I shall begin with the easier notion of undergoing. I assume we mean at least one of the following in clear cases where we say of a person that he underwent something : (*a*) he was acted upon by another agent, perhaps even an animal; or (*b*) in the sense of 'act' that does not concern me here, he was 'acted upon' by an inanimate object or natural force; or (*c*) he acted upon himself, in the sense of 'act' that interests me.

Before I go on to propose a further criterion for the relevant sense of 'act' that appears in my analysis of undergoing, I cannot resist elaborating what I said at the end of Essay I about the connection between

(1) the acts of classes (*a*) and (*b*), and

(2) what happens to a person.

When other people or natural forces act in such a way that something happens to you, these actions are not causes, in any literal sense of 'cause', of what happens to you. The sentence, 'Bill pushed Max; as a result, Max was pushed', is unintelligible, if we give the term 'result' its normal meaning. Why? Perhaps this incoherence is due to the fact that causes must be logically distinguishable from their effects. Although Bill's shove and the resulting motion of Max are separable, the complex event of Bill jostling Max is bound to be identical with Max being jostled by Bill. One could not occur without the other. Consequently these two phrases cannot be descriptions of cause and effect.

It is also noteworthy that the criterion consisting of (*a*), (*b*), or (*c*), as well as the 'non-causal' criterion, give us necessary, but

50

not sufficient, conditions of undergoing. Why? Because some things we do are just as logically bound up with other people's actions as are things that happen to us. If you are knocked down while you are strolling in the woods, it follows that something knocked you down. Perhaps you knocked yourself down by colliding with a tree branch. But similarly for some actions : you cannot duel, play a game of badminton, or lease an apartment without the participation of someone else. And these are unimpeachable cases of action, not undergoing. A duellist may have something happen to himself as a result of the swordplay. He may be scarred or killed. But here we have a causal, not a logical, consequence of duelling.

I propose to call episodes like duelling 'cooperative actions', and I shall neglect them in favour of the central antithesis between more rudimentary actions and things that befall one. Luckily, cooperative and solitary actions have a common feature which sets them both apart from all cases of undergoing. And this common feature is what I hope to capture in the provisional criterion I have promised for verbs of action.

I shall state my criterion first without reference to verbs. The distinctive trait of action I have in mind is revealed by the terms we use to connect a person's deeds with his will – that is, with his desires, aims, decisions, intentions, efforts and conative attitudes. As it turns out, all clear instances of action, including cooperative action, may be intelligibly described in such idioms. Of anything a person does, you may say some of the following : that he did it deliberately, on purpose, unintentionally, under duress, and so on for a broad range of terms which attribute to a person various forms and degrees of control, as well as loss of control, over his actions.

When we discuss performances like walking and stealing, the sort of control, or loss of control, we ascribe to people differs from the equally familiar type of control that an aviator has over his airplane. The pilot sits at the controls. He must push throttles, flip switches, depress pedals and turn the steering apparatus in order to execute the manoeuvres he wants to perform. But when he lands, steps out of his aircraft, and decides to walk home, he does not have to do anything else first in order to walk. The same holds for all the solitary and cooperative actions that concern us.

51

Very generally, we have control of such actions whenever they are things we want to be doing. To say a person lacks control is to say that he is acting under duress, compulsively, unwillingly, or in some other manner that is incompatible with the supposition that he wants to do what he is doing. For instance, a man who walks because someone is holding a rifle at his back does not have much control over his ambulation. The victim of hypnosis has none.

How do control terms and their antonyms furnish us with a criterion for verbs of action? They single out paradigmatic verbs of action because it is always meaningful to use *many* expressions from this family together with action verbs in a statement. Further, when a positive term of control modifies an action verb, the statement is never rendered self-contradictory by the appearance of the positive control term. By contrast, the terms we use for loss of control may have this effect. For example, the statement 'Jane murdered her husband unintentionally' is self-contradictory, because the verb 'murder' means 'unlawfully kill with malice aforethought', and 'with malice aforethought' means, *inter alia*, 'intentionally'.

This last asymmetry between control and loss-of-control idioms is avoidable. We could restrict our criterion to *generic* action verbs such as 'kill', in relation to which 'murder' would be a specific action verb. Our formula would then read: Generic action verbs are verbs that we may use intelligibly and consistently together with many control terms and their antonyms. I prefer the original criterion, because it spares us the work of dividing actions, and the verbs they match, into genera and species.

Before I use these provisional criteria for undergoing and doing to challenge the view that all human events fall into one or the other category, I want to illustrate more fully how my control-term criterion for verbs of action will distinguish between doing and undergoing. Control terms and their antonyms will never carry over from paradigmatic verbs of action to verbs and verb phrases for undergoing. Thus it is meaningful, and either true or false, to say, 'A highwayman *deliberately* took John's watch', 'The highwayman took it unintentionally', and 'The highwayman took it unwillingly, only because his gang leader forced him.'

52

When we turn to undergoing phrases, the situation is radically altered. It is not even false, or for that matter self-contradictory, to describe John himself as being robbed deliberately, unintentionally or against his will. English syntax seems to prevent us from characterizing John, in his role as victim, in any such manner. If we assert, 'John was robbed on purpose', it will sound as if we are talking about the robber, not John, and saying that he had some special reason for picking on John. In other cases, for example, if you say that John was robbed on his own initiative, syntax does not prevent us from using the control term 'on his own initiative' to characterize John. However, the utterance is not intelligible, if we are using the control expression 'on his own initiative' with its literal meaning. As victim, how could John have initiative or any other form of control?

All this might be disputed. Do we not often speak of people as 'willing victims'? The example is irrelevant, because we cannot mean that the victim was being acted upon willingly; we mean that he was willing to be robbed, or more straightforwardly, that he wanted to be held up. This hardly proves that John had control in his role of victim. We shall come later to problems about mental activity verbs such as 'want'; but for now we can say that at least these verbs do not seem to record cases of undergoing. And it is just a contingent matter that what John wants is for something to happen to him. More commonly we want to perform actions.

Now of course I admit that the victim of the robbery may be characterized by means of control and loss-of-control terms, particularly when we talk of how he contributed to his own misfortune. For instance, John may have purposely, or accidentally, wandered into a tough neighbourhood. He may have intended to meet a narcotics pedlar, so that it was contrary to his intention to meet a hold-up man. And when John was robbed, perhaps he surrendered his watch gladly or unwillingly. But these control and loss-of-control idioms are used to depict John's *actions* that helped bring about the robbery; they do not characterize his manner of being robbed.

I hope the distinction between doing and undergoing expressions is clear. A wide range of verbs and verb phrases fall into the pattern we have delineated by means of control and loss-of-control

53

expressions. It makes sense to describe a thief as stealing on his own initiative, or being driven to it by financial pressures; but, as we noticed, it is puzzling to say these things of the person being robbed. Shifting to other verbs, notice that 'The maharajah's bearers strained to carry him in his sedan chair', and 'They carried him effortlessly', are meaningful. 'He strained to be carried' and 'He was effortless in being carried' are not. Again, you can attempt to push someone out of the grocery line; you cannot make an attempt at being pushed from the line. If you try to provoke someone into shoving you, by sneaking into the line ahead of him, this counts as an attempt to provoke, not an attempt to be pushed. Or take the connection between actions and motives: you might have reasons for loaning someone money; he does not have reasons for being loaned the money, although he might have grounds for asking you to loan it.

Finally, consider adverbs we use to depict various styles of conduct. Many of these adverbs also suggest control or its absence. For instance: we say that people walk energetically or listlessly; strenuously or effortlessly; purposefully or aimlessly; willingly or unwillingly; impulsively, conscientiously or carelessly. But are there any corresponding styles of undergoing?

By reference to all these groups of control and loss-of-control expressions, then, we can differentiate action verbs from undergoing phrases. For none of these expressions which connect a man's actions with his desires, choices and goals apply when we report what happens to him. Yet what of sentences such as 'He voluntarily underwent shock treatment' and 'He was forced to undergo it'? There is no question here of the undergoing itself being voluntary or forced. In what way would the shock treatment, or the man receiving it, look different at the time? Our trick sentences are actually reports of what preceded the treatment. 'He voluntarily underwent shock treatment' means 'He consented beforehand to have it.' And 'He was forced to undergo it' means either 'He did not consent beforehand (i.e. he was not consulted)' or 'He refused to have it, but it was administered to him just the same.' Apart from the possibility of consulting with the patient, and his agreement or refusal, it is unintelligible to speak of voluntariness and coercion in connection with the shock treatments he received.

Here is a more difficult example. Not only does a man consent beforehand to undergo hypnosis; but while he is being hypnotized he is eager and cooperative. Is he not willingly hypnotized? No. What is eager and cooperative during the session is not his being hypnotized. He enthusiastically follows the hypnotist's instructions. His actions show no hostility or resistance during the session. This is hardly equivalent to saying that what happened to him showed willingness, or that he displayed willingness in what happened to him.

I hope that this preliminary account and test of our working criteria for verbs and verb phrases of doing and undergoing, as well as distinctions between them, has made the criteria reasonably clear. Now I want to go on and explain, by means of these criteria, why three rather homogeneous collections of verbs appear to stand for events that belong to neither the category of action nor that of undergoing. This explanation will also illustrate further how our criteria help us classify expressions.

2. Initial group of in-between verbs

If a man perspires, flushes, pales, bleeds, trembles, throbs, grows, breaks out in a rash, digests his lunch, freezes or thaws, has he done anything? Control terms sound incongruous with these verbs. We cannot perspire at will. A person can take deliberate steps to make himself perspire, but that is not perspiring deliberately. It is what he does to make himself perspire that is deliberate. If you are cut and you bleed, some purpose might be served by the bleeding. It might prevent infection. However, you do not bleed on purpose. As a first-aid measure, you might try to make your wound bleed, but you would not thereby attempt to bleed. Again, suppose a criminal flushes or goes pale under interrogation. Could he have a motive for reddening? Would it make sense to say that he turned pale by accident? What would it be like to throb energetically, conscientiously or aimlessly? The verb 'grow' appears to deviate from this pattern of incoherence. It makes sense to say, 'I tried to grow a beard last vacation' and 'I grew it on purpose, to shock my business partners'. Yet this hardly sounds like an action. Such *prima facie* counter-examples will be demolished later.

The important point now is that we have all the above-men-

55

tioned reasons for denying that 'perspire' and the other verbs from our initial group stand for actions. Moreover, these verbs are crucially dissimilar to expressions we use to report what happens to people. It seems a contingent matter that people perspire if they exercise violently, and bleed when they meet with injuries. It is conceivable that someone should perspire although no person or thing has acted upon him in such a way that he perspires. On the other hand, it is logically necessary that someone push you when you are pushed, and that someone rob you when you are robbed.

This disparity between cases of undergoing and the events which our first group of verbs describe is very clear in the example of bleeding. The person who bleeds may not have been acted upon. For example, there is no incoherence about the idea of a man having spontaneous stigmata. He bleeds at the hands and feet, but nothing has acted upon him. A pious thinker will assume that God does something to the stigmatist which makes him bleed; a religious sceptic will look for psychological mechanisms. Nevertheless, compare the hypothesis that a person has spontaneous stigmata with that of a spontaneous robbery, namely, the hypothesis that a particular hold-up comprised nothing but the victim's ambush and loss of property, without there being anyone who held him up. You will notice a striking difference. The idea of a spontaneous robbery is incoherent, while the hypothesis of uncaused bleeding is at least a meaningful contender against the causal explanations we listed.

Another point of difference between verbs like 'bleed' and paradigmatic expressions of undergoing has to do with causality. As we noticed earlier, the looter who runs off with the grocery-man's cash-register does not cause the grocer to be robbed; he robs him. If you wish, the looter causes the cash-register to disappear from the store. Still, this episode is not a cause of the robbery, for it is the very same event as the robbery. Now contrast this example of undergoing with the case of someone who bleeds. Suppose your doctor jabs you with a scalpel in order to procure a sample of your blood. His jab is a cause of your bleeding; it made you bleed. Unlike the looter's removal of a cash-register, which is the same event as the grocer's being robbed, your doctor's jab is hardly identical with the bleeding it produces.

56

How shall we summarize the disparities we have uncovered between our first group of verbs – 'bleed', 'perspire', 'throb', 'redden' and so on – and familiar expressions for both doing and undergoing? Call our first group 'bodily process verbs'. From our analysis of these verbs up to this point, it seems that the events they stand for are not things we do, because neither control nor loss-of-control terms will consort with bodily process verbs. More important still, bodily process verbs do not seem to record things that happen to us, because there is no logical connection between such bodily processes and the actions of other agents or inanimate forces, or between them and our own actions.

This latter result deserves a comment, because many contemporary philosophers, among them A. I. Melden ([82], pp. 7, 85, 128–33, 200–15) and Richard Taylor ([114], chs. 5 and 8), assign bodily processions, or 'bodily movements', as they call them, to the category of what a person undergoes. Many more – R. S. Peters ([94], pp. 11–16, 68–9, 85, 87–9, 150–6), for example – concur with Melden and Taylor in accepting the very general principle that doing and undergoing are exhaustive categories. All of these writers assume, in other words, that if any event in which a man participates is not the man's action, then it must be something that happens to him. Here are typical declarations of both of these connected views from Taylor's book, *Action and Purpose*:

'Such things as the beating of my heart and the growth of my hair for example, are motions and changes of my body, but in a familiar though somewhat baffling sense they are not things with which I have anything to do ... [T]hese are physiological processes which I am helpless either to make happen or to prevent from happening in any direct way ... ([114], p. 58).
... [W]hen parts of my body are moving in a manner with which I have nothing to do – as in the case of my heart beating in response to internal impulses . . . . – I am passive, having something done *to* me ... ([114], p. 60).
... [I]n perspiring I am not acting ... this bodily change is simply an automatic reaction with which I have nothing to do' ([114], p. 104).

57

If my analysis of bodily process verbs has been correct so far, then both views are unwarranted. Processes that happen *in* our bodies are not things that happen *to* our bodies or *to* us, because such processes are not instances of anything acting upon us. Secondly, the categories of what we do and what we undergo are not exhaustive, as these philosophers imagine. It appears that we must establish a conceptual orphanage for bleeding and similar events.

3. *A counter-argument*

I think I can remove the sting from the last result, that bodily processes deserve an intermediate category between action and what people undergo. We should realize, first of all, that physiological changes like bleeding are not incidents in the history of a person. They are incidents in his body's history. If we run through the verbs of my initial group, we see that each one of them may be used, without loss of sense or content, to describe an agent's body rather than an agent. The sentence, 'St Francis's feet and palms bled' is no less intelligible or informative than 'St Francis bled at his feet and palms'. Perhaps it is only an accident that we have the latter construction at all. When speaking of blood circulation rather than bleeding, we do not say that a man circulates his blood; we say that his blood circulates through his arteries and veins. But with clear-cut verbs of action, including those we use to describe bodily processes as well as deeds, it makes a considerable difference in meaning if we talk of what a person's body does, rather than of what the person himself does. The assertion 'His legs moved', is plainly not synonymous with the assertion 'He moved his legs', since the former but not the latter may be true of a man with a convulsion.

Another difference between talking about bodies and talking about people is that some verbs of action, and some 'undergoing' expressions, are inapplicable to bodies. It is nonsense to describe a body as walking, stealing or being robbed. And to report, 'Charles's body was carried out of the room', is hardly equivalent to saying 'Charles was carried out of the room'.

The foregoing counter-argument protects the exhaustiveness assumption of Peters, Melden, Taylor and other philosophers. They only have to stress that any episode in the career of a human being must be either something he does or something he under-goes. Since bodily processes seldom rank as episodes in a person's history at all, why should they be either things he does or things he undergoes?

By thus restricting the notions of what one does and what happens to one, we can also refute an apparent counter-instance to our criterion for verbs of action, namely, that verbs of action are those which may be combined with the terminology of con-trol and loss of control. The verb 'grow' troubled us because it makes sense, and may be true, to say that a person tried to grow a beard, that he had a reason for growing a beard, and so on. Now plainly the sprouting of whiskers from a man's chin is not his action. Moreover, the sprouting cannot be described as some-thing he attempted, or for which he had reasons. Where do con-trol idioms sneak in then? One exercises control in allowing one's whiskers to grow, instead of shaving them. You might say that our ability to shave is a form of 'inhibitory control' over the growth of our beards. But it is extremely important not to be misled by this phrase. The inhibitory control one has over the growth of one's beard is altogether different from the power one has over one's rudimentary actions. I stop walking at will; I do not have to do anything in order to bring my ambulation to an end. Yet I do not just stop growing whiskers; I must prevent them from growing by some other action, for instance, by shaving. With this warning about inhibitory control, then, we conclude that it is a man's abstention from shaving, not the resultant growth of his whiskers, that is said to be deliberate, purposeful, and so on. And who would deny that omitting to shave is an episode in the history of an agent rather than of his body?

Unfortunately this move, of dismissing verbs which may be used without loss of meaning to report occurrences in a person's body, will not work against the next group of unclassifiable verbs.

4. *Second group: reaction verbs*
Instead of the previous examples from the bodily process group, 'throb' and 'redden', consider the verbs 'shudder' and 'blush'. To expand the list, what kind of event do you report when you say that a persons yawns, hiccups, chokes, wheezes, vomits or

sneezes? How will you block the inference from active voice to action? You cannot rule out these verbs as merely describing what occurs in a man's body. In fact, it is nonsense to say that a man's body, or part of his body, hiccupped. A person hiccups, not his mouth. To assert 'I didn't yawn; my face did' is a joke. These verbs only depict episodes in the career of a person.

Why not assume that verbs of this second group describe what people undergo? As we noticed already with bodily process verbs, an essential mark of undergoing is absent from these new examples. We agreed that it is inconceivable that something should happen to a man unless another agent, or a natural force, acts upon him, or he acts in such a way that he brings about what happens to him. And just as we saw no absurdity in the notion of a bodily process like spontaneous bleeding, there would equally seem to be no logical contradiction in supposing that a person should hiccup, yawn, blush or shudder, although nothing made him hiccup, yawn, blush or shudder. Consequently these reactions are not things that happen to a person.

I propose to say that 'blush', 'choke' and the remaining verbs of this second group describe people's reactions, although not their bodily reactions. Such responses normally result from various stimuli. People usually choke, for instance, because of some obstruction in their throat, or because they are overcome with vehement emotion. Still, a paroxysm of choking is distinct from these things that cause it, and it could take place without any of them.

Besides this dissimilarity between events like choking and para-digms of undergoing, we notice just as great a dissimilarity be-tween these reactions and our deeds. Like deeds, reactions are ascribed to a person; however, the idioms of control and loss of control, which we use to characterize what a person does, are inapplicable to reactions. It sounds as incongruous to say of a man that he choked at will, on purpose, or unwillingly, as it does to describe his bleeding in these terms. Since we cannot dismiss reactions as merely concerning the body, must be concede that they are on a par with things we do and undergo, but belong to neither category? Possibly there is another way to deal with reactions.

5. *Are control terms necessarily inapplicable?*

We ought to qualify our intuition that it is senseless to characterize reactions as deliberate, accidental, conscientious, careless, and so on. This restriction will also affect our previous ruling that it is absurd to describe such bodily processes as bleeding and digestion in control terms. Our verdicts were reasonable, but they had a specious ring of finality about them. What I intend to demonstrate now is that the terminology of control and loss of control *could* mix with bodily process and reaction verbs, although it does not at present.

To start with, we should return to our example of spontaneous stigmata. We imagined that people bled although nothing caused their bleeding. If that fiction sounded coherent to you, then perhaps you will be able to add further detail to it : our stigmatists no longer bleed at random; instead they often begin and stop when they want to. What is more, they do not have to do anything else first in order to bring about their bleeding, and nothing has to act upon them. I assume, of course, that occasionally they will also begin and stop bleeding as a sequel to the type of event that now makes people bleed and stop bleeding – for instance, as a result of scrapes and clotting, respectively.

What gives these imaginary stigmatists their mysterious power over their bodily processes? What gives ordinary people their power to open and close their jaws, move their limbs and turn their eyes in various directions? These are enigmas best left to physiologists. The philosophical issue is far simpler : Does our story provide a background against which is would be meaningful, and often true, to describe bodily processes in the jargon of control and loss of control? I think so. If one of our stigmatists foresees a benefit from bleeding, and goes ahead, does he not bleed for a reason, on purpose? And if he is unexpectedly hit by something on the nose, and his nose begins gushing, in spite of his efforts to prevent it, would that not be a case of bleeding involuntarily or unwillingly? These seem to be the very circumstances that justify our saying that particular motions of our limbs are voluntary, involuntary or neither. And more conditions of the same kind are easy to imagine, with the consequence that reactions, as well as bodily processes like bleeding, come within the scope of control terminology. Intentional and unintentional choking, deliberate and accidental yawns, conscientious and careless sneezes now seem as intelligible as the counterpart forms of bleeding we invented. I have no idea what goals our fictional heroes might hope to atttain by choking on their food, yawning and sneezing. But if they had some end in view, and did not do anything to make themselves choke, yawn and sneeze, these reactions would be purposeful.

With respect to verbs like 'perspire' and 'bleed', we see that our fantasy promotes them from the category of *mere* bodily process verbs. If people had acquired control over their perspiration and bleeding, it would make a difference whether we ascribe such episodes to an agent or to his body. As things ordinarily stand, it means the same to say that a person sweated or that various parts of his body sweated. In the context of our fable, the two forms of speech would not be interchangeable: it might be true to describe some person as 'sweating in order to cool himself off'; however, this description of his body would be senseless. A standard verb of action should make this point clear: it may be true to say of an ordinary human being, 'He waved his arm in order to hail a taxicab'; but saying, 'His arm waved in order to hail a taxicab' would be incomprehensible.

All these considerations show, I hope, that the verbs I classed as 'bodily process verbs' and 'reaction verbs' are not necessarily ineligible for membership in the category of action verbs. They would migrate into that category under the circumstances I imagined. And this result has some importance for our philosophical understanding of action. All that disqualifies bodily process and reaction verbs from being action verbs, and bars the episodes in question from being things we do, is our belief about human powers. We believe, on good evidence, that people do not have the control over their bodily processes and their reactions which they have over their walking and stealing.

How do these considerations affect our problem about setting up an intermediate category, between doing and undergoing, to house our gangs of wayward verbs? I think we still have a choice. We can disregard bodily process verbs. We can maintain that, given our present knowledge and beliefs concerning the actual capacities of men, these verbs only concern bodies, not agents. Then our choices are: either to admit that reaction verbs stand for some third type of episode in a person's career, not something he does and not something he undergoes; or alternatively, to avoid opening up a new category, on the grounds that our fable proves it to be just a contingent fact that reaction verbs never describe what people do. If we take the second option, we classify reaction verbs as *potential* verbs of action, because our fable provides a setting in which the terminology of control and loss of control would mix with reaction verbs.

I think it hardly matters how we decide about reaction verbs; for the next group of verbs I shall examine will not, under any imaginable circumstances, fit into either of our traditional categories.

6. Breakdown verbs

These verbs resemble the reaction verbs like 'blush' and 'sneeze', inasmuch as they also serve only to describe events in a person's history, rather than his body's history. Yet breakdown verbs differ from reaction verbs in that we cannot specify any situations in which we could use the terminology of control and loss of control to modify breakdown verbs. In this case, the reason we cannot introduce these terms is no longer that they would be altogether unintelligible; it is that positive terms of control would be logically incompatible with breakdown verbs, and terms for loss of control would be either misleading or redundant. What is more, verbs of the present collection do not record things that happen to people.

The latter point is the simplest to establish, and it is proven by the same considerations that led us to deny that bodily process verbs and reaction verbs describe what people undergo. As before, the reason is that breakdown verbs of the following sub-groups,

a 'fumble', 'stammer', 'trip', 'stagger', 'collapse', 'run amok', 'rant',
b 'sleep', 'snore', 'faint' and 'die',

describe events in which it is not necessarily the case that something acts upon the protagonist. As we already noticed with bodily processes and reactions, breakdowns are separable from whatever may have brought them about, as all effects are separable from their causes. Let me illustrate this difference one last time.

63

If a U.S. football star is carried from the field, some person or thing must carry him. Suppose that his admirers do it, by hoisting him onto their shoulders and parading to the nearest exit. Their action of carrying him is indistinguishable from what happened to him, being carried. And it follows that their carrying him is not a cause of his being carried.

Now compare being carried with the breakdowns we might report by using the verbs from sub-groups *a* and *b* above. If the star player fumbled the ball, tripped, staggered, lost his balance, fell, ran amok, raved, fidgeted or fainted, perhaps something acted upon him and perhaps not. If he fumbled the ball because it was covered with mud, this mitigating circumstance is not part of the fumble itself, but only a cause of the fumble. Similarly, if he fainted when another player knocked the wind from him, the other player's action is a distinct event which merely caused him to faint.

Assuming now that the two sub-groups of breakdown verbs we listed do not record what happens to people, why are they not verbs of action? With sub-group (*a*), the reason is that each verb is used to report a lapse in the agent's control over what he is doing. When a football player fumbles, this incident is necessarily contrary to his intentions as a serious participant in the game. Serious participants are out to achieve victory for their team and to avoid such errors as fumbles. When we call the upshot of a play a fumble, we assume a context in which the man to whom we ascribe the fumble wanted to hold on to the ball. In this setting, it would be absurd to report that he tried to fumble, that he fumbled on purpose or deliberately. These and other terms of control are not unintelligible; but they are incompatible with the background assumptions we make when we talk about fumbles. And if we say that the player was *not* trying to fumble, or say that he fumbled unintentionally, then our description of the mishap is worse than pleonastic; it sounds as if it ruled out a genuine possibility, namely, the possibility that our football hero intended to fumble.

But what if the star was bribed to help the opposing team? In that case, when he deliberately allows the ball to slide from his grip, would it not be true to say that he fumbled on purpose? I suppose the scorekeeper would record a fumble. But I wonder how the player's team-mates would describe the incident if they learned of the bribe? Would they say, 'He fumbled deliberately'? I think they would prefer saying that he threw away the ball, or threw the game.

If this example is tenuous, here is a parallel case. Like fumbling, stammering occurs within a particular context, normally one in which a person is talking with others, or perhaps rehearsing a speech he will give to others. As a rule, his aim in speaking or rehearsing will be to make his actual or prospective listeners understand his words. For that purpose, he must intend to speak clearly and fluently. Stammering is called a speech defect precisely because it hinders one from attaining these goals. Consequently it cannot also be one of the speaker's goals to stammer.

You could object to this by offering a counter-example: some actor might deliberately cultivate this manner of talking. If so, we would have to deny that he intended to speak clearly and fluently. We might even regard his speech as defective. My answer is that it is not one of *his* aims to be understood; therefore would we say of this actor that he was afflicted with the speech impediment of stammering? He is simply not being impeded from attaining the standard goal of speaking. I doubt that we would even say that he stammered; only that he deliberately spoke in a difficult manner.

I hope that this examination of typical breakdown verbs from sub-group (*a*) demonstrates why the corresponding control terminology will not mix with such verbs. Now the specimens from the other sub-group, (*b*), mark lapses in a person's information or consciousness, rather than his control, of events. And the patois of awareness, both observational and non-observational, does not mix with these verbs. It is self-contradictory to report that a soldier on parade passed out from sunstroke, and that he knew or believed that he did at the very moment he fainted. He might have had foreknowledge, through a premonitory sensation of dizziness, that he was going to faint; but that is not the same as consciousness of the swoon as he was overcome by it. Furthermore, to report that he fainted unwittingly carries the bizarre suggestion that we think it possible for him to be somehow aware that he has fainted. This latter test is helpful with the controversial examples of sleeping and snoring. You might argue (mistakenly, I believe) that in our dreams we often guess or become certain that we are asleep and dreaming. But would you ever remark that a sleeper did *not* realize that he was asleep, or that he was *un*aware of snoring?

Although these verbs record failures in our awareness, the notion of control retains its primacy. For one thing, it is self-contradictory to say that a man purposely drowned, fainted, slept or snored. 'Deliberately', 'intentionally', 'willingly' and 'energetically' fit no better. But more important is the extra-linguistic tie between awareness and control. Normally, the episodes we count as a person's intentional actions, and hence as being under his control, are also events of which he is aware – often without observation. The converse does not hold, incidentally: people sometimes know, with or without observation, what is happening to them; but that does not concern us.

The conceptual/logical link between control and awareness is this. A man may be ignorant of some details of what he is doing, but he must have an idea of what type of action he is performing; otherwise his action is not under his control. It may be true to say that a pickpocket deliberately took an alligator-skin purse containing £10·54, a salary cheque for £45·83, such-and-such credit cards, photographs of friends and relatives, and various cosmetics, from Jane. And this description is correct even if the pickpocket had no specific knowledge or beliefs about the handbag and its contents, and no idea who Jane was. But he must have had minimal awareness of what he was doing. If the purse-snatcher was unaware that he was taking another person's property, then it is false to say that his act was voluntary, deliberate and so on. If this minimal degree of consciousness must accompany various forms of control, that is enough for our thesis about breakdowns of awareness. Since the verbs in sub-group (*b*) rule out any degree of concurrent awareness, these verbs must also rule out control as well.

You might ask, incidentally, whether there are any features of the setting in which the concepts of control and awareness flourish which link them together in this manner. Perhaps the conceptual connection is due to our habit of deliberating and deciding beforehand about our important actions, rather than plunging into them on the spur of the moment. And it is essential to this kind of reflection and planning that we should later be able to carry out our design. But how could we subsequently execute our decision unless we are then aware, in some degree, that what we are doing fulfils our antecedent decision?

Apart from this, it seems clear that breakdown verbs are ineligible for membership in both our familiar categories. Moreover, we cannot imagine circumstances under which breakdown verbs would migrate into the category of action verbs. You will recall that we dismissed the first collection of recalcitrant verbs as concerning only events in a person's body. And the second family, reaction verbs, did not absolutely compel us to set up an intermediate category, between action and undergoing, because we managed to specify changes in the powers of human beings which would allow reactions of theirs, such as yawns and sneezes, to count as things they do. But no similar changes would affect the status of fumbling, collapsing, running amok, fainting and other lapses of control or awareness.

You might object here that imaginary changes are uncalled for, because breakdowns ought to be classified as actions on different grounds, which I have already supplied. Halfway through section 1 of this paper, I briefly mentioned a special group of actions, from which I took murder as an example, that are by definition under our control. I noted that it is self-contradictory to report that a man unintentionally murdered someone. Now is there not a compelling analogy between actions like murder, and breakdowns, of which it is self-contradictory to say that they are intentional, or in any other way under our control? If murder is necessarily intentional, should we not hold that breakdowns are necessarily unintentional, and hence just as much actions as murder?

I can think of two replies. One is that in the case of murder we can say what is necessarily intentional, namely, killing. And killing is plainly an action. But this pattern of analysis does not hold for every breakdown. Are drowning, fainting and sleeping necessarily unintentional? If so, what exactly is unintentional when someone drowns, faints or sleeps? No verb comes to mind. And furthermore, any verb that we are inclined to suggest does not sound like an action verb, as 'kill' does. My second line of reply to the argument that breakdowns are actions is far more speculative. It would start with the metaphysical contention that control is somehow a more basic feature of action than loss of control. In other words, although it is always intelligible to modify action verbs with control and loss-of-control terminology, one limitation we must set upon action verbs is that it should never be self-contradictory to join them with some control terms. Why? Here my conjecture is that part of what we mean by an action is something we can deliberate about, decide upon, and carry out. But the latter, executive, stage can occur only if we have control over the action. However, loss of control does not seem to be tied up in this way with action. It does not seem to be true that what we can deliberate about, decide upon, and carry out, must be something over which we could lose control, and do unintentionally, by accident, unwillingly or unawares. This is what I mean by the speculative counter-argument that control is more basic to action than loss of control. My two replies reinforce each other, inasmuch as the first reply challenges the objector to say what action it is over which he loses control when he figures in a breakdown; and the second reply challenges the objector's assumption that loss of control is conceptually linked with action, in the way that control is.

I hope this neutralizes the objection that breakdowns ought to be classified as necessarily unintentional actions, at the opposite pole from necessarily intentional actions like murder. A different complaint would be that breakdowns are trivial exceptions to the well-established dichtomy of events into things we do and things that happen to us. Why should they merit a new category in addition to the familiar pair we have? One reason I have for giving such dignity to breakdowns is that they are intimately connected with action, even if they are not themselves actions. Breakdowns are some of the ways in which agents fall short of the goals they have in a particular action. Many breakdowns can only occur when agents pursue such goals. Thus when a football player carries the ball, one of the ways his action might be spoiled is if he fumbles. His action of running will be marred if he trips. What is more, he cannot possibly fumble unless he is carrying the ball, and it is equally impossible for him to trip unless he is running or moving in some manner. One exception to this pattern is running amok. A man who goes berserk, and fires his revolver at random into a crowd, need not have been engaging in any particular forms of activity. Apart from such exceptions, breakdowns are supervenient occurrences : they only take place when we are performing certain actions; they are extra events, over and above the actions; and furthermore, they are unwelcome upshots of the actions we are performing. Would we fully understand the actions if we did not know that they could have these vexatious endings?

7. *Near analogues to breakdown verbs*

Another reason for not dismissing breakdown verbs as unimportant freaks is that many other philosophically prominent verbs exhibit some resemblances to them. I shall take examples from two groups of verbs that I originally included in my collections (*a*) and (*b*). I only realized my initial error when I got a pre-publication version of Donald Davidson's essay 'Agency' ([38]). These troublesome examples are :

(*a′*) 'miss', 'bungle', 'botch', 'blunder', 'spoil' and 'fail';
(*b′*) 'overlook', 'misplace', 'misjudge', 'miscalculate', 'mistake', 'misidentify', etc.

Returning for illustration to the football star, imagine that he misses a tackle. The analogy with our breakdown case of fumbling is impressive. Whatever caused him to miss his tackle – mud, a tricky manoeuvre by the ball-carrier – is clearly separable from the faulty attempt. Moreover, control terms and their antonyms do not consort with the verb 'miss'. Both 'He missed on purpose' and 'He missed by accident' sound odd. Finally, botching a tackle, like fumbling, must occur while one is doing something – in this case, lunging at the ball-carrier. However, the parallel collapses at this stage. For missing the tackle is not an extra event that accompanies or continues after one's lunge at the ball-carrier. To say that the would-be tackler missed is not to record a sequel, such as the ball escaping in a fumble. It is to evaluate the lunge, by reference to the agent's intention of felling the ball-carrier.

A similar analogy and disanalogy turns up with verbs from the (*b′*) group, for instance 'miscalculate'. One must be computing how much one owes the Inland Revenue when one miscalculates one's income tax. One cannot deliberately, or inadvertently, miscalculate – although one can deliberately write down an arbitrary or an incorrect total. But the miscalculating is not a supplementary occurrence, over and above what one does by way of figuring out the total, in the way that the escaping football is a supplementary occurrence when the player's grip loosens.

The last near analogue of a breakdown verb I shall take from groups (*a'*) and (*b'*) is by far the most interesting; the generic verb 'fail'. Perhaps someone will object straight away that there is not the slightest consanguinity between the notion of failing and notions like fumbling, which do not mix with control or awareness terms and the antonyms. After all, the objection would go, do not people often deliberately fail to perform their duties, and inadvertently fail to attend dances? I agree, but in these illustrations, 'fail' does not mean anything like the quasi-breakdown of failure; it means 'omit'. And as we remarked already, with regard to a man's abstention from shaving (section 3 above), an omission *is* a deed. Omissions may be characterized in the terminology of control and loss of control.

I want to deal instead with the sense of 'fail' that crops up when we speak of people failing *in* their actions. Thus imagine that a daredevil is engaged in the action of swimming across the English Channel. Admittedly, from this characterization of his behaviour, it does not follow that he intends to reach the other side. After all, he might be ignorant of his whereabouts. Or he might not have set any particular goal for himself; he is perhaps only after exercise. It is even compatible with the report, 'He is swimming across the English Channel', that he positively intends to swim less than the full distance across. However, what interests me is that it sounds flatly self-contradictory to describe him as both swimming across the English Channel and intending to *fail* in this action that he is performing.

If he intends to fail at a particular task, then it surely follows that he is not engaged in that task. So, to vary the example, suppose that a desperate-looking gunman orders our swimmer to cross the Channel. He intends to thwart the gunman by feigning exhaustion after a short distance. In these altered circumstances, it is not true to describe him as 'swimming across the Channel but intending to fail in what he is doing'. What would be a suitable characterization? Perhaps 'swimming toward the other side, but intending to fail at the task the gunman has set for him', or 'pretending that he is doing his utmost to reach the other side'.

So much for the impossibility of intending to fail. My reasoning presumably shows at the same time that the notion of '*un*intentionally failing in what one is doing' is odd. And to this extent the notion of failing is like the genuine breakdown concepts of stammering and fumbling. But as we remarked already with the 'quasi-breakdowns' of botching and miscalculating, there is no supplementary occurrence in the case of failing at the task one is performing. The swimmer who fails in his action of swimming the Channel merely stops. He figures in no further event beyond the swimming which qualifies neither as an action nor as something that happens to him. Swimming is something he does. Failing is not a further identifiable event at all. Therefore failing diverges from the pattern we found in the previous cases of genuine breakdowns, as well as reactions and bodily processes. Each group was composed of events that are separately identifiable, in space and time, from any actions the person might happen to be engaged in when he bleeds, or blushes, or stammers.

I gave these near-analogues to prove that the full-fledged intermediate verbs we isolated, particularly breakdown verbs, are not trivial exceptions to the traditional dichotomy of doing *versus* undergoing. Other philosophically significant verbs as well bear less striking but still noticeable resemblances to breakdown verbs. I shall only list them, without supporting explanation : first a whole range of 'success' verbs, that obviously correspond to 'fail' : verbs like 'complete', 'perfect', 'reach', 'conclude' and 'carry out'. And finally a number of 'mental activity' verbs, such as 'ache', 'itch', 'think', 'guess', 'remember', 'know', 'hope', 'envy', 'admire', 'hate' and 'enjoy'. Verbs from both these groups particularly resemble intermediate verbs inasmuch as they will not consort with most terms of control and awareness. Some remarks on this will appear in section 5 of Essay IV, and section 18 of Essay X.

Summing up

That breakdown verbs stand for events of neither category seems to be beyond doubt. But even the other groups of verbs we found not to require an intermediate classification have some importance for our long-range analysis of doing and undergoing. We disproved the current assumption that bodily process verbs describe things that happen to people. We showed that saying that a man perspired is only saying that something happened *in* him, or in his body. Furthermore, we noticed that there is nothing about perspiring and similar episodes to bar them from the category of action. To sweat is not to act only because one happens to lack control, and therefore happens never to lose control, of the process. But it is conceivable that one should gain control, and consequently risk losing it at times. On similar grounds, we erased all permanent lines of demarcation between reaction verbs like 'hiccup' and indisputable verbs of doing, such as 'walk'. It sounded unintelligible to say, 'She blushed on purpose' and 'He hiccupped by accident', only because we are convinced that people do not have the power over their blushes and hiccups which they have over their gestures. As for the control terminology itself that has served throughout this paper as a mark of action verbs, all I have shown is that it works fairly well for this purpose, and that it also reveals the oddities of bodily process, reaction and breakdown verbs. I regret that I have not been able to say what control and loss of control are.

III

ARE THERE NON-CAUSAL EXPLANATIONS OF ACTION?

ORIGINALLY CO-AUTHORED BY ARNOLD B. LEVISON

In the last two essays, the topic of causality and action has been treated in an oblique and critical manner, with the result that I appear to exclude causal concepts altogether from the panorama of human agency. The present study, for which I am grateful to my colleague Arnold B. Levison for his collaboration, should help to restore some balance and give causality a fairer run.

We begin at what looks like a well-travelled philosophical dead end. For more than a decade, theorists have bickered about whether an explanation of someone's behaviour can be causal in form. In particular, when the person's behaviour is accounted for by reference to reasons he had for acting, is the account of it ever causal? Our hope is to reconcile the disputants, and to offer concrete suggestions regarding at least one non-causal form of explanation. For this purpose, we shall take on trust a widely accepted but somewhat psychologistic general notion of explaining an event. The generic notion is that you explain a particular occurrence when you make it seem more intelligible and less surprising to your listeners than it was before they heard your explanation. How does your account render the occurrence less puzzling? It reveals how the event conforms to a pattern which is familiar to your audience. Given this overall scheme, causal explanations will belong to the species which dispels mystery about a particular event by placing it in the mosaic of other events and standing conditions that preceded or accompanied it. A causal explanation will inform you of the role these played in bringing about the occurrence that interests you. Presumably causal accounts will include true law-like statements that similar antecedents and similar conditions are always followed by events like the one that baffled you.

These assumptions are more or less standard. And one upshot of our discussion will also seem hardly novel: that a person's behaviour is amenable to causal explanation, and that many deeds result, in part, from the agent's reasons, desires or motives. Our other verdicts will be new: first, that philosophical opponents of causal explanation are still right, in so far as they contend that there are further things worth saying about a man's reasons for acting, which render his action more intelligible than it was. These complementary forms of explanation, according to us, are never causal, and causal accounts will not replace them. This disparity will be found even if, during a non-causal explanation of someone's deed, the reasons, desires or motives that come into the picture were also causal factors. Our second new verdict concerns a widely recognized but much disputed feature of reasons for action, namely that an agent's knowledge of his reasons is not inductive or observational. Since all other causes are known inductively, and certified through observation, how can reasons be causes? We argue that there is no inconsistency between according a privileged status to an agent's report of why he acted, and counting his reasons among the causes of his deed. No contradiction arises, because the agent's description of these causal factors may very well differ from the description of them which appears in a relevant causal law; and such a law forms the backbone of any full-fledged causal explanation of what the agent did. In other words, the agent may not know the cause of his action as this cause would be specified in a scientist's account of the deed.

Our conciliatory theses all hinge upon a distinction between explaining an event by fitting it into a general cause-effect pattern, and another manner of making the event intelligible, which we dub 'essential explanation'. Roughly, to propose an essential account of some incident is to delineate those qualities or aspects of the incident which figure in our criteria for saying what *kind* of occurrence it is. You could later go on to give an essential explanation of the kind of occurrence itself; this would be a philosophical analysis, or, borrowing a phrase from one recent writer on this topic, Geoffrey Maddell [77], an 'elucidation' of the concept of that type of occurrence. The difference in levels should be obvious. First you might say what makes your wife's

74

activities in the kitchen this afternoon an instance of following a recipe. Then you might elucidate the notion of following a recipe, showing how it is connected with the more general notions of obeying rules, skill and knowledge.

Just to make sure that our quasi-technical term, 'essential explanation', is understood, here is a childishly simple case of one that is offered for a particular event. The situation is that during a recent storm in the vicinity of Chicago, many buildings were blown apart, while immediately adjacent buildings were unscathed. Why? An essential explanation of the incident would run : the storm was a tornado, and tornadoes consist of violent winds of small extent that touch the ground only in certain places along a narrow path. Now you recognize the storm, and the destruction it left, as instances of a familiar type of natural catastrophe. And clearly the account you received does not list preceding events or standing conditions which brought about the violent winds, nor does it cite laws of nature to explain how these winds demolished buildings. Seeing the incident as a type of windstorm that blows down things along a narrow path is not at all the same as discovering that it exemplifies a causal regularity, namely, the regularity of strong winds bringing about a sudden and extreme reduction of air pressure within a small region, which in turn causes structures within that region to fly apart. An essential explanation of a particular tornado is therefore quite independent of a causal explanation of the tornado and its effects. To be sure, both forms of explanation may be infelicitous. You might say something false – or incoherent, vague and incomplete – when you specify how a storm was brought about; and you might be mistaken in similar ways when you explain the puzzling characteristics of the storm. Moreover, this example, and others we shall give from the arena of human action, should make it clear that an essential explanation is not just a trivial matter of replacing one description of an event by a synonym or a dictionary equivalent. Such accounts of an individual occurrence are designed to inform you of the characteristic it has which qualify it as the sort of event it is.

Is there anything common to both essential and causal explanations? Professor Donald Davidson has suggested to us that both explain by 're-describing'. An essential account of an occurrence furnishes a new description of it in terms of its properties that make it a certain kind of event, and a causal account re-describes it as having resulted from such-an-such antecedent happenings or standing conditions.

We are more intrigued with dissimilarities between causal and essential explanation. Suppose you grant these differences, and you admit that essential accounts are not merely lexical. You might still ask why causal explanation has bulked so large, often hiding its congener. With regard to non-human events at least, the answer is that careful observers, who have a good command of their native language, hardly ever need essential accounts of things that go on around them. For an inhabitant of the American Midwest, there is no question about what made some event a tornado; instead, he would like to know what made it occur, and how it brought about damage, so that he and others could predict similar storms in the future, and take protective measures.

Essential explanation assumes more importance when we turn to human goings-on. We are often baffled precisely because we lack an essential account of someone's performance; and it would not ease our bafflement to find out what produced his behaviour. Travellers in exotic countries experience this puzzlement from time to time. In the hills of Kabylia, for instance, you notice a group of Bedouins who calmly play flutes, tap drums and smoke their pipes while a boy gyrates about, periodically stabbing himself in the legs and arms. What is up? Is he berserk? Are the bystanders allowing him to commit suicide? Nothing of the sort. An essential explanation would be that you are witnessing a religious ritual, part of a forbidden animistic cult; the youth is performing a sacred dance. You might want to hear other salient details of the cult and this ceremony. And once you have this essential explanation of the behaviour you witnessed, you might also inquire about causes. What made the participants engage in the ritual at this particular time? What historical events and conditions produced this cult in the first place? But, as we already saw, the causal explanations you would get in reply are entirely distinct from the original specification you received of what was going on, and what made it the sort of event it was.

So much for our distinction. What bearing does it have upon the philosophical wrangle about explaining human behaviour

76

which we intend to resolve? Before we demonstrate how our distinction will advance a compromise, we must briefly examine one element of the dispute. The source of controversy that interests us is the familiar fact that any item of human behaviour, such as the Bedouin ceremony recorded above, may be described in a variety of idioms. Worse than that, the terms we can choose from may belong to quite different systems of discourse. For instance, we could use physiological terms, the jargon of anthropology or psychoanalysis, and either mentalistic or rigidly behavioural language of ordinary life. These alternative vocabularies at our disposal may not be intertranslatable. A true report of the incident in one of these idioms will not be synonymous with true reports of it in others. And this creates trouble when we get around to explaining the behaviour we observed. Characterized in one set of terms, the behaviour is made intelligible by further statements in the same idiom. But it becomes no more intelligible than before when the description of it is accompanied by statements in another terminology.

How has needless controversy about explanation developed, and particularly about the supposed incompatibility of causal and non-causal explanation? Because, it would seem, many philosophers have mis-diagnosed the situation. They have imagined a thorough-going incompatibility between causal explanation and the other things we find worth saying about human behaviour. We find a mere incongruity between expressions ordinary folk use to report the behaviour, and expressions we can take from other systems of discourse when we attempt to explain the behaviour.

Here is an illustration of how multiple descriptions for the same item of behaviour create headaches. The illustration also shows, we hope, why the standard philosophical diagnosis of the distress cannot be correct. The scene of action is a Florida beach. We notice several holidaymakers basking in the sun: others are afloat in the surf; and a lifeguard is on top of his watchtower. So far we have seen nothing worth dignifying with the name of action. Then a bather goes under, and action begins. We report faithfully that the lifeguard dashes into the water and hauls the bather to safety. So far, our rudimentary narrative is in the everyday language of gross material objects, human agents and their activities. But you could report the very same incident without these terms. You might single out the same event, and enable your listeners to identify it for purposes of further discussion and investigation, if you limited yourself to the vocabulary of physics and physiology. For instance, you might record the geographical location and the posture of certain organisms, the condition of their bones and muscles, the operation of their nervous systems, and the various changes of position, posture, neural activity, and so on, that ensued over this particular stretch of time. An attentive listener could then pinpoint the event you referred to. He would be able to visit the scene and gather more information about the episode, even though you had not uttered words like 'bathing beach', 'lifeguard', 'swimmer in danger' and 'rescue'.

What would an essential explanation of the incident sound like? That depends upon the description of it that you begin with, and upon your interest in it. If you were a physiologist, no doubt you would start with a report of some bodily motions, and you would demand more details about them, so that it would become clear to you exactly what sorts of bodily processes took place. If you were a newspaper reporter, a lawyer or a sociologist, you would not be satisfied if an eyewitness gave his testimony in physiological terms. Even if you knew physiology, you would want quite a different essential account of the episode. You would want to hear about its legal, social, moral and emotional aspects.

Suppose you begin with this report: 'A swimmer was in danger of drowning, and the lifeguard on duty rescued him.' According to your purposes and your antecedent knowledge, an essential explanation of the event, so described, would provide answers to questions from one or more of the following groups:

1 Questions about the lifeguard:
   a What is it to be a lifeguard?
   b What tests does one pass to be a lifeguard?
   c What does a lifeguard have to do with people who are swimming at the beach where he is stationed?
   d What is it to have the duty of saving people?
   e By means of what institutions do governments protect people from harm?

78

2 Questions about the bather :
  a What is it to be on holiday?
  b What is it to have the right to be protected from drowning?
  c What is drowning?
  d By what standards do we judge that a person is in danger of some harm, such as drowning?
  e Had the bather himself neglected to take some customary precautions against drowning?
3 Questions about the action :
  a What makes the event an act by one of the participants in the event?
  b With regard to the action thereby selected, i.e. the lifeguard's performance, what features of it make it the specific action of rescuing?

Depending upon your ignorance of the society in which this incident took place, these and similar inquiries would be worth pursuing. Only (2*c*) could be answered satisfactorily by a witness who limited himself to the terms of physiology. All the other questions in groups (1) and (2) call for essential explanations of normative features of the incident. The notions of being a lifeguard, being stationed somewhere, having an obligation towards people, government, danger, harm, safety and precautions, are normative notions in the straightforward sense that they only apply to things when there is a society with various types of norms. If a number of men are not members of any social group, then it is impossible that one of them should be a lifeguard, an employee of the municipal government, and responsible for the others' safety on a particular beach; nor could another of them neglect safety measures and risk drowning. These relationships, and the lifeguard's action of carrying out his duty, require a setting of laws, customs, authority, and participation in common activities such as holiday-making. It would be mad, therefore, to demand from physiology an essential explanation for these aspects of the incident. It follows that a causal explanation, in physiological terms, of the various bodily motions that took place during the rescue will never elucidate its normative features.

But our sketch of an essential explanation shows a lot more

than a clash between (i) causal explanation of bodily processes, and (ii) essential explanation of the actions that comprised these bodily processes. In fact, these forms of explanation are not really incompatible. How could they be, since they are both correct explanations of the same event? Explanation (i) will not do the same job as (ii), and conversely. But who expects them to replace each other? The point is that while (i) and (ii) are both explanations of the same episode, each accounts for different features of it, and in a very dissimilar manner. There would be just as much of a clash, and just as little, between *either* (i) *or* (ii) and (iii), an essential explanation for the bodily processes which figured in the rescue – namely, a physiological account of what sorts of processes these were – as we found *between* (i) and (ii).

This last consequence deserves elaboration. Presumably the bodily processes that occur during the rescue are not human actions. But they resemble actions inasmuch as they may be reported in a variety of idioms, and these reports are not interchangeable. A physiological description of a bodily process is not synonymous with a description of the same process in everyday non-technical language. Furthermore, explaining how the process was brought about is not the same as identifying what sort of process it is. So even when we are dealing with events that are not actions, such as bodily processes, it is also true that a causal explanation will not replace an essential explanation of them, and that a particular essential explanation is suitable only when the event has been described in the same family of terms as the explanation. Thus it is not a peculiarity of actions that essential and causal explanations for them will never stand in for each other. Moreover, the peculiarity is not just that we are unable to substitute a causal for an essential account of an action or a bodily movement. Essential explanations that are stated in mutually exclusive idioms are just as unsuited to replace each other. For example, if you want to know what gross bodily movements took place during the rescue, and you have no interest in physiological minutiae, then an essential explanation in physiological terms would be useless to you.

Returning now to the topic of action, how does this long-winded story of the rescue help reconcile philosophers who disagree about the possibility of causal explanations for what a person does? All disputants seem to believe that a physiologist could give us a causal explanation of the bodily movements that go into actions like the rescue. Our illustration shows that the physiologist would not thereby give us any kind of explanation – causal or essential – for the normative features of the very same event. However, we also outlined an essential explanation which brings these normative features into relief. Finally, the example proves that the essential explanation we sketched is perfectly compatible with the physiologist's causal account of non-normative elements, and also compatible with any essential explanation he might propound for these non-normative elements.

For that matter our story illustrates why an essential account of the normative features of the rescue cannot block a causal explanation of these very same features. Naturally you would not substitute the causal account for an essential explanation; for you must understand what the social and institutional background of the rescue is before you explain what caused the background to develop as it did. And presumably such a causal account of the norms that enter into the lifeguard's performance will not be restricted to the official vocabulary of physiology. But otherwise, why rule out causal explanation of these elements *a priori*? Do not historians, anthropologists, sociologists and political scientists already offer some causal accounts of norms? An explanation does not have to be complete and unalterable; it ought merely to provide some fresh insights into the social conventions that you are studying.

So far we have not examined actions that are unconnected with social institutions. Can we also demonstrate that they are amenable to both causal and essential explanation? For convenience, we shall resume our story of the rescue, except that we shall now delete the normative background that has been the focus of our essential explanation of the incident. At present, that is, we shall forget the rescuer's job, his qualifications, his duties, and accepted standard of safety and danger. Is anything left over when we suppress these factors? Can we call our protagonist a rescuer any more, and his performance a rescue? Yes, if we paint in some fresh background, which is free of institutional overtones. Our story will be amended as follows. Our protagonist is not a lifeguard any more; he is a noble savage, uncontaminated by society. He comes upon a beach, notices another noble savage drowning, and pulls him to shore. This still sounds like an action – a rescue, in fact – although it is plainly *not* a case of someone carrying out his official duties, keeping others out of danger, or performing a feat of heroism over and above the call of duty.

An essential explanation of the occurrence would have to deal with the inquiries of the type we listed in group (3) above. It would thus settle two questions: (3a) Why does the episode count as an action by the rustic rescuer, instead of being either the action of some other participant, such as the drowning man, or else not an action at all, but possibly something that happened to one or more of the participants? (3b) What marks the incident as the specific act of rescuing?

At this juncture, reasons and particularly desires move to the centre of the stage. We could propose either of two mutually compatible essential accounts which provide at least logically necessary conditions:

($3a_1$) The episode is an action because it is under the rescuer's control; more vaguely, it conforms to his desires at the time;

($3a_2$) The episode is an action by our unpolished protagonist because it is caused by his desires and beliefs.

Then we would go on to explain, (3b), that the event counts as the specific act of rescuing because the protagonist's chief desire was to remove the other man from the waters in which he was visibly drowning. But how about alternative ($3a_2$)? Why do we declare in our essential explanation of this particular deed that it was brought about by the agent's conative attitude?

Perhaps we should formulate the challenge more precisely: Why does an event rank as an action when it comprises motions of the rescuer's body which resulted from his desires and beliefs? We put it this way because you might hold that the desires and beliefs on which a person acts are part – integral components – of the total event which is his action. Motions of his body would be further elements. However that may be, we admit that we are presently unable to set out a causal account of the kind that is required to clinch answer ($3a_2$). We have not yet heard from scientists *how* a man's desire and belief might produce motions of his body. We lack relevant details and causal laws, of the type scientists present when they explain how flashes of light make

one blink. Nevertheless, until this causal hypothesis is either filled
out or refuted, we suggest this sort of connection between desire
and deed, because otherwise the link will remain baffling. The
most persuasive backing for this essential account of the relation
between desire and deed appears in Donald Davidson's important
essay, 'Actions, Reasons and Causes'. Davidson writes :

> 'A person can have a reason for an action, and perform the
> action, and yet this reason not be the reason why he did it.
> Central to the relation between a reason and an action it
> explains is the idea that the agent performed the action *because*
> he had the reason ([34], p. 691).
>
> If, as Melden claims, causal explanations are "wholly
> irrelevant to the understanding we seek" of human actions,
> then we are without an analysis of the "because" in "He did
> it because . . .", where we go on to name a reason. Hampshire
> remarks, of the relation between reasons and action, "In
> philosophy one ought surely to find this connection altogether
> mysterious" . . . Hampshire rejects Aristotle's attempt to solve
> the mystery by introducing the concept of wanting as a causal
> factor. . . . Failing a satisfying alternative, the best argument
> for a scheme like Aristotle's is that it alone promises to give
> an account of the "mysterious connection" between reasons
> and actions [34], p. 693).
>
> One way we can explain an event is by placing it in the con-
> text of its cause; cause and effect form the sort of pattern that
> explains the effect, in a sense of "explain" that we understand
> as well as any. If reason and action illustrate a different pattern
> of explanation, that pattern must be identified' ([34], p. 692).

Yet is it not question-begging to incorporate into our essential
explanation of a deed the provision that the deed resulted from
reasons the agent had for acting? One question which may be
begged is whether the *only* unproblematic account we can have
of the connection is causal. At any rate, notice once more that
even if we incorporate the causal link, we have not yet furnished
the causal explanation itself of *how* reasons produce deeds – or
the bodily motions which figure in what people do. Whether
desires and beliefs are ghostly, non-physical goings on, or whether
they are cerebral processes, they have not been identified. And

neither introspectionists nor neurophysiologists have formulated general laws which specify the circumstances under which desire and belief are followed by intentional action that is directed toward the same goal as the initiating desire. We are assuming, with Hempel [56], that a causal account of an occurrence must contain true law-like generalizations which delineate the conditions under which similar occurrences are always observed. In the absence of such generalizations, all you can do is report the antecedent event or condition that is a cause of a particular action. But naming causes is a far cry from providing causal explanations.

We have strayed from our provision, in part $(3a_2)$, of our essential account of the rescue, that the unlettered rescuer's desire caused this event. All we want to argue is that this method of making him the author of the incident, and thus making it his action, is free of serious obscurities and inconsistencies. A parallel case, from outside the sphere of human action, will demonstrate why there is no absurdity in this procedure which we have adopted from Davidson. The parallel case is the event of a person's skin becoming suntanned. An essential explanation of this tanning process would specify, *inter alia*, that the process results from exposure of one's skin to sunlight. That is what it is to get a suntan. The condition of one's epidermis would not be a suntan if it were the effect of something else or if it were spontaneous. An 'artificial suntan', resulting from application of a lotion, or from exposure to an ultra-violet lamp, is no more a suntan than synthetic diamonds are diamonds. And furthermore, this essential explanation of someone's suntan is not a causal explanation of how the sun's rays brought about changes in the pigmentation of his skin.

If you accept our latest distinction, between making causality a part of your essential explanation for some event, and formulating the causal explanation of the event, then it does not matter that we are presently unable to explain how a man's reasons or desires might cause him to act. For we have shown the compatibility between essential and causal explanation of a person's behaviour, in terms of the very same factors, his reasons or desires.

Shall we leave the argument at this stage? It is not enough to notice the foregoing connection between essential and causal accounts of someone's deed. We should point out that essential explanations are quite trivial if they only inform us:

($3a_2$) that a particular incident was so-and-so's action because it resulted from the reasons he had for acting; and

($3b$) that the incident was the specific act of Xing because so-and-so's desire was to X and he knew that he was Xing.

What should be added to an essential account? The other things worth saying will also concern the agent's reasons, but they will not concern only the causal relation between his reasons and his deed. A final look at our untutored rescuer will clarify this. A more helpful thing to say about the man's desire would be that it is by reference to his desire that the native himself understands his behaviour. Moreover, his view of what he did, as defined by his desire, has a special primacy for other people who report his action. In other words, the native's performance fulfils a purpose or intention that he would acknowledge as his own. He would describe what he was up to in terms of this purpose or intention, if he had occasion to be candid with us. Furthermore, it is this description of his behaviour, the one he is disposed to give when he is open and truthful, which makes what he did the type of act it is, rather than some different type. For instance, if we are unsure how to characterize his performance of removing the other fellow from the surf, we would ask about his reasons. Was one of his reasons for hauling the swimmer from the water that he wanted to kill the man himself? Was it his plan to cook the wretch for dinner that evening? Did he expect that the fellow would give him something valuable? If so, then he did not exactly rescue the swimmer.

The agent's candid description of what he did, in terms of his reasons, is particularly indispensable when his performance appears to be marred in some way. How could you prove, for example, that he *failed* to get the other man out of the water, unless you establish that he wanted to get him out? If there was some error on the native's part – if, for instance, the man he removed from the water was not drowning after all – then this false belief, which was among the native's reasons for acting, must be mentioned. It is in this sense that the agent's own description of his deed and his reasons is so crucial. If we describe the native's behaviour as an act of rescuing a stricken bather, we assume that this is how he would report it if he were sincere. And if his report were at odds with ours, we would have to withdraw ours, or bring it into line with what we have discovered regarding his desires and beliefs.

These remarks about the primacy of an agent's own description of his deed, in terms of his reasons for acting, must sound woefully incomplete. What counts for our argument, however, is that when you report someone's behaviour as you think he understands it, the explanation you furnish is an essential rather than a causal one. The pair of events you are concerned with, his reasons and his deed, may be causally related. But even if your essential explanation of his deed specifies that they are, it does not qualify as a causal explanation of his deed, since it fails to set forth the law-like causal pattern to which these events conform. Why does the essential explanation you derive from the agent's avowals fall short of a causal account? No doubt he too is ignorant of the causal uniformities which this case exhibits. The descriptions under which he reports his act and its cause probably do not appear in any accepted or plausible law-like generalization. His action and the event he is reporting when he announces his reasons may have to be reported in different terms, perhaps from another system of discourse, before the result and these antecedents can figure in a causal explanation of what he did. Yet even if you must deploy the jargon or neurophysiology in order to give a detailed account of how his reasons caused his body to move, they remain causal factors.

Philosophical opponents of causality are vindicated to a large extent by our conclusions. They were wrong in supposing that if a particular event is a human action, it is exempt from causal explanation. But they were right in maintaining that other non-causal forms of explanation are indispensable for our understanding of what people do. They were right in saying that when a man discloses his reasons for acting, he does not provide a causal explanation of his need. We add, however, that the agent may still have reported things which are causes of his action, although the assertion that they are causes is a relatively unimportant part of the essential explanation of what he did.

IV

SOME PUZZLES ABOUT EFFORT

ORIGINALLY CO-AUTHORED BY SUZANNE MCCORMICK

The notion of control was prominent in the analyses of what it is to act which were given in Essays I and II. Essay III dealt at length with the specific control notion of having reasons for acting. Now we should focus on another specific aspect of control, which also has firm conceptual ties with reasons for action.

A theory of action must have a lot to say about human endeavours. You could hardly analyse most of the things people do without mentioning their successful and unsuccessful efforts. Mental states, such as a person's desires and decisions, also find expression in his attempts. And turning again to the controversial topic of the self-knowledge one is supposed to have without benefit of evidence and observation, there is no better example than one's knowledge of what one is trying to do.

Although trying is such an important action-concept, little attention has been directed to it, because it has appeared to be philosophically trouble-free. After all, isn't trying simply exerting yourself – mentally or physically – as a means of bringing about some result you want? And just as you can think of anything under the sun, can you not try to do anything under the sun? Both of these natural views of trying come up repeatedly in such excellent books as *Thought and Action*, by Stuart Hampshire ([48], pp. 107–13, 134, 170–87). A characteristically terse statement of the 'no limits' view is given by Kurt Baier in an abstract, "Acting and Producing" [15]. He writes: 'I doubt whether there are any species of action in which it is impossible to distinguish between on the one hand the attempt and on the other success and failure.'

Plausible as they sound, these and other connected doctrines about trying call forth a swarm of minor but challenging problems. To begin with the cause-effect model of endeavour: there are at least three more relevant species of trying besides the

87

perennially bewitching causal, or means-end, pattern. We shall not take time to belabour the suggestion that trying is merely bracing yourself inwardly, while manifesting your subcutaneous movements through your behaviour. Richard Taylor's book, *Action and Purpose* [114], thoroughly refutes this 'internal non-physical cause' theory. Still, the mentalistic interpretation of trying raises genuine problems. Is trying only overt bodily behaviour? Without worrying about mind-body dualism, one can also ask whether a man's attempt is anything more than the event of his having certain intentions and beliefs. In jurisprudence, according to Herbert Morris ([86], pp. 354-6), many serious writers hold this view, and so conclude that 'the sole purpose for requiring conduct in the law of attempts is to establish *mens rea*' or criminal intent.

As for the natural assumption that you can try to do anything, a random survey will indicate that there are unsuspected limits. For instance, it sounds absurd to describe a person as attempting to choke, to misplace something, to feel pain, to regret, to become annoyed or discouraged, to have a particular motive, to know or believe something. The problem is: why are these events beyond the range of trying? Perhaps, as Wittgenstein suggests in a famous passage ([121], Part I, Sections 622-3), most of our everyday activity is incompatible with trying. Wittgenstein declares: 'When I raise my arm I do not usually try to raise it.' Then, discussing the statement, 'At all costs I will get to that house', he remarks: 'But if there is no difficulty about it – *can* I try at all costs to get to the house?'

A tussle with these and similar questions should deepen our understanding of trying and its conceptual ancestor, action. A good starting-point would be a short catalogue of the relevant meanings of the verb 'try'.

1. *Species of Trying*

In order to illuminate the concept of agency, we should focus on situations where we say that a person is trying to do something, or trying more or less vigorously, in the course of accomplishing some task. Thus we can neglect the senses of 'try' in which a judge tries a law-breaker, an experimenter tries out vaccines, a gourmet tries a sauce, a shopper tries on hats, a gambler tries his luck at baccara, or a child tries one's patience. In the remaining cases that we must analyse, a striking feature is the agent's overt activity. One exception will be discussed later : the case of a man who is totally paralysed below the neck. He may justifiably assert that he is attempting to wiggle his toes, although no visible behaviour reveals his attempt. Otherwise we see that ordinary specimens of trying may be grouped according to the behaviour they comprise. This method of grouping is perfectly compatible with the assumption that all types of trying share certain non-behavioural characteristics. And since a person's activity on some occasion might exemplify more than one type of trying behaviour, our categories will overlap. Bearing these complications in mind, we may profitably distinguish four senses of the verb 'try', or kinds of trying :

(a) Exertion, the least interesting category. A man who executes some feat with a striking display of energy and concentration is said, in this sense, to be trying hard – perhaps 'trying too hard', as when an acrobat's laboured style mars his performance. If he does his stunts effortlessly, he is said not to be trying at all.

(b) Causal trying. This paradigmatic use of try and attempt occurs when we discuss what people do – with or without exertion – in order to bring about more or less distant results. Thus as you mail a bomb to your worst enemy, you might confide, 'I am attempting to blow him to pieces'. Since the explosion is many days off, and may not scathe your foe when it occurs, you would be over-sanguine to assert that you are presently blowing him to pieces. Although your contribution to the crime is over when you dispatch the explosives, you cannot say, 'I have blown him to shreds' until later. The causal link between your contribution and the subsequent blast may be described in various ways : 'By sending him a bomb, I blew him to pieces'; 'I caused his death (caused him to die) by sending him a bomb', and so forth. But it would be puzzling to talk as if there were a causal relation between two successive actions of yours, and say, 'By sending him a bomb, I caused myself to (or made myself) blow him to shreds'. There is not a pair of actions here. Rather, your dispatching the bomb is the first link in the chain that eventually includes a fatal blast. If we wish to emphasize your *modus operandi*, we say that mailing the bomb was your action, the blast its effect;

if we wish to underscore your responsibility for the tragedy, we say that your action was blowing your enemy to shreds, and that you did this by mailing him dynamite.

(c) Initiatory trying. Here no spatial or temporal crevasse divides attempt from accomplishment, as in causal undertakings. If a hiker succeeds in his attempt to scale a precipice, reaching the summit is a *terminus*, rather than an effect, of his climbing. Bruises, fatigue or exhilaration would be effects of his attempt. Another way to make this distinction is to note that if the mountaineer has not scaled the cliff by the time his contribution to the attempt is over, he cannot succeed *in* his attempt. What if he stops trying, but a sudden gale carries him the rest of the way? Despite his extraordinary luck, he cannot brag that he reached the summit through his efforts. His endeavour failed, but he got there just the same. In causal attempts, however, it is precisely the events that intervene between the agent's contribution and the end-result that explain how his activity brought about the effect he desired.

(d) Procedural trying. This sense of the verb is prominent when we relate the activity of people who carry out the prescribed routines one must follow in order to lease an apartment, qualify as a commercial pilot, marry, or perform any other conventional operation. These operations, and the procedures by which one accomplishes them, are conventional because they must occur within a setting of custom, authority, rank, ceremonies and regulations. How does this feature single out procedural trying? With causal trying, the means we use to produce effects gain acceptance because they have already worked, or shown promise of working; whereas procedures cannot possibly work – as procedures for leasing land or marrying – unless they are already accepted by a community. The same contrast holds between initiatory and procedural endeavours. It is inconceivable that a man should succeed in an attempt to qualify as a commercial aviator, while refusing to go through established procedures. Another, but less significant, peculiarity of procedural trying is that, in *some* cases, correctly going through all the formalities guarantees success. For instance, if you do everything one normally does in trying to register an automobile – fill out applications, submit documents and procure a certificate of registration – then you have registered your car.

90

Yet no matter how flawlessly and conscientiously you execute a causal or initiatory attempt, the attempt could miscarry.

2. Requirements of Trying: Environmental and Epistemic

Now we should turn to Wittgenstein's illustrations, quoted above. They reveal an obvious requirement for exertion trying. How could you strain in lifting your arm when you are in a normal, unhindered condition? Something must hamper you. The hindrance would be external if you are holding an immense bar-bell that makes you toil as you raise your arms above your head. Perhaps the impediment is inside you. You might have a painful stiffness that makes you struggle to move your arm. Wittgenstein's second example reiterates this point for more complex initiatory attempts with exertion. Unless there is some obstacle – a snowdrift, a pack of wolves – between a man and the house he is trying to reach, nothing he does will distinguish a listless from an all-out attempt to get there. The impediment may be psychological : some unwarranted fear that he must overcome. If the path is clear, and his mind as well, is he prevented from forging ahead 'at all costs'? It is more accurate to say : a necessary condition for intelligible talk of exertion is that a hindrance should be present.

Closely allied to this condition is an epistemic requirement for meaningful discourse about causal, initiatory and procedural trying. When an agent acts with the intention of accomplishing some task (call it 'Xing' for short), there must be some doubt that he will manage to X, before we can talk of his attempt to X. More precisely : we say that a person is trying, or will try, to X, when we think he may be unable to X. Normally, our reason for doubt is that we have some obstacle in mind, which may prevent him from Xing – and not merely force him to exert himself in Xing. But we may be uncertain without having any stumbling-block in view. Xing might be a long-range project; who knows what will turn up, or whether the agent will carry it through?

Besides suggesting the likelihood of failure, rather than the necessity of struggle by the agent, this epistemic requirement differs in another significant way from the obstacle requirement for exertion. The epistemic criterion is asymmetrical with regard to tenses of the verb 'try'. A procedural illustration will clarify this.

It was certain, as far as anyone could tell, that Green would purchase a ticket for the opera when he set out to do so yesterday morning. Tickets were plentiful, Green had funds, and he arrived at the box office as it opened. With no reason to expect failure, we would *not* have said, 'Now Green is trying (or will try) to purchase a ticket,' but 'He is purchasing (or will purchase) one.' Yet at the moment the cashier was handing him a ticket, and Green was giving her the appropriate number of notes and coins, a gunman appeared, and absconded with all the money and tickets. Green was not attempting to buy a ticket, but since he did not complete the transaction, he attempted to buy a ticket. In other words, talk of *past* attempts does not presume that there *was* any doubt that the agent could carry out his intention.

3. *The Incompleteness Criterion*

This last example suggests another criterion of causal, initiatory and procedural trying, as well as a different analysis of Wittgenstein's remark, 'When I raise my arm I usually do not *try* to raise it.' The criterion is : we can only speak of an agent 'trying to X', in the causal, initiatory or procedural sense, when the agent can do something short of Xing, by way of attempting to X. It should be possible to describe what the agent does as 'trying but failing to X'. When Green started to purchase a ticket, and the transaction was interrupted by the gunman, what Green did fell short of a purchase, although it was an appropriate first step toward that end. But when your arm is in a healthy, unhindered condition, you cannot do anything less than move it; there is no room for any prefatory deed which qualifies as 'what you do *first* in order to move your arm'. For what would you do by way of a causal attempt to make your arm move, or an initiatory attempt to inaugurate its motion? If you grit your teeth or squint, that would not be relevant enough to moving your arm, and will not constitute 'what you do first'.

Is it impossible for an unencumbered person to try moving his arm because he has 'direct' control of his limbs? As far as trying is concerned, this power is irrelevant. It does not matter how you happen to move your arm; what matters for trying is that it should be possible for you to do something of which we could say, 'You tried but failed.' We can illustrate this point by considering an activity which does not exemplify the sort of direct control one has over one's gestures: the activity of pretending. Pretending is vastly more complicated than moving your limbs; it often requires special talents and training, which are wholly unnecessary for moving your limbs; yet trying to pretend is even more absurd than trying to move your limbs. Under no circumstances could you attempt to pretend, in the causal, initiatory or procedural sense of 'try'; whereas you could try to move your arm if it were 'asleep' or tied up.

An objector might describe the following as an attempt to pretend. On a dare, Brown agreed to visit a near-by housewife, and pretend that he is a debt-collector. If nobody is at home when he drops by, is he attempting to pretend? No : Brown only attempted to call upon the woman, with the ultimate aim of pretending; but he did not try to pretend. Well, assume that Brown meets her. His disguise is inadequate and he threatens her half-heartedly. Is that trying but failing to pretend? It sounds like pretending, but unsuccessfully. Brown's failure *in* pretending is not a failure to pretend, but a failure to *deceive* the housewife, perhaps due to his lack of skill. A final possibility is that he calls on the woman, but does not bother to disguise himself, to menace the woman about her unpaid bills, or to do anything else with the purpose of portraying a debt-collector at work. Here he failed to pretend, but what will you count as his attempt to pretend? To say that Brown failed to pretend is merely to say that he *did not* pretend; it is hardly to say that he tried unsuccessfully to pretend. Thus it seems that any deed of Brown that you nominate as an instance of 'trying but failing to pretend' will be either an attempt to put himself in a position where he can pretend, or else it will be a case of incompetent pretending.

Admittedly these claims do not hold good for a closely related activity – 'pretending to oneself' or 'making believe'. But this disparity serves to reinforce the incompleteness criterion we are examining. Brown can attempt to make believe just because it is possible for him to do something which falls short of making believe, so that what he does will qualify as an unsuccessful attempt. He might take Baudelaire's advice, and eat hashish so that he can make believe that he is a god. If the dosage is too weak, and he does not undergo the illusion he sought, he has tried, vainly, to make believe.

These remarks hardly give a complete account of pretending and making believe. Most of the nuances have been captured already in the symposium 'Pretending', between J. L. Austin and G. E. M. Anscombe [12, 2]. However, one of Austin's examples must be mentioned here, because it appears to refute our thesis that you cannot try to pretend. He supposes that during a party you are challenged to pretend to be a hyena. 'You proceed to jump around powerfully on your hind legs, boxing with your fists and fondling something in your pocket,' says Austin. 'You are meaning or trying to pretend to be a hyena, but actually behaving like a kangaroo : this is the correct and the shortest accurate way of describing the situation. There is no short answer to the question "Is he pretending to be a hyena or isn't he?" ' Now if we assume, with Austin, that you *meant* to pretend to be a hyena, we must conclude that you were indeed pretending, although your gestures were singularly inappropriate. Consequently you were not trying to pretend. If Austin cannot give the short answer that you were *not* pretending to be a hyena, how will he maintain that you were only trying? ([12], pp. 213–15).

It would be interesting to digress further, and ask why a person cannot try to engage in activities like pretending. Here is a conjecture : pretending is already a form of trying – trying to dissimulate, to mimic, to deceive, according to the circumstances; and the notion of 'trying to try' is surely incoherent.

4. *Trying to Try*

Suppose, for the moment, that pretending is a form of trying. Would that make an attempt to pretend impossible? Perhaps the absurdity of 'trying to try' is merely verbal, due to stylistic inelegance. If so, then we should be able to specify a context where it would be intelligible to state that a person tried to try. Here is a promising situation : Grey is driving to a department store to be interviewed for a job. He is going there in order to try to get the job. While driving along, he has a puncture. As he struggles with the tyre, he explains to a passer-by, 'I am trying to try to get a job.' Isn't this statement elliptical, however, for 'I am trying to change this tyre so that I can (put myself in a position to) try to get a job'? If this analysis of Grey's statement is correct, we do not have an attempt to try to X, but an instance of 'trying to W with the ultimate purpose of trying to X'. The ellipsis is more glaring if we suppose that Grey is fortunate in his attempt to change the tyre, and then he heads for the nearest billiard-hall, instead of going on to the store. By successfully trying to try to get the job, has Grey tried to get the job? In this story, the answer is far from obvious. Yet ordinarily, when a person successfully attempts to do something, he does what he was attempting to do.

Here an objector might rejoin: Wasn't Grey trying to get the job from the moment he set out for the interview? Driving, as well as grappling with the tyre, on this interpretation, would be 'early stages' of Grey's attempt to get the job. So even if he loses interest after replacing the flat tyre, he has tried to get the job. This analysis refutes the charge of ellipsis against the notion of 'trying to try', but creates deeper troubles for it. On the 'early stage' view of Grey's efforts with the tyre, it is pointlessly redundant to call this an *attempt to* attempt to get the job, for Grey is already trying to get the job. In fact, this locution may be more than pleonastic; it may lead to self-contradiction. The reason is that in standard attempts to X, the agent does not X until his attempt to X is successful. If it fails, he does not X at all. On the 'early stage' view of Grey's attempt to try to get the job, however, he is already Xing (= trying to get the job) before he has tried, successfully, to X (= try to get the job).

So much for the impossibility of trying to try. What remains speculative is the link between our earlier conclusion, (i) We cannot attempt to engage in certain activities, namely to pretend, because nothing we do will fall short of the activities themselves; and our present conclusion, (ii) Trying to try to do something, namely trying to try to deceive, is impossible. These claims are individually sound. However, we are not warranted yet in asserting, for example, that trying to pretend is impossible *because* pretending is already a form of trying. Other instances of the same pattern are easy to multiply. Groping for your garage key is trying to find it, and you cannot try to grope for it. Reaching for a drink is trying to get hold of it, and you cannot try to reach for a drink. Until we explain clearly the sense in which these and other activities are forms of trying, however, we are not entitled to a 'because'. We must be able to explain, for example, why it is more plausible to say that pretending is an attempt to deceive or imitate, rather than, for instance, an attempt to entertain or impress someone.

Instead of tackling these larger problems, we shall continue towards the more limited objectives we began with, of delineating the notion of trying, and thereby gaining some insights into the generic notion of agency. Before we digressed to show that a person cannot try to try to do anything, we examined the incompleteness criterion, which specifies that one can only attempt actions which one might not succeed in performing. This criterion has a significant 'opposite number' which will explain a few more of the difficult cases we noticed at the outset.

5. The Requirement of 'First Steps' in Trying

Why can't someone try to ache, to get furious, to have particular motives, intentions and beliefs, to know, to be mistaken? Intuitively speaking, a man whose goal is to experience aches, or any other sensations, should try to do something else first. Whereas there could not be any intermediate steps to take by way of trying to pretend or trying to move one's limbs, in the present case the agent seems to be omitting a preliminary step. If he wants an ache, he must try to do something that will bring about that kind of sensation; he might try running a mile.

Is the impossibility of attempting to experience aches and other sensations, without doing anything else first, due to the fact that sensations are 'mental' states or processes? No, because there are countless physical episodes that cannot be the object of a 'direct' attempt. Choking is a perfect illustration. A person might try to swallow a huge mouthful of food, so that he will choke; but in that case his attempt is directed toward a first step. He is attempting to make himself choke, a different story from attempting to choke.

You might reply to this by appealing to what was said in Essay II about the impossibility of trying to choke. There it was argued that the impossibility is merely contingent. Is it not conceivable, after all, that as a result of mutations, people should

96

acquire the same power to choke and to experience sensations that they now have over their elementary gestures? Without pausing to prove the cogency of this fiction, we must still deny that these people can try to choke and ache. The reason is different now. It is now precisely because these imaginary people have direct control over their choking and their sensations that we should deny that they can attempt these things. For they could not try unsuccessfully, any more than they can at present try to move their arms. So even if it makes perfect sense to imagine people choking and experiencing various sensations at will, it would not make sense to describe them as 'trying to choke' and 'trying to ache'.

With the other 'mental' states we listed along with aching, it sounds *prima facie* unintelligible to suppose either that people try to be in these states, or that they put themselves into such states at will. How would you try to be furious? Would a man's emotion be described as 'rage' if nothing made him angry? You simply cannot get angry in the direct way you get up from a chair. The necessity of 'first steps' is obvious : you cannot attempt to fly into a rage, but you might attempt to do something – read about or witness a shocking injustice – that will make you boil with anger. The same holds for motives and intentions. Suppose a man were questioned about his reasons for buying shares in the Poor Farmers' Co-operative. Would it make sense for him to reply, 'I tried to invest from profit-seeking motives alone, rather than from sentimental motives'? He might try to make a profit out of this investment; he might attempt to discover reasons for expecting that this venture will pay fat dividends; and of course he might try, in all his business activities, to be hard-headed. Nevertheless he could not attempt to have a particular reason for this purchase. With intentions, too, it is nonsense to speak of trying to have them. However, we may attempt to form them by doing something else first. If you have not yet planned your spring holiday, you might try to make up your mind by examining travel folders. With all these cases, incidentally, the incompleteness criterion, as well as the 'first steps' requirement, is satisfied. The measures a person takes in his attempt to procure various sensations, and to produce certain emotions, motives and intentions in himself, often fail to bring about the result he desired.

The would-be holiday-maker might become less certain where he should go, as a result of reading travel folders.

First steps are unavoidable when your efforts concern your own beliefs. With the possible exception of matters of religious faith, you can neither assent to propositions 'at will' nor attempt to believe them. It is part of our conception of belief that one's opinions are normally the upshot of preliminary activities such as observing, gathering information, sifting evidence, consulting experts, or perhaps having the truth revealed to one in mystical experience. Therefore all a person can try to do is to engage in these preliminary activities, with the purpose of arriving at a verdict on some issue. For similar reasons, one cannot attempt to know something, and the idea of 'knowing at will' is altogether incoherent. However, people do try to devise proofs and gather conclusive evidence for various propositions; and there is no oddity in saying that a person who tries to learn something, to make sure whether some proposition is true, or to remember something, is directing his efforts toward knowledge. Once again, the person's attempt will concern means, or 'first steps', rather than knowledge itself.

Can a person's endeavours be aimed, even indirectly, at error? It sounds very strange to say that a man attempted to have – or to take steps toward – a mistaken belief. How could he make an effort to think erroneously that he knows something? What would it be like to try to misremember? These are only trickier cases of the preceding type. If you suspect or know some proposition is false, evidently you cannot try to believe it. However, you might try to put yourself in situations where you will unwittingly accept, and perhaps think you know propositions which are in fact false. The most plausible cases would be situations where you cannot afford to suspend judgement, but you are aware that you risk assenting to falsehoods which you cannot detect at the time. This last feature does reveal a significant dissimilarity between 'indirect' endeavours towards false belief and ordinary attempts. When you try, successfully, to prove something, it is possible for you to say, 'Now I've done what I've been trying to do'; but you could not possibly take note of your 'success' in acquiring a mistaken belief.

Are there cases where circuitous attempts of all kinds are impossible? Generally speaking, any performance that involves a breakdown of will or awareness cannot be the object of an attempt. Trying to do something by accident, against your will, unintentionally, involuntarily, inadvertently, and so on, appears self-contradictory. If you attempt to place yourself in circumstances where people tend to break down in such ways, this attempt would entail a degree of awareness and purposiveness that is incompatible with the foregoing description of your resultant behaviour.

6. *Further Conditions of the Agent and his Environment*

Before we examine more closely the place of belief and intention in trying, we should take note of some additional criteria that apply to specific attempts. Procedural attempts, of course, require suitable conventions and rules. During the Dark Ages, nobody could set up a bank account for himself, or try to do so. A far-sighted person might have tried to establish a bank, and to make others accept the necessary rules, so that he could have a bank account – but that is a different undertaking.

In any event, rules are not always enough. For a particular agent to take advantage of the rules and engage in many procedural attempts, the agent himself must have official status. Until Tom secures a place in an Olympic team, nothing he does will rank as a victory, a defeat, or an attempt to win an Olympic medal. If Tom sneaks on to the field during the Olympic high jump, and leaps over the bar before he is taken into custody, he might believe that he is trying to win a medal, but this is surely a delusion. If his heart is set on Olympic fame, he can attempt to get into the team, so that he will then be in a position to try winning a medal. These undertakings are quite distinct, however; for he might attain his goal in one without beginning the other. Tom is fortunate in his attempt to get into the team, for example, but develops heart-murmur before he tries for a medal during an Olympic event.

In other cases, the agent may be debarred from trying because he lacks some minimal ability, rather than status. If a showoff has never studied Tibetan, and he is unable to pronounce Tibetan phrases from a dictionary, will anything he does qualify as 'trying to converse in Tibetan with a native speaker'? Should he

99

emit squawks and gurgles, all you can say is that he is attempting to sound as if he is conversing in Tibetan. At best the showoff can try to acquire a sufficient mastery of Tibetan, so that he will later be in a position to try conversing in it.

Often trying is impossible because the agent is literally not in a position to try. Suppose an adventurer is hundreds of miles from the ocean. Then he cannot attempt to dive for sunken treasure. He might get his equipment ready before leaving for the coast. But even if we include his inland preparations under the general rubric of an attempt to get rich by *finding* treasure, we cannot say that he is already trying to *dive* after treasure.

Paradoxically, there are other cases where an agent is in a position, the necessary rules are established, the agent has appropriate status and ability, but he still cannot try. Often the attempt is impossible unless the agent possesses certain instruments. For example, if a man is at the tennis court, knows how to play tennis, and so on, but has no racquet, he cannot try to play tennis. He might try to play or invent some new game, using his hand as an ersatz racquet; he might hang around the tennis courts all the morning in the hope of borrowing or filching a racquet. It would then be true to say that he tried to get into a game. But as long as he lacks the essential means for playing tennis, nothing he does will count as an attempt to play.

7. *Must the Objects of Trying Exist?*

In contrast to means that figure in an attempt, such as a tennis racquet, we might speak of the 'objects' toward which a man's endeavours are directed. When Ponce de Leon tried to locate the Fountain of Youth, the Fountain of Youth was the object of his undertaking; it was what he tried to discover during his explorations of Florida. From this example, it seems reasonable to say that, unlike the instruments that are sometimes essential, the object of any attempt need not exist. Must the agent believe that a suitable object exists? Pragmatically speaking, yes, for it would be a waste of energy to attempt to find the Fountain of Youth if you doubted that there was one. However, as long as Ponce de Leon made a conscientious search of Florida, keeping his eyes open for a spring with rejuvenative powers, he would be

100

attempting to discover the Fountain of Youth. He might declare, 'I doubt that there is such a Fountain, but I am trying to find it, on the odd chance that it does exist; after all, what can I lose?' A person's efforts, then, may be directed toward something he does not believe to exist.

Is this possible? The trouble here is that the agent cannot expect to do what he is trying to do, since the item he requires for success is presumed not to exist. Let us consider this larger problem: does an attempt to do something require either (a) that there should be some likelihood of success, or (b) that you believe you will do what you are trying to do?

8. *Trying and Expectation of Success*

Here is a fanciful but difficult case. At the end of August we notice a man on the beach who is performing unusual dances and intoning prayers. He asserts that he is thereby attempting to make the summer weather last throughout the autumn. Of course we doubt that his mummeries will influence meteorological phenomena, but do we want to say that he is trying? Assume, for simplicity, that this man is the only practitioner of these rituals; otherwise we could regard his antics as a procedural undertaking, with accredited but ineffective procedures. For a causal attempt, must there be some chance that the agent will do what he is trying to do?

Now suppose the man will not admit that his prayers and dances are ineffective. He might say, 'Little do you know,' jarring our already shaken confidence in the absolute number and nature of causal techniques. Yet if we concede, because of what he says, that he is engaged in a causal attempt, we forgo a useful distinction between trying and merely thinking one is trying.

We cannot disqualify this man's activities by any of the criteria we have considered thus far. There is doubt of success. What he does can fall short of making the summer weather last. He is not omitting any 'first steps'. He has the opportunity and ability to perform the dances and prayers that constitute his attempt. Still, there is something odd about his endeavour. Possibly we can explain the oddity, and also show why his activity nevertheless ranks as a genuine causal attempt, by introducing one more requirement for causal, as well as initiatory and procedural,

attempts : namely, that some sequel of his attempt would count
as success in his attempt.

9. *The Logical Possibility of Success*

This requirement for trying has two parts :

(i) We must be able to describe some outcome of the agent's
current behaviour as 'succeeding' or 'doing what he tried to do'.
Perhaps the outcome will not in fact occur; but the statement
depicting it cannot be self-contradictory, and must also be compatible with other statements that describe the agent, his activity
preceding the outcome, and relevant features of his surroundings,
as noted in sections 2, 3, 5 and 6 above. This provision reinforces
many of our previous verdicts. For example, it is not self-contradictory, nor inconsistent with any relevant statements about
Florida, that Ponce de Leon should come across a spring whose
waters restore his youthful appearance.

(ii) Another provision is that for a person's behaviour to qualify
as an attempt to do something, the outcome that would constitute success must be a success *in* his attempt. The preposition
'in' brings out the connection between what the agent does by
way of trying, and the happy sequel to what he does. We do
not want to describe coincidences as 'doing what he tried to do'.

Our difficult case satisfies both provisions. There is no absurdity
in supposing that unseasonably mild weather follows our protagonist's dances and prayers. Provision (ii) will be satisfied too,
but in a way that leaves us uneasy. How shall we show that the
unusual weather was anything more than a fluke, that is, that we
can count it as the man's success in his attempt? Unless he offers
a cogent theory about the effect of orisons and dances upon
meteorological phenomena, we are free to put down the subsequent weather to chance or quite extraneous causes. His ignorance, and ours, of how his actions brought about the atmospheric
irregularity deprives us of grounds for demonstrating that he
succeeded in his attempt. Nevertheless the claim that his
endeavours produced the unseasonable weather is neither falsified
nor emptied of meaning by our inability to demonstrate the connection between his mummeries and the weather. At least we
understand what it means for him to claim there is a causal
relationship here, even if we have no idea what it could be.

102

The present criterion of success in an attempt is useful for resolving the case of the totally paralysed man, which we took note of in section 1. The first half of the success criterion is met, because it is conceivable that his toes should wiggle a moment after he mutters, 'I'm trying to wiggle my toes.' The second half of the requirement is hard to fulfil, because there seems to be no activity we might identify as the attempt which led to success. Going back to the incompleteness criterion, neither can we find any activity to call his attempt, in case he fails to wiggle his toes. So whatever happens, we are disinclined to speak of an attempt, successful or futile. However, we cannot flatly reject his assertion that he is trying. How did the man make sure he still could not move his toes, except by trying? Is this not a test the physician might use to establish that the man remains paralysed? Either we demand an exception for this unique attempt, or else we speak of his mysterious 'concentration' upon his toes as his attempt; perhaps we conjure up even more elusive cerebral activities to fit the bill. At any event, we should not deny that an attempt occurred.

Now aside from the problems about the paralytic's attempt, there may be objections to our choice of the weak requirement, that success should be logically possible. Why not require that success is believed likely, by the agent and perhaps by others? Possibly belief is unnecessary, because of the fact, mentioned in the case of the paralytic, that trying and failing often serves as evidence that a man cannot perform some task. You might hesitate over this example, arguing that if the paralytic himself lacks confidence, or belief, in his ability to wiggle his toes, he doesn't really try. To get out of this impasse, let us shift to an uncontroversial example. John is convinced that the crystal of his watch is shatter-proof, that nothing can break it. Consequently he believes that he could not break it. He confirms his belief by trying to crush it and failing. This test would not be a confirmation of his belief unless he was really trying. A half-hearted attempt would be useless. Thus doubting that one can do something (smash the crystal) is compatible with an attempt to do it.

This same example will help us investigate a final point about trying.

10. *Must One Intend to Do What One Tries to Do?*

The example indicates a negative answer. Indeed, there is a sense in which we would *deny* that John intended to break the watch-crystal. This sense of 'intend' entails desire, and it is clear that John had no desire to shatter the crystal, although he desired to test it. Nevertheless, if he pounded the watch vigorously with a sledge-hammer, he both attempted and intended, in some other sense, to break the crystal. For if the glass disintegrated, would it not be true to say that John broke it intentionally? The unwanted outcome was within the scope of the intention he had in testing the watch. John pounded it in order to see if the crystal would shatter. The unwelcome result was one he considered possible, although it was not what he expected or desired to bring about.

This restricted type of intention fills out our sketch of trying. More about the relation between people's attempts, intentions and beliefs will be said in the following essay. For the present, we should briefly retrace the argument in terms of the generic concept of action.

11. *Trying and Doing*

We contended that before you can try hard in performing a task, something must impede you. That is, exertion in trying demands an obstacle. With causal, initiatory and procedural attempts, there must be some doubt that you will do what you are attempting to do. Normally you have some expectation of success, but total doubt seems logically compatible with trying. With regard to the activity that constitutes an attempt, it must be such that it could fall short of what you attempt to do. With some actions that one sets out to perform, trying is impossible, because whatever one did by way of an attempt would be the action itself. With other goals, one must direct one's efforts at something else first, as a means towards one's goal. We listed some miscellaneous requirements that give content to the notion of 'being in a position to try'. Among the circumstances we included rules, minimal capacities and instruments, when appropriate; but we denied that it was necessary for any objects of a man's attempts to exist. Finally, we concluded it need only be logically possible for you to do what you attempt to do.

V

CAN ONE INTEND THE IMPOSSIBLE?

This study will cover some of the ground that was surveyed in the preceding essay. In particular, sections 7–10, which were concerned with conceptual bonds between trying and intending, will again be helpful. Also the fuller analysis of other elements in an attempt will provide clarification and support for the cases I've devised here of people intending to reach a goal that they expect not to attain.

Since a number of excellent contemporary works have dealt with the general topic of intending, I shall narrow my sights. A manageable and interesting enigma about intention springs from the following kind of situation. I can aim to transform lead into gold, to make myself invisible, or to write down all the fractions between zero and one. That is, I can have all these schemes as long as I am ignorant that it is impossible for me to accomplish them. But when I recognize insuperable hindrances to my designs, can I still intend to carry them out? The verdict of one eminent writer who has noticed this problem is lucidly and emphatically unfavourable. Stuart Hampshire's opinion goes:

'To intend something to happen (as the result of my activity) is at least to believe that it may and could happen. It would be self-contradictory to say "I intend that to happen, but I am sure that it will not" or "I believe that it is impossible" ' ([48], p. 134).

Miss G. E. M. Anscombe takes the contrary view. She writes:

' "I am going to . . . unless I do not" is not like "This is the case, unless it isn't. . . ."

In some cases one can be as certain as possible that one will do something, and yet intend not to do it. . . . A man could be as certain as possible that he will break down under torture, and yet determined not to break down' ([1], p. 93).

With a view towards exploring the boundaries of intention, I shall argue for Miss Anscombe's position. I shall concentrate on two questions: (a) Is the notion of 'knowing it is impossible' clear enough to serve as a limiting case of 'intending'? (b) If a person can *try* to reach goals which he knows to be unattainable, why can he not intend to succeed in his attempts? For the purposes of the argument, I shall assume that men have undertaken, and do attempt, enterprises which they know to be hopeless. I have in mind a glorious array of desperate causes, from the Spartans at Thermopylae and Roland at Roncevaux, to the last-ditch resistance of the Warsaw Jews. If you wish an inglorious attempt, consider the French Army trying to quell the Algerian revolt from 1958 to 1962.

Before I defend my claim that there are actions, which the agent knows to be impossible, that he can intend – not just yearn or hope or wish – to perform, I want to restrict the discussion:

(1) I concede that a man cannot *promise* to attain results which he believes are beyond his powers. Consequently, the intentions with which I shall be concerned are not intentions for which one is entitled to give one's word.

(2) I shall neglect intentions to perform actions which the agent knows to be logically impossible, such as counting all the fractions between zero and one, drawing a five-sided hexagon, or demonstrating the validity of an invalid syllogism.

(3) By 'impossible' I shall mean two kinds of actions or events: (a) Those whose occurrence is incompatible with the truth of natural laws in which the agent believes; thus, according to my beliefs about aerodynamics, it is impossible for me to fly by flapping my hands. (b) Actions or events for which the agent has no technical means; in this sense, it is impossible for physicians to cure various diseases.

(4) I shall elide distinctions, vital in other contexts, between a number of terms of epistemological appraisal: 'knows', 'is sure', 'is convinced', 'realizes', 'is aware', 'is persuaded', 'assumes', 'thinks' and 'believes'. The only point upon which I insist is that the agent possess what he considers sufficient grounds for believing he cannot execute his design. His state of mind cannot be merely speculation upon, or imagination of, insurmountable difficulties. Finer distinctions are irrelevant for this investigation. A prisoner

106

who intends to flee Devil's Island will hardly have the time, the laboratory apparatus or reference-books to decide whether to say : 'I have incontrovertible evidence that I can't make it' or 'It looks pretty hopeless'.

The initial quotation from Hampshire actually contains two theses : (i) 'If you intend to do something, then you believe it is possible', and (ii) 'If you intend to do something, then you do not believe it is impossible'. The apodoses seem equivalent because the idiom 'I do not believe it' frequently expresses disbelief rather than lack of belief, as in 'I don't believe it will rain'. Thesis (i) is the stronger. I might lack the belief that it is impossible for me to swim the English Channel, although I have never come to the opinion that I can do it. In that case, thesis (i), but not thesis (ii), would disqualify me from intending to swim the English Channel. In practice, (ii) entails (i) : if we cross-examine a man to determine why he has *not* formed the opinion that he cannot ascend K–2, he must decide what to believe. He will have to find evidence that he might be able to do it, or else he will have to admit our evidence that K–2 is beyond his capacities.

When I maintain that a person can intend to do something which he believes to be impossible, I reject thesis (i) as well as (ii) : believing that X is impossible rules out believing that X is possible. Why do I deny that it makes an essential difference in what one can intend, when one realizes that a goal is out of reach ? One reason is that our criteria for saying 'He thinks it's impossible' are impossibly vague. For the majority of hazardous enterprises, there is at least one example of past success. So probability of success is greater than zero. And if we are concerned with a venture in which all previous attempts have failed, let us say stealing the gold in Fort Knox, we can draw upon analogies, like the Brinks robbery, to make our prospects seem more favourable.

A promising model of an impossible action might be the following : an alchemist, after years of fruitless experimentation, decides that lead cannot be transformed into gold. If he thereby accepts the doctrines of modern chemistry regarding the elements, then, from his viewpoint, there is no chance of success. However, he could still argue that there is nothing sacrosanct about the theory that elements are irreducible; it was established by systematic

107

observation, and future experience might disprove it. In that case his decision, that he cannot transmute lead into gold, could mean that he has lost patience with such a difficult enterprise, and would rather try making a name for himself in medicine. But it remains conceivable that he should persist with his alchemical project.

If 'impossible' does not mean 'zero probability', might it be defined as some very low probability? I do not think that a figure can be found which is appropriate to every situation. If there is only one chance in ten that a platoon will overwhelm an enemy pillbox, most commanders would say, 'It's not humanly possible'. On the other hand, people who buy lottery-tickets do not hesitate when the odds are infinitely less favourable.

You might argue that the foregoing considerations lose their persuasiveness if we speak of subjective probability. In subjective probability theory, a man's willingness to invest in a Daily Double ticket at the horse-races, together with his declaration that he intends to win, constitutes our criterion for saying that he believes he might win. If the better goes on to declare that he cannot possibly win, then he must be speaking of objective probabilities. The fact that he is betting must indicate that he has chosen to ignore objective evidence, such as the past record of the horses, or that he relies on a hunch which would have no probative value for other gamblers. But this argument begs the question, 'Should we accept your criterion of "believing an event is possible" in cases of this sort?' Why, after all, should we rule that an apparently sincere avowal of intention, together with belief that one's goal is unattainable, is self-contradictory? The notion of 'intending the impossible' sounds less odd than alternative explanations of the horse-player's state of mind: 'He is ignoring evidence of which he is aware', or 'He trusts evidence that he recognizes to be generally unacceptable'. In saying this I am not proposing that we discard subjective probability theory; since gamblers in fact prefer to wager when they expect they might win, its criterion for their beliefs is empirically justified.

Perhaps there is another way to characterize impossible actions, such that 'intending the impossible' will be revealed as a self-contradictory notion. The following conversation between a physician and a faith-healer suggests an appropriate criterion for impossible actions:

108

Physician : Why are you kneeling by that child?

Faith-healer : I'm praying.

P : Why?

F : She's got leukemia, and I intend to cure her.

P : What makes you think that prayers might cure her?

F : That's the mystery.

P : But how can you intend to cure the girl by prayer when you have no idea how your actions might cause her to get well? There is no statistical basis for expecting your orisons to have that effect. And are you able to explain the process by which your mummeries could reduce the number of white corpuscles in the child's bloodstream?

F : I agree that it's impossible, but I intend to cure her. After all, don't you scientists ever use techniques whose operations you do not comprehend, which seem to produce the intended result only by chance? How about electric shock-treatment for schizophrenia and radiation in cancer-therapy?

P : Well, neither of those techniques is very scientific; besides, we use them only in desperate cases.

F : Isn't leukemia desperate enough? Furthermore, when you employ your 'unscientific' methods, don't you intend to cure the patient?

P : No; we only *hope* to; and of course we try our best.

Before I question the physician's re-description of intentions to do the impossible as 'merely hoping and trying', I should note that my argument is independent of three important facts : (1) Most people strive for goals they deem attainable; (2) We rely more upon a man to carry out his project when he has informed himself about its feasibility, and we tend to distrust the man who plunges blindly into all sorts of undertakings; (3) We take minute planning and careful investigation as evidence that a man's intentions are firm. Such facts are woven into the pragmatic background against which we use the notion of intending. If these circumstances did not obtain, our concept of intending would change, perhaps to the point of unserviceability. But notice that these facts and similar ones are only *general* conditions for having the concept of intention that we have. Consequently it does *not* have to be true in each particular case of a person with some goal : (*a*) that he expects to reach his goal, (*b*) that he has even bothered to learn

109

what his chances are of reaching it, or (c) that his intentions are serious in proportion to the amount of information-gathering and planning of action that he has done. We must also leave room for the intentions of uninformed, impulsive and unsystematic people.

Now we should scrutinize the kinds of attempts in which a man might display his intention to do something that he believed impossible. Would we ever say of such efforts that the agent intended, or only that he wished desperately to do what he was trying to do? This question will require that we look at various conceptual connections between trying and intending.

Hampshire appears to countenance attempts to do the impossible. 'It seems,' he writes, 'I can always try to bring about a certain effect, even if, knowing myself and the circumstances, I am more or less certain that I will in fact fail' ([48], p. 112). In such cases, however, Hampshire maintains that one cannot intend to succeed in one's attempt. Hampshire's general formula therefore runs: 'To try to do something is necessarily to intend to do it, or to intend to come as near as possible to the achievement in view' ([48], p. 134).

Hampshire's final clause, which provides that in hopeless undertakings the agent only intends to 'come as near as possible' to doing what he is attempting to do, will not fit some everyday cases. Take this one. A recently drowned swimmer is washed up at the seaside. A lifeguard arrives. Despite the apparent futility of it, he gives the victim artificial respiration. The lifeguard presumably believes he cannot bring him back to life, but he is trying to revive the swimmer. Does he intend to revive him? What would it mean to deny this, and maintain that he only aims 'to come as near as possible'? In this case there is no intermediate result, closer to reviving him than failing. The compromise view of Hampshire's is inapplicable here, and Hampshire would either have to assert flatly that the lifeguard cannot intend to revive the drowned man, or that he can intend to. The latter verdict sounds most plausible in the circumstances, particularly because there is a well-established routine R, which is both designed to and fairly likely to bring a water-soaked person back to life. This goal is so intimately associated with engaging in this routine that it does not matter what thoughts and desires are going through the life-saver's mind. To execute the routine R in a conscientious manner is to attempt to revive a drowned person, and also to have the built-in goal of the routine, however pessimistic one is about attaining the goal.

If you object that the life-saver cannot be really trying, that he must be merely going through the motions of artificial respiration, I would call that an excessively strong logical consequence of your analysis of trying. What is your evidence that the lifeguard is careless and unenergetic? At most it could be a contingent truth, about the effect of one's belief upon one's endeavours, that a man who is convinced he is going to fail never tries his best. It cannot be true by virtue of what we mean by 'try' and 'believe' that a person who believes he is going to fail will only try half-heartedly.

Another objection to my defence of trying and intending the impossible would be that it is always more plausible to suppose that the agent has other aims instead of one that he believes to be unattainable. For example, why not suppose that the lifeguard merely intends to placate the drowned man's distraught widow by administering artificial respiration to him? Or perhaps he is only following regulations, which specify that every person who appears to have been immersed less than six hours must be given artificial respiration, however hopeless it looks. My answer to this line of reasoning is that these other intentions do not rule out an intention to do the impossible. The lifeguard may have these other aims as well as the aim of reviving the drowned man. In fact, these other aims could give him all the more reason to try, and consequently to have the intention of making the drowned man breathe. It would be precisely because he has the goals of placating the victim's widow, and of conforming to regulations, that he gives the victim artificial respiration, with the intention of making him breathe.

This is my main argument from trying to intending. However, I should add a few qualifications about this general form of argument. It cannot be used to vindicate hypotheses about every sort of impossible intention. The reason is that there are some actions we can intend to perform, but cannot attempt. In these cases the evidence for attributing the intention to an agent would have to be something other than his efforts.

This qualification is in conflict with Hampshire's view that an

111

agent can make an attempt to perform any sort of action. A fuller treatment of these points is given in sections 2, 3, 5, 6 and 9 of the preceding essay, but I shall give one illustration here of an action that someone could intend but not attempt. A healthy man, armed only with a pen-knife, who manages to approach within ten feet of a dreaded dictator, can both try and intend to assassinate him. Now suppose that the would-be assassin is either bedridden with paralysis, or locked in a prison cell. He might still plan and scheme to kill the tyrant. But there would be no course of action presently open to him which would translate his intention into an attempt. That is, nothing a paralysed or imprisoned man could do, in the absence of the dictator, will qualify as 'attempted assassination'. Colloquially speaking, he cannot even make a stab at it.

Hampshire disagrees. He writes of situations in which the agent is not able to perform the behavioural routine which constitutes an attempt:

> [The agent] 'might have tried to get himself into the required position to make the attempt, and this could be counted as making the attempt, because he is taking the first steps towards the achievement in view' ([48], p. 171).

But I find it more plausible to describe the agitations of the paralysed man, and the machinations of the imprisoned man, respectively, as 'trying to get out of bed' and 'trying to get out of jail'. If we asked them what they tried to do in the course of the day, it would be hyperbolic of them to claim: 'I was trying to kill the dictator'.

As I suggested above, there might be grounds, other than attempts, for saying that our imprisoned hero intended to assassinate the dictator. He could be filing at the bars of his cell, that is, trying to escape, with the ultimate intention of killing the tyrant – even though he admitted that the dictator was much too well guarded. The evidence – a plan, for example – does not constitute as convincing a proof of intention as an attempt. It is hard to decide whether the plan expresses a fixed determination rather than a dream or hope, until the man is in a position to perform actions which are specifically directed towards bringing about the death of the dictator.

My final point will be that the principle 'If you try to X, then you intend to X' applies to a striking range of attempts to do the impossible, and that there are good reasons not to invent some other, attainable purpose for the agent, simply to avoid saying that a person intends the impossible. One representative case should be sufficient to refute Hampshire's doctrine that the agent cannot ever intend to succeed in a hopeless undertaking.

My argument will consist in showing the untoward consequences of always saying that when a person attempts the impossible, he lacks the intention to succeed. Imagine a heroin addict who yearns to free himself of his habit: he knows, from having failed in earlier attempts to resist his craving, and from having studied the case-histories of other addicts, that he has practically no chance of accomplishing the feat. Suppose that the addict makes a sedulous attempt to cease taking his anodyne, and – contrary to all expectations – manages to quell his agonizing desire for the drug. If his friends congratulate him on his amazing reformation, should he declare, 'Don't praise me; I tried, but I didn't really intend to stop taking narcotics'? His statement expresses more than modesty; it borders on paradox. In the face of the man's persistent efforts, can we say that he lacked the intention to stop taking heroin, that he only hoped to cease?

The notion of 'hope' or 'mere longing' is misplaced in this context. To quote Miss Anscombe: 'A chief mark of an idle wish is that a man does nothing – whether he could or not – toward the fulfilment of the wish' ([1], p. 66). If we rule that the heroin addict did not intend to succeed in his attempt, will we say that his successful reformation was *unintentional*? That is an incongruous way to characterize the man's action of curing himself. It is more appropriate to describe his sustained manifestation of self-control, his plainly goal-directed efforts, as a feat he intended, rather than to say, 'He only hoped to rid himself of the craving'.

If anyone complains that this last example is illegitimate, because the drug addict didn't really know, but only thought he knew, that he could not cure himself of heroin addiction; then I should repeat the animadversions of my opening remarks regarding the notion of 'impossible'. What counts is that the agent be convinced, when he takes the first steps toward a goal, that he cannot attain it. In cases like that of the heroin addict, an agent might be surprised at his success; but there need not be any lack of concentration in his efforts, or lack of satisfaction at their results, to differentiate his attempt from attempts to reach attainable goals. In the latter cases, we do not hesitate to ascribe intention to succeed – except when there is evidence of some ulterior purpose to the attempt. Therefore unless we have evidence of some ulterior purpose to a man's attempt to do the impossible, why should we not say that such a person also intends to do the impossible? At any rate, we should reject Hampshire's view that it is 'self-contradictory to say "I intend that to happen, but I believe that it will not" '.

VI

HOW IS ABILITY RELATED TO PERFORMANCE?

We have approached human behaviour from a number of angles, some of them familiar, others relatively novel. Causality seems to be an inevitable theme, whether we discuss the relations between an agent and his deed, the contrast between doing and undergoing, explanations of behaviour, trying and doing, or intention. The next topic I shall consider, what it is *to be able to* carry out one's intention, to try or to succeed in an attempt, must seem excessively familiar. And sure enough, causality will turn up again. Philosophers have raised such questions as whether one's ability might be a cause of one's performance; whether it means the same to say 'John can do X' and 'If John wants (decides, tries) to do X, that will cause him to do X'; and whether it is consistent to assert both, 'Something caused John to do X', and 'Nevertheless he could have done something other than X.'

In tackling the subject of human powers, I believe that I shall get the most useful results if I evaluate and develop further a justifiably influential but extremely difficult essay by the late J. L. Austin, 'Ifs and Cans' ([11]; subsequent page references in parentheses are to this paper). I am going to narrow my attention to his views of the connections and contrasts between having an ability and performing the kind of action one has the ability to perform. This will be especially germane to the other topics in the present collection of studies.

A good jumping-off place will be an apparent clash between two of Austin's remarks on ability and performance. The remarks which sound incompatible are: (i) 'It follows merely from the premiss that [a person does something], that he has the ability to do it, according to ordinary English' (p. 175); and (ii) 'There are . . . good reasons for not speaking of "I can lift my finger" as being directly verified when I proceed to lift it, and likewise for not speaking of "He could have done it" as being directly verified by the discovery that he did do it' (p. 172; see pp. 170 and 173, fn.). Austin's proposals sound inconsistent because whenever the premiss 'I raised my finger' entails the conclusion 'I had the ability to raise my finger', as (i) provides, then the discovery that I raised my finger should directly verify, or suffice to prove the truth of, the same ability statement, which goes against (ii).

After I sketch in some indispensable background for discussion of these issues, I shall demonstrate the compatibility of Austin's remarks (i) and (ii). Then I shall show the bearing of both these suggestions upon Austin's much debated thesis, (iii), that statements specifying what a person *can* do are not to be analysed into hypothetical or conditional assertions. In particular, I shall use my interpretation of his remarks (i) and (ii) as a means of assessing the version of his thesis (iii) which reads : 'So-and-so can do X' never means the same as 'So-and-so will do X if he tries'. I shall have to look into Austin's famous counter-example against this kind of hypothetical analysis of a golfer's ability to sink an easy putt. But I shall offer a new account of the moral he draws from this challenging example. For convenience, call this moral 'thesis (iv)'. This is Austin's view that our abilities are 'inherently liable not to produce success, on occasion', even when we try our best and nothing causes us to fail (p. 166, fn.). This moral is naturally tied up with Austin's notorious concluding remark, (v), that the assumption of determinists, that our successes and failures always have causes, 'appears not consistent with what we ordinarily say and presumably think' about our powers (p. 179). I attempt to show that Austin's confusions regarding (iv) will explain why he need not have maintained (v). Finally, I shall say something positive about the logical and pragmatic relations between ascriptions of ability and conditional statements. My verdict will be that ability statements resist translation into conditional form; nevertheless they have hypothetical overtones : they always entail one or another type of conditional statement. Still, I salvage part of Austin's theory in connection with (iii), that conditionals like 'So-and-so will do X if he tries' never state causal hypotheses.

So much for plans; now down to details.

1. *Stage setting: various senses of 'can' and 'being prevented'*
My discussion of ability will be limited in several respects. I shall

not investigate what it means, in general, to assert that some-thing can happen or that a person can perform some task. As Wittgenstein noticed, 'can' is not univocal. All that seems to be constant, from situation to situation where we say that a person can do something, is that we exclude one or another impediment. Wittgenstein's dictum goes:

'When we ask a doctor "Can the patient walk?", we shall sometimes be ready to substitute for this "Is his leg healed?" – "Can he speak?" under some circumstances means "Is his throat all right?", under others (e.g. if he is a small child) it means "Has he learned to speak?" . . . We use the phrase "He can walk, as far as the state of his leg is concerned", especially when we wish to oppose this condition for his walk-ing to some other condition, say the state of his spine' ([123], p. 114; see also [122], Part I, §§ 182–3).

Austin himself, in 'Plea for Excuses', set out a similar theory of what we mean when we say that a person is acting freely, which presumably entails that he *can* act differently. Austin's account of this kindred notion begins:

'While it has been the tradition to present ["freedom"] as the "positive" term requiring elucidation, there is little doubt that to say that we acted "freely" (in the philosopher's use, which is only faintly related to the everyday use) is to say only that we acted *not* un-freely, in one or another of the many hetero-geneous ways of so acting (under duress, or what not). . . . "Free" is only used to rule out the suggestion of some or all of its recognized antithesis' ([10], p. 128).

The uses of 'can', as well as 'acting freely', that interest a philosopher, occur mainly within contexts of judicial, moral and similar forms of evaluation. Typically, the 'can' of ability crops up when someone has not done what he ought to have done. My doubles partner in a tennis match does not return a serve. Your neighbour does not alert the police when he hears a prowler force open the door of your apartment. At that moment, an out-of-state policeman wanders by, but does not arrest or shoot the intruder. More dramatically, there is a child drowning in the river, and the only bystander at the scene does not rescue the child. Before we censure these people, we should ask whether they *could* have acted as we think they ought. Against this evaluative backdrop, what meanings has the verb 'can'? We already noticed that it rules out one or another impediment. On the positive side, however, we might be asking the very general question : 'Was it within the power of these agents to do what they ought?' This is not equivalent to asking whether they had any specific powers, such as powers of concentration, of endurance, or persuasion. Specific powers like those are abilities. Asking vaguely whether the agent could have acted in a certain manner might be a request for at least four other more definite kinds of information, besides information about his abilities. We might want to know, for instance,

'Was the agent in a position to do what he failed to do?' (Here we would be using the 'can' of opportunity.)

'Was he aware of relevant features of the situation? For example, did the bystander notice that the child was in danger?' ('Can' of knowledge or awareness.)

'Did he have the necessary equipment to act? For instance, was a telephone available to your neighbour? Was the police officer carrying his revolver?' ('Can' of means.)

'Was he entitled to act? Are policemen from another state authorized to detain or shoot suspected lawbreakers?' ('Can' of right or authority.)

When a person is to blame for not doing what he ought to have done, presumably it is true, in *all* five of these senses of 'can', that he could have performed the action. To say that it was within his power, from every standpoint, is to say that he could have acted, in what Austin calls the 'all in' sense of 'can'. Often we inquire only about someone's ability, opportunity, knowledge, means or rights, because we assume it to have been within his power, from other standpoints, to act.

Now I want to connect these senses of 'can' with the various impediments I mentioned above. It seems to me that in 'Ifs and Cans', Austin does not sufficiently emphasize how each sense of 'can', beginning with his 'all in' sense, serves to 'rule out' one or another obstacle to action. Clearly one thing we always mean, when we ask whether the people in my illustrations could have done better, is: 'Were they prevented?' I shall try now to

118

elucidate this notion of being prevented. It has as many senses as 'can'. What qualifies as an obstacle will depend upon at least three factors : (a) which sense of 'can' we are using, (b) how important the action was that the agent did not perform, (c) what consequences he might have faced if he had performed it. If we are using the 'all in' sense of 'can', then every type of impediment is ruled out whenever we assert that a man could have done something. The more restricted senses of 'can' exclude hindrances of their own level. With respect to factors (b) and (c), it is noteworthy that many circumstances which may have influenced the agent, perhaps causing him to fall short of his duty, will not count as obstacles which prevented him from doing what he ought. Causes are not hindrances if (b) the action was urgent or (c) the consequences of action were negligible. Imagine that my tennis partner declares : 'I couldn't return that serve because I was overcome by muscle cramps.' Plainly the cramps interfered with his ability. On the other hand, if he complains, 'There was a puddle on the court between me and the place where the serve landed, so that I would have got my new shoes wet if I had gone after the ball'; then surely we would deny that he was disabled. Did the puddle deprive him of the opportunity to return the serve? That depends upon the importance of the match. If it was purely recreational, all right; but if it was a grudge meeting, or a championship, then the water was no impediment, even if it caused my partner to let the serve go.

The gulf between mere causes and impediments is especially noticeable when we turn to the bystander who does not haul a drowning child from the river. Suppose that he tells us : 'I was wearing a brand new suit; it would have been ruined if I had plunged into the water; and by the time I stripped, the child had disappeared.' We would deny that the danger of ruining his clothes deprived him of an opportunity to help the child. The task was too serious, and the consequences for his clothing were too trivial. But now suppose that the child did not fall in; it let a toy sailboat drift out into the current. Then once more we would rank the danger to the man's suit as a circumstance that prevented him from going into the water.

The hindrances I have catalogued so far are causes, but some obstacles are not. The legal status of being from another jurisdiction cannot bring it about, in a causal sense, that the policeman had lost his power of arresting wrongdoers. Heavy drinking might disable him temporarily or permanently; but travelling to another state cannot operate on him as alcohol might. The disparity between causal and non-causal hindrances will emerge clearly if we recall that any event which causes another might conceivably fail to produce its regular upshot, although other conditions remain as before. Thus it is not self-contradictory to suppose that the policeman should consume a gallon of gin and yet for the first time suffer no loss of ability. But is it conceivable that, without any change in our laws and customs, the officer should cross the state line and, contrary to all our previous experience in these matters, retain his authority to arrest people? If that sounds absurd, then this kind of impediment upon one's rights is not a cause. Incidentally, I am not denying that there are causes which prevent policemen from making arrests. For instance, a policeman might trip while chasing a culprit, with the result that the culprit escaped arrest. In that case, however, tripping did not limit or cancel out the policeman's authority; it prevented him from exercising the authority he had.

My distinction between impediments and causes goes beyond saying that not all obstacles function as causes. What I wish to underscore is that not all circumstances which cause a person's failure to accomplish some task rank as circumstances which prevented him, so that he could not have accomplished the task. This distinction will help us reject Austin's indeterministic theory of abilities (iv), and his conclusion (v) that determinism conflicts with the common-sense view of abilities, which Austin believes to be indeterministic.

Before we stray into that familiar arena of debate, however, we should explore Austin's other doctrines regarding abilities, for they are original and challenging. Just as I have had to neglect many connections between the concepts of ability, opportunity, awareness, means, rights, and hindrances, I must overlook many nuances in our concept of ability. Thus I shall blur distinctions between specific ability terms: aptitude, talent, flair, fitness, capacity, competence, knack, skill, proficiency, even dexterity and strength. My only concern will be the relation between all species of ability and action.

120

2. *Ability and being able*

Recall Austin's remark (i), 'It follows merely from the premiss that he does it, that he has the ability to do it, according to ordinary English.' If this principle of 'ordinary English' were correct, it would support Austin's thesis (iii) that ascriptions of ability are not hypothetical, but categorical assertions. Take as a premise this report of Brown's performance at the shootng gallery: 'He hit three bull's-eyes in a row'. This assertion is categorical enough; so if it entails the proposition, 'Brown had the ability to hit three bull's-eyes in a row', at least some ascriptions of ability are categorical. But is this inference valid? I admit that we are entitled to conclude, 'Brown *was able* to hit three bull's-eyes in a row'. I deny, however, that this conclusion is equivalent to asserting that Brown has a certain degree of ability at target practice.

The non-equivalence becomes noticeable if we expand our account of Brown's display of marksmanship: 'Before he hit the three bull's-eyes, he fired 600 rounds, without coming close to the bull's-eye; and his subsequent tries were equally wild.' This amplified record of Brown's performance in no way compels us to retract our assertion that he *was able* to hit three bull's-eyes in a row. He was able to do it, but without any regularity. Therefore he does not have this sort of ability at target shooting.

This story reveals the ambiguity of expressions from the 'being able' family. A similar story would uncover the same ambiguity of 'being unable', 'not being able' and 'could not' – which would prove that it never follows from the fact that a champion *once* could not (was not able to) hit a bull's-eye that he lacked ability on that occasion. 'Was able' sometimes means 'had the ability', and sometimes means 'did'.

Here is an illustration with 'will be able'. It may be irrational, but it is not self-contradictory to declare: 'Regardless of his meagre skill, I have faith that Brown will be able to hit three bull's-eyes tomorrow.' This concept of 'being able', which does not entail ability, should be quite familiar. Examples of it would be: 'The village sorcerer was able (Heaven knows how!) to cure my lumbago'; 'The dude managed to ride a ferocious bronco'; 'Somehow or other, the castaway survived for ten days without food or drink'; 'The ill-prepared rebels brought off a *coup d'état*';

121

'The inexperienced kidnapper contrived to elude an FBI drag-net.' On the negative side, a skilled portrait painter might exclaim : 'I just cannot get the shadows right today !'

For simplicity, call the 'being able' and 'being unable' in these examples the 'being able' and 'being unable' of managing and not managing, respectively. These expressions carry the hint that the subject had a lucky break or a bad break; but that is imma-terial. What matters for us is that our distinction will explain why Austin allows (i) that in 'ordinary English', 'He did it' entails 'He had the ability to do it', and nevertheless maintains (ii) that there are 'good reasons' for blocking these inferences. Perhaps what Austin had in mind is the fact that colloquial discourse seldom discriminates between the 'ability' and the 'managing' senses of 'being able', and thus sanctions invalid arguments of the form : 'Brown hit three bull's-eyes in a row; so he was able to do it; therefore he had the ability to do it'. Exegetical con-siderations aside, the distinction is crucial to an understanding of ability. Before we go on to that, however, I anticipate one criticism.

3. Objection: the person who manages to do something must have a momentary ability

A philosopher might agree that Brown, as well as the sorcerer, the novice rider, the castaway, the rebels and the inexperienced kidnapper did not have enduring abilities; but he might insist that they necessarily had some kind of short run ability at the moment they succeeded. On this view, my 'managing' sense of 'being able' collapses into the 'being able' of ability – in these cases, an ability which only lasts a moment. Now what sort of ability is this? Is anything to be said for this notion of an ability that 'just comes and goes', except that it again permits inferences from action to ability?

Now standard proficiencies and skills come and go in the sense that they develop, wane and disappear as time passes. But they do not 'just come and go'. In particular, when a man is suddenly disabled, it is never the case that his ability just deserts him. Various identifiable circumstances deprive him of his powers : fatigue, vehement emotion, illness, heart attack, injury. There was no hint of any disabling circumstance like this in our story

122

of Brown's target practice. Nothing is said which explains how his ability might have 'gone' after he shot three bull's-eyes. The sudden ripening of his skill, at precisely the instant he hit the first bull's-eye, is also inexplicable if we accept the 'momentary ability' hypothesis.

A more positive reason for denying that Brown was endowed with momentary prowess is that one of the things we always mean when we attribute an ability to a man is that one can rely on him, in normal situations of opportunity, knowledge, equipment, and right, to perform a certain kind of task. We want fairly consistent success from a person with ability. A wine-taster whose powers of discrimination 'just come and go', a typist with 'momentary proficiency', or a wrestler who possessed strength for two minutes during the middle of a bout, would be totally useless to us. Since these pragmatic requirements permeate our notion of an ability, this notion will not stretch to allow for momentary abilities on which we cannot rely. Having thus dismissed the objection against my 'managing' sense of 'being able', I want to explore further the relation between ability and performance.

4. Criteria for competence

How frequently must someone succeed, and how many catastrophic miscarriages are tolerated by our standards for ascribing ability to him? The answers will vary with the task that we say a person has the ability to execute. A race-track tout who predicts one-tenth of the season's Daily Double winners would rank as a skilled prognosticator by anyone's standards. A surgeon who loses one-third of his patients when he does appendectomies would be declared incompetent, unless there were peculiar conditions, such as the unavailability of a scalpel and sterilizing equipment, which explained these failures.

Often we decide that someone has an ability without waiting to count up his successful and faulty performances. All we require is success at analogous tasks in testing situations. Thus a young lieutenant might be judged fit to lead a platoon in battle, merely on the strength of his handling of problems during manoeuvres.

What about rudimentary performances such as lifting one's fingers? Is it not ludicrous to imagine tests, and ratios of success to failure, as criteria for ascribing to someone this kind of ability?

Of course it would be ridiculous, *when* we already know that a person is in normal condition. Normalcy includes the power to move one's limbs! But if we intend to establish whether someone is normal, tests are in order. A person whose hands are crippled with arthritis visits Lourdes. He dips his hands into the holy water of the grotto, and his fingers begin moving. Has he regained the ability to lift his fingers? Surely we need more than a single display to be convinced.

5. *Success, failure and effort*

Here is another crucial element in our notion of ability. When we speak of a person's successes and failures, in testing situations and in settings where he has the opportunity, the necessary information, the equipment and the right to do something, we make assumptions about his will. That is, we take it for granted that he wants to execute the task, that he prefers doing it rather than alternative tasks, that he intends to do it, or that he is attempting to do it. The very concept of success incorporates assumptions of this kind regarding his conative attitude. Why? An example will clarify the point. A man might unintentionally put a radio together – while distractedly juggling the components. But it would be self-contradictory to report that he *succeeded* in assembling the radio, if he knew that he did not intend to. Therefore success entails intention. The same holds for unsuccessful actions. The report, 'John did not succeed in assembling the radio; but he made no attempt to, and had no intention of putting it together', is also self-contradictory.

What if, instead of saying, 'He did not succeed,' we say, 'He failed to assemble the radio, but he neither tried nor intended to'? Then we shall avoid contradiction. That is because the verb 'fail' is ambiguous, as we noticed in previous studies. Transposing those earlier remarks into the present context, we see that the ambiguity of 'fail' consists in the fact that, in one sense, to fail to assemble a radio is simply to omit the whole undertaking; and omitting to assemble it entails neither trying nor intending to assemble it. Failing by omission is not even trying to do it. The cases of faulty action I imagined in section 1 of this paper, beginning with the doubles partner who does not return a serve, were all instances of omission-failure. The other sense of 'fail', which

124

alone has relevance for this brief digression on the concept of success in action, is equivalent to what we mean when we say that a person does *not* succeed. This other sense of 'fail' turned up in the anecdote about Brown at the shooting gallery, who consistently failed to hit the bull's-eye, even though he tried his best.

How is this relevant sense of 'fail', and the sense of 'succeed' which pairs up with it, germane to the analysis of ability? They are important when we appraise people's behaviour in testing situations. As we have argued, one successful attempt to do something, during a test, hardly ever proves that the person has the ability to do it; and one failure never proves inability. Therefore it seems that success and failure are related to ability as follows: If a man usually succeeds, under allowably difficult circumstances, he has the ability; if he usually fails, then he lacks it. To say that he has the ability to perform a particular act, here and now, in suitable conditions of opportunity, and so on, is to say, *inter alia*, 'He will *probably* succeed.' And the evidence you need to refute the forecast of probable success is just the same as you need to refute the original ascription of ability: regular failure in optimum conditions similar to the present ones.

This digression on failure, success and ability has considerable bearing upon some of the controversial remarks by Austin that I set out to examine. The foregoing part of our analysis, together with the account of impediments and causes in section 2, equips us to grapple with a celebrated Austinian footnote, in which he defends the views I numbered (iii), (iv) and (v). Austin is beleaguering hypothetical interpretations of 'He can' as meaning 'He will if he tries'. We are to imagine Austin on the golf course. Conditions are ideal. Austin faces a short putt. He attempts to knock the ball into the cup, but fails. He remains firmly convinced that he had the ability, then and there, to hole it. If Austin's belief is correct, the hypothetical analysis is refuted; since 'He will sink the putt if he tries' is falsified, while 'He can' seems to have been true. Austin argues:

'Indeed, further experiments may confirm my belief that I could have done it that time although I did not.

But if I tried my hardest, say, and missed, surely there *must* have been *something* that caused me to fail, that made me unable to succeed? So that I *could not* have holed it. Well, a modern belief in science, in there being an explanation of everything, may make us assent to this argument. But such a belief is not in line with the traditional beliefs enshrined in the word *can* : according to *them*, a human ability or power or capacity is inherently liable not to produce success, on occasion, and that for no reason (or are bad luck and bad form reasons?)' ([11], p. 166).

Numerous commentators on this passage have missed Austin's confusion between two species of cause, which our analysis has repeatedly distinguished : (*a*) causes 'that made me unable to succeed,' so that 'I could not have holed' the ball; and (*b*) other causes for my failure. Causes of family (*a*) are impediments, which either incapacitate a golfer, spoil his opportunity, interfere with his awareness, rob him of the means he requires, or perhaps invalidate his right to play on that golf course. What would constitute a non-hindering cause of type (*b*)? Slight nervous tension, which makes the golfer swing less accurately than usual; or an imperceptible ridge in front of the cup, which deflects the golf ball. Austin's error is to reason that, since the golfer might fail without being hindered by any cause from group (*a*), on those same occasions there is no cause at all, not even a cause of type (*b*), for the bad putt. This *non sequitur* plainly reinforces Austin's beliefs (iv) and (v) that determinism clashes with the assumptions we encapsulate in our everyday uses of the terms 'ability' and 'can'. For if it were true that a man with an ability might try and fail, but nothing caused his failure, then this action (his failure) was uncaused, and determinism is false. On the other side, if determinism were correct, and failures like this always have causes, then Austin's reasoning would lead one to deny that the golfer could have sunk the putt he missed. It is needless to add that this whole line of argument is drawn from an assimilation of all causes to hindrances.

6. *Chisholm's reply to Austin*

In his perceptive discussion ([25], pp. 20–5) of 'Ifs and Cans', Roderick M. Chisholm criticizes Austin's short putt example in quite a different way. According to Chisholm,

126

'If Austin's golfer really could have holed it that time, then there was something such that, had he tried to do it along with the other things he did do, then the absent condition (e.g. applying more pressure with the thumb) would have been supplied, and he would have holed the ball.'

Chisholm's counter-argument goes as follows. Chisholm provisionally reinstates, as the general analysis of 'He can do X', a hypothetical proposition: 'There is something Y such that if he tried to do Y then he would do X.' One point is unclear, however, if we apply this analysis to Austin's putting example: what action Y is the golfer supposed to *try* to perform, with a view toward sinking the putt (Xing)? If the golfer has normal control over his thumb, and nothing interferes with him, does it make sense to say, 'He is trying to apply more pressure with his thumb'? Chisholm surely does not mean that the golfer will sink the putt if he tries, in the sense of exerting himself, and presses as strenuously as he can with his thumb upon the golf-club. That form of trying would certainly wreck his shot. Successful putting demands a relaxed grip. Perhaps what Chisholm means is that the golfer should try harder to sink the putt, and that his 'trying harder' would *consist* in pressing more firmly with his thumb. If so, then the golfer's attempt to do Y is the same as his attempt to do X, in this case; and it seems, in the quotation I gave, that Chisholm is merely begging the question against Austin's claim that the golfer tries his best and fails.

Chisholm's objection to the short putt example avoids confusion between hindering causes of type (*a*), and other causes of type (*b*) which account for a wild shot. However, Chisholm does appear to think that a skilled golfer can overcome every cause of type (*b*) by means of a sufficiently careful attempt to sink the ball. This is a dubious assumption. Would we say that a golfer who leaves out extra thumb pressure only made a half-hearted attempt? A conscientious or 'full-fledged' attempt to exercise your putting skill consists in guarding against the most frequent, noticeable and fatal causes of inaccurate putting which figure among (*b*)-type causes: for example, extreme nervousness; gripping the golf-club very tightly; gross irregularities of the terrain. Thus, even if Chisholm does not think that extra thumb pressure is comprised in a proper attempt to hole the ball, he seems to believe that precautions of this kind will always enable you to succeed in your attempt. Following Austin here, I disagree. Are there not minor causes of inaccurate putting that a skilled golfer will not detect in advance? If so, they would not count as hindering causes of type (*a*), due to their rarity and comparative innocuousness; still, they would make him miss occasional shots, and he could do nothing to neutralize them. Therefore we must reject Chisholm's doctrine that if a man with ability tries and fails, additional effort on his part would have resulted in success.

Chisholm's reply to Austin's golfing story is offered in defence of one hypothetical analysis of 'He can do X' which Austin is challenging. The analysis is that 'He can do X' means 'He will do X if he tries (to do Y)'. Although Chisholm denies that Austin's story has refuted this hypothetical interpretation of 'can', Chisholm offers independent reasons for discarding hypothetical accounts. Chisholm's statement of these reasons in his discussion of 'Ifs and Cans' is laconic but interesting :

> 'The statements "He does X if and only if he tries to do Y" and "He *cannot try* to do Y" are inconsistent with "He can do X", but they are not inconsistent with our *analysans* – they are not inconsistent with "There is a Y such that if he tries to do Y he will do X". (There are, of course, many acts which one cannot even *try* to perform.) . . . If this difficulty is genuine, then it applies not only to the present formula, but also . . . to any attempt to define "can" in terms of "will if". For any such attempt will presumably introduce a verb of which "he" may be made the subject; it will then be grammatically permissible to insert "can not" between the subject "he" and the verb; and then it will be possible to describe a situation in which the *analysans* is true and "He can" is false' ([25], p. 25).

In a subsequent paper, entitled 'He Could Have Done Otherwise", Chisholm spells out this objection of his against 'He will do X if he tries (to do Y)' and similar hypothetical interpretations :

> 'In saying "You could have arranged things this morning so that you would be in Boston now," are we saying : . . . "There

are certain things such that, if this morning you had undertaken (chosen, willed, tried, set out) to bring it about that those
things would occur, then you would be in Boston now"? . . .
Consider . . . those things which are such that, if this morning
our agent had undertaken (chosen, willed, tried, set out) to
bring them about, then he would be in Boston now. And let
us suppose (i) that he *could not* have undertaken . . . to bring
any of those things about and (ii) that he would be in Boston
now only if he *had*. . . . These suppositions are consistent with
saying that he *would* be in Boston now *if* he had undertaken those things, but they are not consistent with saying that
he could then have arranged things so that he would be in
Boston now' ([27], p. 411).

From the rest of his essay, it is evident that Chisholm believes
any standard *cause* of his protagonist's not taking measures to be
in Boston now *prevents* him from taking those measures, so that
he could not take them. Chisholm writes: 'If our agent had it
within his power . . . , then . . . at 10 o'clock this morning there
was no sufficient causal condition for his not then undertaking
those things.' ([27], p. 413; see his definition (D1) on p. 414;
and pp. 415–17.) Now Chisholm's reply to Austin was free of
the confusion we found in Austin's golfing anecdote between (*a*)
causes which disable or otherwise hinder one, and (*b*) other causes
of one's action. But Chisholm is guilty of the same mixup in 'He
Could Have Done Otherwise'. Chisholm there assimilates causes
of group (*b*) to those of group (*a*), when he offers his own refutation of the view that 'He can' means 'He will if'. A sign that he
has made this assimilation is that he nowhere describes a case of
someone being rendered *powerless* to elect some course of action,
in contrast to simply being caused not to elect the course of
action.

Since this muddle is so pervasive in discussion of human
powers, I shall risk redundancy and excavate it from Chisholm's
argument. A slight elaboration of Chisholm's example will bring
out his confusion. Imagine that the would-be traveller was standing alongside a train at ten o'clock this morning. He knew that
the train would arrive in Boston by this time. He had a ticket.
He had a right to visit Boston, in contrast, say, to visiting Havana.

What caused him not to board the train? If a negligent conductor dropped an immense suitcase on him, and knocked him unconscious, then he was indeed prevented from taking the appropriate measures to be in Boston now. It would be true, under those causal conditions, that he could not have taken the measures. But this is more a case of being powerless to *go* to Boston than of being powerless to choose or try, as Chisholm says it was.

Instead of a hindering cause, consider this: the prospective traveller recognizes a long-lost college chum and decides to go over and talk with him, since there will be a later train to Boston. Did the appearance of the friend cause the traveller not to take measures which would have put him in Boston by now? Decidedly. Was he disabled, or impeded in any way from boarding the train, as he would have been if a suitcase felled him? Heavens no. Although there was a sufficient causal condition for his not taking measures to be in Boston now, we should not conclude, with Chisholm, that the traveller was powerless to take these measures. He simply did not. He could have stepped on to the train, and so he could have got to Boston by now.

7. Chisholm's answer to me

In a paper written since I first raised this objection, Chisholm agrees that the traveller was not powerless in the second case ([28], pp. 43–6). But Chisholm will not rank the traveller's meeting with his friend as a sufficient condition, or even 'an essential part of a sufficient condition of the man's not being in Boston at this time.' Deploying a brand-new distinction, Chisholm's verdict is that the encounter only 'contributed causally' to the traveller's delay. Chisholm explains:

> 'If S is a sufficient causal condition for E, then we may say, among other things, that S is a complex set of events which is such that it is a law of nature that . . . for any time t, if S occurs at t, then E will either occur at t or later than t; it is not a law of nature that, for any time t, if S occurs at t, then E will occur prior to t; S and E are logically independent of each other; and it is not a law of nature that S does not occur' ([28], pp. 44–5, including fn. 12).

This is a standard characterization. There is also no novelty when Chisholm provides for *one* sense in which an event C may contribute causally to E: 'C may be essential to a sufficient causal condition of E', namely the conjunction of events D and C, where D alone is insufficient for E. But then Chisholm propounds a bewildering *second* sense of 'contribute causally':

> C may be essential to *preventing* a sufficient causal condition of not-E . . . C occurs along with D . . . such that . . . D and not-C . . . would be a sufficient causal condition of E's not occurring. . . . If E does occur, then . . . C contributes causally to E.

This second sense of 'contribute causally' appears tailor-made for Chisholm's assumption that causes – sufficient causal conditions anyhow – prevent a man from acting otherwise. He writes: 'C may be a contributing cause in the second of these two senses even though there occurs no event S such that S is a sufficient causal condition of E.' Turning to the debated example, Chisholm writes:

> 'the appearance of the friend . . . prevent[ed] there being a sufficient causal condition for the man then *not* stopping and talking with any friend. In other words, the man was in this situation D: the conjunction of D and the nonappearance of his friend [not-C] would have been a sufficient causal condition for his not then stopping and talking with any friend [not-E], but D itself was not a sufficient causal condition. . . .'

Chisholm then sums up boldly: his analysis 'is consistent with saying that there was no sufficient causal condition for [the traveller's] . . . stopping and talking with his friend'.

Taking this last point first, we must ask: Is mere consistency enough to vindicate Chisholm's 'disabling' assumption? No, because he has already admitted that the traveller could have done not-E; boarding the train was up to him. Thus Chisholm must hold categorically that there is no sufficient causal condition for E. His doctrine is that there *cannot* be sufficient causal conditions for free acts like E. I agree with Chisholm that 'it is possible for us to say that a man's act has no sufficient causal condition'. As long as it is only possible that there was no sufficient causal condition for the admittedly free act E, then it is equally possible that there was a sufficient causal condition for E. Hence saying the traveller could have boarded the train (not-E) is compatible with the presence of a sufficient causal condition for his remaining to chat instead (E).

I have another grumble regarding Chisholm's revised analysis of the debated example. Event C, the appearance of our traveller's friend, sounds to me as if it were 'essential to a sufficient causal condition of E'. In circumstances D, C occurred and was followed by E (stopping and chatting). In D alone, E would not have occurred. I cannot satisfy Chisholm's demand for a 'law of nature' that covers this sequence of D and C followed by E. But I assume there is one to be constructed by social psychologists or neurophysiologists. After all, when encounters like this one take place, do we not expect the participants to alter their usual routine as the traveller did?

Perhaps Chisholm's analysis of how the encounter only contributed causally, in his peculiar second sense, to our traveller's delay, may be revised to meet these objections. But at this stage it seems clearly unwarranted to suppose that when a man could have done something other than what he did, there was no cause of the action he performed.

8. *Back to the hypothetical analysis of 'can'*

I agree with Chisholm that many causal factors prevent a man from choosing, or even from contemplating, a particular line of action. If the would-be traveller had been hypnotized, and had retained the post-hypnotic suggestion that he must change his mind at the last moment about going to Boston, then I concede that he could not have chosen to take all the necessary measures to be in Boston by now. The man could not have stuck to his decision that he would leave for Boston at 10 a.m. Therefore the hypothetical interpretation of 'can', as 'will if he decides', is refuted; since it is true that he will go if he decides, but false that he can go. To accommodate such cases, however, we may repair the hypothetical analysis, and list *ad hoc* exceptions of various types. All we have to say is: ' "He can do X" means "He will probably do X if he undertakes (chooses, tries, decides, etc.) to do Y; and provided that, in case he does not undertake to do Y, his omission is not due to hypnosis, uncontrollable impulses, brain-washing and similar volitional impediments".' The hypothetical analysis, so revised, yields no explanation why these abnormal states of the agent deprive him of his power to act; but neither does the categorical analysis, which specifies that statements of the form, 'He can do X', simply record the present condition of an agent. If you maintain the categorical interpretation, you must also take it as a brute fact that hypnotized people lack certain powers.

9. *Could desires be hindering causes?*

Before I return to Austin's attack upon the hypothetical analysis of 'can' statements, I think it worth noticing one further peculiarity of Chisholm's anti-hypothetical reasoning. He seems to believe that a person's desires are hindering causes, just like posthypnotic suggestions and pathological urges. Chisholm does not say anything which directly implies that the traveller's desire to converse with a long-lost friend has rendered him unable to *choose* or *undertake* to begin his journey to Boston. Nevertheless, Chisholm appears to believe that such volitional factors would prevent a traveller from going to Boston. His belief comes out in a much earlier essay, 'Freedom and Action' [26]. There Chisholm focuses upon a parallel case: a killer has desires and beliefs which cause him to shoot someone. Chisholm begins by saying that there is no important difference between this man and a hypnotized killer. Chisholm declares:

'If what we say he did was really something that was brought about by a second man, one who forced his hand upon the trigger, say, or who, by means of hypnosis, compelled him to perform the act, then, since the act was caused by the *second* man, it was nothing that was within the power of the *first* man to prevent. And precisely the same thing is true, I think, if instead of referring to a second man who compelled the first one, we speak instead of the *desires* and *beliefs* which the first man happens to have had. . . . Since *they* caused [his action] *he* was unable to do anything other than just what he did do' ([26], pp. 12–13).

Later on Chisholm evaluates a hypothetical interpretation of 'The killer could have acted differently'. He argues :

'What the murderer saw, let us suppose, along with his beliefs and desires, *caused* him to fire the shot; yet he was such that if, just then, he had chosen or decided *not* to fire the shot, then he would not have fired it. . . .

. . . Suppose, after all, that our murderer could not have *chosen*, or could not have *decided*, to do otherwise. . . . Then he could not have done anything other than just what it was that he did do' ([26], pp. 15–16).

Why suppose 'that our murderer could not have chosen . . . to do otherwise'? Presumably because his desires and beliefs caused him to make the choice he did make. It seems that, in Chisholm's view, they prevented him from electing a different course of action. At any rate, Chisholm reports no other causes of his actual choice except for his desires and beliefs, and so nothing else seems to be a candidate for a hindering cause. Now if Chisholm does hold that ordinary attitudes and thoughts, which have not originated from hypnosis, brain-washing or cerebral lesions, prevent us from choosing otherwise, and thereby render us powerless to act otherwise, he is unjustified. What entitles Chisholm to assume that desires whose origin is not abnormal will prevent a man from choosing or acting differently? He must demonstrate their similarity to circumstances which disable or otherwise hinder a person.

There is a hint in 'Ifs and Cans' that Austin has committed the same error as Chisholm. Austin denies that 'I can' means 'I shall if I choose'. He also denies that 'the meaning of "I shall if I choose" is that my choosing to do the thing is sufficient to cause me inevitably to do it' ([11], p. 159). What is Austin's point here? A swimmer who is caught in a riptide drifts inevitably out to sea. Even if he desires and struggles to reach the shore, he cannot avoid drifting seaward. The current stops him from returning to the beach. Now look at someone who is not in the grip of a current. He floats or strokes away from the shore because he wants to. Perhaps we would rank his choosing or desiring to do this as a cause of his seaward motion. But it sounds incongruous to assimilate this case to the riptide situation, and to say, 'Even if he desired or struggled to go back, his choosing would cause him inevitably to move out to sea.'

This error of assimilating all causes to hindering causes has received more than enough attention. I hope that it is clear how Austin's indeterministic theses (iv) and (v) is nourished by this confusion. In the remaining section of this paper, I want to scrutinize a kindred, but less pernicious assumption, which appears both in 'Ifs and Cans' and in Chisholm's commentary: the assumption that every conditional statement of the form, 'He will if he chooses (tries, etc.)', must record a causal relationship.

10. Non-conditional 'if's, causal 'if's and non-causal but conditional 'if's

Among the five remarks by Austin on ability that I began with, I have said very little about (iii), his thesis that statements specifying what a person can do are irreducibly categorical. At present I want to investigate Austin's denial that such assertions may be translated into hypothetical form. As before, I shall focus on ascriptions of ability. My modification of Austin's thesis will read: An ability statement is not equivalent to one or more conditionals, but it must entail one or more; however, such conditionals need not specify causal relationships. Austin, and Chisholm as well, seem to overlook the possibility that a conditional assertion might not describe a cause-effect sequence. Austin therefore appears to believe that his disproof of the view that 'He will if he tries' is a *causal* conditional automatically also proves that a statement of this form is not a conditional of any sort. Moreover, Austin seems to assume that just because 'can' statements are not analysable into hypothetical form, they are logically unrelated to statements of that form. Actually these are minor errors in such a ground-breaking paper as 'Ifs and Cans'. But we shall not have a satisfactory account of human power, and how causality bears upon it, until we correct them.

My study of the connection between having an ability to do something and doing it, in sections 1 to 5, demonstrated why having an ability does not guarantee success, even under ideal circumstances. Furthermore, it seemed that a person might not succeed even though he was unhindered by disabilities and similar interferences. That is, the man's failure never proves that he

could not do it then and there. However, one's failure may still
have causes, of the non-hindering variety. For these reasons, I
suggested that when you ascribe an ability to someone, in a
situation that is free of impediments, you imply that if he sets out
to do what he has the ability to do, he will *probably* succeed.
The degree of likelihood to which you commit yourself will vary,
as I noted in section 4, with the type of action that concerns you.

How do these conclusions affect Austin's thesis (iii)? We must
interpret (iii) at greater length. His doctrine, that ability statements are categorical, is not a grammatical remark. He gives
many compound sentences which contain an 'if' clause as examples
of sentences which are used to make categorical assertions. His
paradigm is: 'There are biscuits on the sideboard if you want
them'. He allows that a statement of this form might be analysed
into another statement which will contain the 'can' of entitle-
ment or right: 'There are biscuits on the sideboard which you
can (or may) take if you want them'. However, Austin maintains
that the latter statement is equally non-conditional. I think that
one might use Austin's paradigm, 'There are biscuits on the sideboard if you want them', to ascribe an ability as well as a right.
For example, one might mean: 'You will find biscuits on the
sideboard if you want (or bother trying) to find them'. Anyway,
besides his paradigm of a non-conditional 'if', Austin presents the
following ability statements as non-conditionals:

> I could have walked a mile this morning in 20 minutes, if I
>   had chosen;
> I am capable of doing it (if I choose);
> I could have ruined you this morning (if I had chosen);
> I could have won if I had chosen to lob.

With what is Austin comparing these 'if's? He gives a paradigm of a causal 'if'-statement which does not contain a 'can':
'I pant if I run'. The only causal ability statement he gives is:
'I can squeeze through if I am thin enough', of which he reports
that it includes 'an ordinary causal "if"' (p. 158). He mentions
a number of other conditionals having to do with ability:

> He could shoot you if you were within range;
> I could do it if I had a thingummy;

I could have ruined you this morning, if I had had one more vote;

I could, or should have won if he had chosen to lob (or to let me win).

Austin never says whether the 'if'-clause in these examples specifies a cause; but it is significant that he fails to mention the possibility that it does not, and that the statement should still be conditional.

For Austin, the distinctive features which set apart all such conditional 'if'-statements from their non-conditional counterparts are these. You may deduce a contrapositive from conditional 'if'-statements, and not from the others. Non-conditional 'if'-statements allow you to infer, or detach, the main clause; but this is forbidden with conditional 'if'-statements. Austin explains:

'From "If I run, I pant", we *can* infer "If I do not pant, I do not run" (or, as we should rather say, "If I am not panting, I am not running"), whereas we can *not* infer either "I pant, whether I run or not" or "I pant" (at least in the sense of "I am panting"). . . . These possibilities and impossibilities of inference are typical of the *if* of causal condition: but they are precisely reversed in the case of "I can if I choose" or "I could have if I had chosen". For from these we should not draw the curious inferences that "If I cannot, I do not choose to" or that "If I could not have, I had not chosen to" (or "did not choose to"). . . . But on the contrary, from "I can if I choose" we certainly should infer that "I can, whether I choose to or not" and indeed that "I can" period: and from "I could have if I had chosen" we should similarly infer that "I could have, whether I chose to or not" and that anyway "I could have" period. So that, whatever this *if* means, it is evidently not the *if* of causal condition' (pp. 157–8).

The inference pattern Austin sketches is distinctive. However, his final sentence suggests that Austin believes the pattern to mark off only two kinds of 'if'-statement: causal conditionals and non-conditionals. What about non-causal conditionals? It seems doubtful to me whether there is 'an ordinary causal "if" ' in 'I can squeeze through if I am thin enough'. How does being thin

137

enough bring it about that I have the ability? And it is even more questionable whether being thin brings it about, in any causal sense, that I have the opportunity, the knowledge, the means or the right to squeeze through. Austin's other conditionals sound just as uncausal as the squeezing one, by a similar test.

I am particularly interested to see whether Austin has established that statements of the form, 'He will probably do X if he chooses (tries, etc.) to do Y' are non-conditional. I agree that they are not causal. You do not cause yourself to sink a putt by trying or choosing; you only cause the ball to tumble into the cup, by striking it in a certain manner.

An example will help us focus on the issue of conditionality. Suppose it is probable that if Green tries hard to beat Thomas at ping-pong, Green will defeat Thomas. There are no hindrances around to bother Green. Isn't it equally probable, in this case, that if Green does not win, his attempt was faulty? At any event, the statement, 'It is probable that if Green tries hard to beat Thomas at ping-pong, he will', does not conform to the inference pattern of non-conditional 'if'-statements; for it hardly entails that Green will defeat Thomas whether he tries to or not, and that Green will probably defeat him *tout court*. So this 'if' is at least different from non-conditional 'if's.

How is this sort of conditional linked with ascribing skill to Green? In the following way, I think: if you credit Green with the ability to defeat Thomas, you must be prepared to accept some hypothetical statements of this form, although you will have considerable choice among antecedent clauses. Also you must be prepared to reject the sub-contraries of these conditional statements. It would be very odd for an admirer of Green to declare: 'He has the ability to smear Thomas, but I have no idea whether he will win, even if he puts his heart into the game.' That is: if you believe Green has this ability, you must believe that there is some condition, perhaps even Green's relaxing and not caring, which is more likely to presage a victory by Green than a loss. The likelihood of his triumph does not, of course, exclude the possibility that it is Thomas's lucky day, and that he will manage to turn the tables on his more skilled opponent.

This revision of Austin's theory about the entailment relations between an ability statement and non-causal, but conditional, probability statements deserves more scrutiny than I shall give it here. I believe that the entailment in question is partly pragmatic. When you ascribe an ability to someone, perhaps you thereby commit yourself to accepting some hypotheses and not others about the conditions under which the agent will do what you say he has the ability to do. Why have philosophical adherents of hypothetical accounts in the past so often favoured 'if'-clauses which specify quasi-psychological conditions of the agent, such as trying and choosing? I think that this unexamined assumption is justified by the fact that our concept of an ability is the concept of a power which is under the control of its possessor. By contrast, the corrosive power of nitric acid is not within the acid's control.

The principal error I find in previous accounts of an agent's control is the further assumption that the only way you ever control an event is by causing it to occur, to continue, to stop or not to occur. If we carry over this latter assumption to the case of doing what you have the ability to do, we get the absurd result that you bring it about that you sink a putt by first desiring or trying to sink it. With regard to Green's victory, the causal assumption suggests to us that Green's method of defeating Thomas consisted in his wanting or attempting to defeat him. But the questions, 'How did Green triumph?' and 'What caused his victory?', are not always answered if you say, 'He wanted and tried to win.'

If the connection between quasi-psychological states of the agent, such as desire or endeavour, and his doing what he has the ability to do, is not always causal, what is it? Perhaps it is wiser to keep silent, rather than feel obliged to propose a surrogate for the dubious causal view. My own hesitant conjecture about the relation is this. The 'if' we find in 'Green will defeat Thomas if he tries (to defeat him, to keep him running from side to side)' introduces a supposition. In other words, when you credit Green with skill at ping-pong, you are committed to predicting a certain kind of performance by Green, under some range of conditions. These conditions must be conditions of Green, since you are talking only about his ability, not his opportunities, rights and so on. Among conditions of Green that are relevant to his winning are his desiring or making an effort to win. You have great latitude in specifying these relevant conditions, and for this reason your statement that Green has the ability to defeat Thomas is not synonymous with any particular 'if-then' statement. Nevertheless, your ability statement, together with the supposition that the condition obtains, which you have selected as relevant to Green's victory, gives you reason to say that Green will win. On this conjectural interpretation, 'Green has the ability to beat Thomas at ping-pong' entails some statement of the form 'If Green . . . ; then probably he will win'. Your evidence for all these assertions is the frequency of Green's success, under a wide range of similar circumstances in the recent past.

Austin presents a clever argument to dissolve this epistemic bond, through common evidence, between ability statements and the sort of non-causal conditional I want to connect with them. Austin's argument is directed against the analysis in Professor Nowell-Smith's book *Ethics* [88]. Should we, as Nowell-Smith proposes, conclude from the evidence of a man's earlier success in reading a certain book, not only that he *could* have read it yesterday, but also that he *would* have, if his conative attitude had been suitable? Austin replies that considerations of the man's attitude and probable actions are out of place. He explains:

> 'Whether or not we should describe our conclusion here as "categorical" it seems that it should still be a conclusion of the form "he *could* have done so and so", and not in the least a conclusion concerning what he *would* have done. We are interested, remember, in [someone's] abilities: we want to know whether he could have read [the novel] *Emma* yesterday: we ascertain that he did read it the day before yesterday, and that he does read it today: we conclude that he could have read it yesterday. But it does not appear that this says anything about what he would have done yesterday or in what circumstances: certainly, we are now convinced, he *could* have read it yesterday, but *would* he have, considering that he had read it only the day before?' ([11], p. 172).

Far from severing the tie between ability, attitude and performance, Austin's reasoning actually strengthens it. Austin's closing rhetorical question implies that the reader of *Emma* is the sort of person who cannot bring himself to wade through the same novel two days in a row. Then we have excellent grounds to deny, both that he would, *and* that he *could*, have read *Emma* yesterday. Of course he had the ability to read classics of English literature, but his uncontrollable aversion towards reading the same book again hindered him from reading *Emma* yesterday. His distaste worked analogously to a post-hypnotic suggestion. He lacked the ability to read that novel then and there, because of his temporary loathing for it. He could have read a similar novel yesterday. And today, after his respite from *Emma*, he has recovered his ability to read it. All this reinforces the connection between 'could' and the 'would' of probable action, as well as the 'would' of volition. If both of these 'would's were logically independent of our ascription of reading ability to the fellow, why does Austin bother 'considering that he had read [*Emma*] only the day before'? This fact would be irrelevant to our report of the man's ability at a particular time, unless it affected the man's present desires, and these had some bearing upon his action.

I conclude, in appraisal of Austin's much-debated thesis (iii), that he is right to deny that ability statements are synonymous with conditionals, especially causal conditionals; but he is misguided in denying that ability statements are connected in any way with any sort of conditionals. His remark (i) and (ii) proved mutually consistent, and undercut the indeterministic view of ability and action we found in (iv). By (i) and (ii), we see that ability does not guarantee success, even in perfect conditions, and failure does not prove inability. However, it hardly follows (iv) that the failures of a skilled person, in optimum conditions, are uncaused. Nor will it follow, from the contrary assumption that a man's failures have causes, that these causes prevented him from exercising his ability, or that they disabled him. Again, if we admit that his failure to do what he had the ability to do, or for that matter his success, had one or more causes, we are not thereby admitting that his desires and efforts were among these causal factors. And even if a person's conative attitudes do operate as causes of his behaviour, along the lines suggested in Essays III, IV and V, it would be grossly fallacious for us to conclude that they prevent him from acting differently. Only some desires and decisions, such as those resulting from hypnosis, render one powerless to do anything else. With other circumstances that

141

might qualify as causes of one's behaviour, some do and some do not hinder one. When we assume there was a cause of a man's failure to do what he has the ability to do, we are far from conceding that, after all, he could not have done it. Naturally these conclusions invalidate Austin's famous remark (v), that the ordinary concept of ability is inimical to a deterministic outlook on human conduct. Whether people's actions, including their doing and not doing what we say they *can* do, are causally determined, remains totally independent of questions about what we mean by 'can' and 'ability'.

VII

CAN OUR WILLS BE FREE?

In section 6 of the preceding study I found difficulty accepting an argument of Chisholm's against the 'soft' determinist's equation of 'He can do X' with 'He will do X if he chooses to do X'. From the quotations I gave, it seems that Chisholm intends to demonstrate the non-equivalence of these statement-forms by supposing, with regard to a particular agent N, that

   i N would do X if he chose to do X,
   ii N would do X *only* if he chose, i.e. N would *not* do X if he did not choose to do X,
   iii N *cannot choose* to do X.

According to Chisholm, the *analysans* proposed by the determinist, premise (i), along with Chisholm's suppositions (ii) and (iii), entail (iv), 'N *cannot do* X'. Therefore (i) obviously is not equivalent in meaning to 'N can do X'.

I shall not go over Bruce Aune's interesting detailed critique of Chisholm's deduction (see [9]). For the sake of argument, *pace* Aune, I shall suppose that there is no deductive or no 'modal' fallacy if you infer (iv) from (i), (ii) and (iii). What I want to do in the present study is focus on statements like (iii), which ascribe some volitional incapacity to the agent. If a premise of this type is to figure in a non-trivial deduction of (iv), we need a reasonably precise account of conditions that hinder a man's will. If (iii) records conditions which prevent N from *doing* X, your deduction of (iv) is trivial. We want a proof that one circumstance, his inability to choose, leads to another, his inability to act. And as I argued at length in the foregoing study, you beg important questions if you infer, from the fact that N *does not* choose to do X, or from the fact that something causes N not to choose to do X, the truth of your premise (iii) or your conclusion (iv). Not choosing is hardly being powerless to choose, and not all causes leave you powerless. In this study, I want to approach

143

this crucial concept of a volitional impediment, along quite general lines, beginning with a tiny dose of historical background.

Hobbes's deterministic analysis of choosing and doing provoked the same response you hear nowadays. During his famous debate with Hobbes, Bishop Bramhall contended that if a person's

> 'will do not come upon him according to his will, then he is not a free, nor yet so much as a voluntary agent. . . . All the freedom of the agent is from the freedom of the will. If the will have no power over itself, the agent is no more free than a staff in a man's hand' ([85], p. 44; [57]).

Bramhall's fears are echoed in a new book by Richard Taylor, *Metaphysics*. Taylor asks

> 'whether the causes of my actions – my own inner choices, decisions, and desires – are themselves caused. . . . If they are, then we cannot avoid concluding that, given the causal conditions of those inner states, I could not have decided, willed, chosen, or desired otherwise. . . .' ([113], p. 49).

It is unimportant, adds Taylor, whether these volitional events occur because an 'ingenious physiologist' has tampered with one's brain; whether they result from one's addiction to narcotics, from baneful 'hereditary factors, or indeed from anything at all.' Ultimately, the agent has no 'control' over his conative states. So even if the agent has strength, skill, endurance, opportunity, implements and knowledge enough to engage in a variety of enterprises, still he lacks mastery over his basic attitudes and the decisions they produce. After all, we do not have occasion to choose our dominant proclivities. For Taylor, our inability to guide our own will appears to invalidate our freedom of action; he thinks we 'cannot but act in accordance' with our current preferences. ([113], p. 45).

Outcries like these, to the effect that determinism entails that our wills labour under some kind of bondage, find some provocation in the words – if not the thought – of Locke ([74], Book II, Ch. XXI), Hume ([61], pp. 313, 408), Schlick ([107], p. 155) and others who move along in the wake of Hobbes. These champions of universal causation often write as if, given the motivational state of an agent who is considering what to do, he is somehow forced to reach the decision which terminates his deliberations. This is one of Hobbes's conclusions during his interchange with Bramhall ([85], pp. 50–1). Hume and Schlick also seem to hold that we are deprived of control over our wills.

Another line Hobbes takes is that the whole question raised by Bramhall and other anti-determinists, 'Are men ever free to will as they will?', is 'absurd speech' ([85], pp. 42, 48–9). Locke begins his famous chapter on power with a similar outlook, arguing that it makes sense to attribute power to an agent, but not to his will. Later on in his analysis, however, Locke begins to worry that we might be slaves of our own desires; and he wonders if, by cultivating some of our desires and suppressing others, we might acquire the very sort of power over our wills that he had declared nonsensical. Mill, finally, offers a perfect illustration of the difficulties you run into when you take a generally deterministic outlook, but then try to find a place for control and freedom on the level of desires and decisions (see his [83], Ch. XXVI).

Against this historical background, I want to bring some coherence into the dispute. I would ask philosophers who share the anxieties of Bramhall and Taylor : Just what sort of 'power over' their wills are men supposed to lack? Is it at least conceivable that men should not have laboured under this deficiency? We should try to describe a universe in which men can will as they will. In the world we know, presumably a man's inclinations and resolutions are affected by earlier circumstances that he could not have influenced – the composition of his genes, or experiences he underwent during infancy or military duty. Why does it follow that he 'could not have' developed different proclivities, that he cannot help deciding as he does now? And how could things be different? If I cannot accomplish certain feats because I am out of condition, awkward, untrained, timid or uninformed, the remedies are obvious. Whether or not a cure is feasible, that is, we know what would constitute a cure for my debility, and so on. But what circumstances would give me the proper dominion over my will? Even if, *per impossibile*, I had the chance to select my hereditary traits, my childhood environment and formative experiences, my present desires and personality, the same problem arises : what caused me to take the character I picked for

K   145

myself? Either my selection was arbitrary, in which case I exercised no control over the outcome; or it was determined by some mysterious prior inclinations, which presumably escaped my control.

We must formulate the problem more precisely. Count some, but not necessarily all, of the following as states and operations of our wills: planning, forming intentions, resolving, deciding, vacillating, changing our minds, sticking to our resolutions, considering alternative courses of action and estimating their advantages or risks; perhaps even the covert actions that go under the impressive titles of 'willing', 'performing acts of volition' and 'setting ourselves'. Now our aim is to understand what would constitute possession or deprivation of liberty for these phenomena. So we must consider the horde of idioms we find rallying about the banner of liberty. Most prominent are expressions we use to describe the way people act, such as 'willingly', 'voluntarily', 'knowingly'; terms we use to describe agents, such as 'liberated': and terms we use in specifying what people can, could, and will be able to do, such as 'power', 'capacity', 'opportunity', 'means', 'know-how', 'authority', 'privilege' and 'right'. The diverse antonyms of these terms, beginning with 'coercion', merit particular notice, because they delineate the heterogeneous ways one might lack freedom. My plan will be to assume that this vocabulary has sufficiently clear meaning in the context of our reports of agents and their undertakings. Hence my chief question is going to be simply, 'Do these terms have some application to the wills and decisions of human agents?'

I realize that many philosophers have declared that by a free will they mean precisely a will whose states and dictates are to some extent causally independent of surrounding conditions, including the agent's proclivities, and thus occur 'by chance'. I shall not examine this view here. Countless others, from Hume [61, 62] to Nowell-Smith [88], have demonstrated how the absence of causes for our deeds and preferences is bound to *lessen* our control over both. Consider one analogy: in so far as the tuning of my FM radio is not determined by the pressure I exert upon the knobs, or by any other happenings inside or outside the wireless, I have no way of tuning my radio to this or that broadcasting station. Thus to the extent that no correlation, positive or negative, holds between my resolutions and preceding circumstances – for instance, between my decision to enlist in the Navy and my antecedent yen for a seafaring life – neither I nor anyone else can hope to guide my will.

Getting back to the main inquiry, I shall have to postpone analysis of terms like 'free agent', 'free will', 'free to do' and 'free to decide', in order to recall the intricacies of 'acting freely'. This may illuminate one facet of our question about free will, namely: 'Do people ever deliberate and make up their minds freely, or can they not help deciding as they do?'

In his 'Plea for Excuses', Austin contends that a satisfactory account of 'acting freely' should set out the outstanding 'breakdowns' to which human endeavours are susceptible. Austin declares, in a passage from which I have already quoted:

'While it has been the tradition to present this as the "positive" term requiring elucidation, there is little doubt that to say we acted "freely" (in the philosopher's use, which is only faintly related to the everyday use) is to say only that we acted *not* un-freely, in one or another of the many heterogeneous ways of so acting (under duress, or what not). . . . "Free" is only used to rule out the suggestion of some or all of its recognized antitheses. . . . "Freedom" is not a name for a characteristic of actions, but the name of a dimension in which actions are assessed. In examining all the ways in which each action may not be "free", i.e. the cases in which it will not do to say simply "X did A", we may hope to dispose of the problem of Freedom ([10], p. 128).

I wonder, following Austin, what sorts of mishap we mean to 'rule out' when we talk of liberty at the deliberative and planning stage? Some parallels between doing and deciding may be dismissed straight away. To start with the dimension of awareness or intelligence: at times we know what we are doing, and sometimes we act unwittingly, because we are misinformed, inattentive, dazed or asleep. For instance, I jostle the person ahead of me in the grocery line, but fail to notice that I do. Could I make up my mind to nudge him, but remain unaware of my decision? The idea is baffling. A postman might hand over a registered letter to an imposter, mistaking him for the addressee.

Could anyone make a decision by mistake – resolve to fish next Sunday instead of resolving to weed the lawn – because he confounds the former with the latter decision? Neither recognition nor misidentification appear to have a role in these proceedings. Travellers often leave their baggage along the way because of distraction or absent-mindedness; but it is absurd to suppose that people should make plans while they are totally preoccupied with something else, or while their minds are blank.

Another kind of behavioural slip has no counterpart on the deliberative plane. Many of the things we do are accidents. Because of a freakish rebound, one tennis player accidentally drives the ball into his opponent's eye. What would it be like to decide by accident? The setting of coincidence, ricochets, unexpected collisions, sudden appearances, short circuits, jammed machinery and ineffective safety devices, which makes it possible for us to hurt people and damage their property by accident, cannot be found in the volitional sphere.

For somewhat different reasons, it sounds absurd to suggest that decisions, like deeds, might be unintentional, or intentional either. I am concerned with the restricted use of these terms in discourse about the preparations, aims or expectations of an agent. We can meaningfully ask, for example: 'Did the rapist mean to bring about the death of his victim? Did he have reason to expect she would take poison because of his assault? Could that expectation have been one of his grounds for attacking her?' It makes sense to claim or to deny that he intentionally caused the woman's death. In addition, alternative circumstances can be imagined in which the assailant neither desires nor anticipates the suicide of his victim. Nothing of either sort is possible for decisions. For example, would it not be self-contradictory for a man to claim that he had no idea his deliberations would terminate in a decision? An assault need not be expected to result in the victim's death; but when a man considers what to do, it is necessarily one of his aims, or at least one of his expectations, that he will make up his mind. That is part of what we mean when we say he is deliberating.

A more difficult comparison is between involuntary motions which result from muscle spasms, blows, flashes of light, noises, chills or the like, and certain types of decision. Assume that whenever people receive some particular drug, or hypnotic spell, or whenever some part of their brain is tickled by a probe, they are struck by the thought of going for a stroll. Would this upshot count as an involuntary decision? We may readily grant that these stimuli give people an urge to walk, and that this urge appears to be involuntary. However, we notice a telling difference between this phenomenon and the sorts of resolutions people make impulsively, neglecting to survey alternatives and consequences. With regard to any impulsive decision, it is conceivable that the agent should have paused instead to reflect; we have some idea how this reasoning might have proceeded. This possibility is excluded, however, by the foregoing account of urges and sudden 'thoughts of doing' which result from drugs, hypnosis or probes.

But now assume that these stimuli dispose people to reason systematically and critically about a walk. Just those individuals who would normally make up their minds to walk do so, and with good reasons, in these imaginary test-conditions. Given this revised narrative, it sounds all right to speak of a decision, but odd to call the decision involuntary. Why does 'involuntary' sound alien? Because when we use this term to characterize someone's blinks and winces, one thing we mean is that these reactions occur *regardless* of his concurrent thoughts and deliberations. An intense light flashes into my eyes and, no matter what I am thinking at the time, I squint. By contrast, when the drug or whatnot produces careful and plausible deliberation, and a decision to walk only in case the agent sees some benefit to it, the decision is a prime example of a state of affairs that *is* influenced by the agent's thoughts. The origin of his decision now seems of secondary importance, and would not compel us to call it involuntary.

If the notion of willing 'freely' cannot intelligibly be used to rule out deciding 'unwittingly', 'by accident', 'unintentionally', 'involuntarily' and their immediate kin, is it altogether empty? No, for there seem to be noteworthy points of resemblance between deeds people execute and decisions they reach under compulsion; while suffering great pain; during intoxication; while overcome by vehement feelings; and because of provocation, blackmail, flattery, indoctrination, brain-washing or habit. Besides

149

these mishaps, another type of breakdown has a parallel in deliberation. Normally our duties and obligations require us to perform certain tasks; but sometimes decisions are required. A trustee of another person's fortune may be obligated to plan in advance for various contingencies, e.g. decide which securities must be sold if the cold war ends, even though his decisions never happen to be translated into deeds. Consequently the trustee is no longer free to plan or not, as he chooses. In general, then, to assert that someone's will is free is to deny that it is presently subject to these impediments and pressures. Since we understand how coercion and the like diminish a man's intelligence, caution, and his sense of right and wrong, if he is considering what to do, we would deny that a decision he made while in such circumstances was free.

Each of the pressures we catalogued is also likely to impair a man's freedom in his actions. Therefore, unless there are some further conditions for willing freely, which I have overlooked, it seems that no special precautions are needed to secure freedom for an agent's volitional movements. As a matter of fact, since there is no possibility that the agent should ignore his own decision, no chance that he will make up his mind unintentionally, by accident or involuntarily, fewer safeguards are required. If someone reaches a decision while he is untroubled by any of the disturbing influences we listed above, we would be mistaken to argue : 'If his decision is due to anything else at all – his schooling or his desire for wealth – then he still cannot help deciding as he does.' We have not managed to uncover anything as positive as 'power' or 'control' by an agent over his deliberations; but at least helplessness and unmanageability appear not to be logical consequences of determinism.

Concepts of the freedom-cluster apply to agents, as well as to the deeds they perform. So we can profitably survey a few analogies between ascriptions of liberty to people and things we might say about their wills. Here again we should expect as many dimensions and contrasts as we find in the notion of 'acting freely'. A primitive example will help at the start : imagine that the waterpipes in my house freeze over. I ring a plumber, and he informs me that he will not be free until tomorrow afternoon. His remark has a definite enough meaning in the setting of my request, and it has nothing to do with the current or future state of his will. The plumber is not at liberty now, we may assume, because he is tied up with other work. Even if he decides to repair my pipes today, all the same, he is not thereby released from his previous commitments, and thus remains not free. What is more, he will be at liberty as soon as his previous commitments have been met, whether or not he makes up his mind to work on my house. That is: although he is going to be free tomorrow, perhaps he will forget my request, or choose to spend the afternoon skin-diving, rather than repair my frozen pipes.

Ascriptions of liberty to someone like the plumber, then, are not covertly about the person's will. But one thing is plainly involved in such statements: a background of various possible restrictions, such as the plumber's current work-schedule, which have roughly the same status as 'breakdowns' in action. We must presuppose some environment of constraints, regulations and prerogatives. Within this sort of context, a free person stands in contrast to a captive, a serf, a ward, a dependant, a person under some legal, financial, professional, social, religious or moral obligation. In complex settings, a person may be free *vis-à-vis* one set of restrictions, but not another. For example: a drunken merry-maker who is incarcerated for disturbing the peace, and then turned loose on bail, is at liberty – pending his trial at any rate. By the same token, other lawbreakers who are condemned to remain under lock and key are deprived of liberty. Now suppose our reveller is a citizen of a repressive dictatorship, whose ruling officials assign work and lodgings to the populace, ration food and clothing, ban political parties, prohibit elections and censor all communications media. If we consider these additional restrictions, we should deny that our reveller is a free man.

Can we extract any general pattern from such talk of liberty and restrictions? It sounds plausible to say: until he is freed on bond, our celebrant is not at liberty *to* leave the jail, but even when he acquires this liberty, he is not free *to* dwell where he pleases, to quit his job, and so forth. Although we cannot catalogue all the things a free agent is free to do, such inventories are linked with the concept of personal liberty. It would be absurd to declare: 'The pupils of this progressive school enjoy considerable freedom, but they are not allowed to destroy anything, to swear, to read whatever strikes their fancy, to stay away from classes, to participate in sports or abstain from them; in fact, most of the pupils' time is consumed by prescribed activities.' Because of this liaison between 'free' and verbs, we might characterize this adjective as 'infinitive-hungry'. Speaking in the material mode : human freedom has some activity or achievement as its object.

Ascriptions of personal liberty, in this respect, are like ascriptions of power, capacity, skill, opportunity, right and prerogative, as well as statements about a person's knowledge and means for undertaking some course of action. When we say someone is talented, able, privileged and so forth, a verb is in the vicinity. People are able or unable to bend their knees, to concentrate; they are gifted or inept at safe-cracking; they have or miss an opportunity to smoke hashish; they have the privilege of parking their automobiles in a loading zone; they are equipped or unequipped, and have or lack the knowledge one needs for oil prospecting. Freedom is also connected with these other notions in a more significant way : whenever an agent is at liberty to do something, he must be *able* to do it, in at least one – but not always the same one – of these other senses of 'able'. In discussing the plumber, we took it for granted that he was qualified and outfitted to repair my water-pipes; our concern was with his opportunity to perform the task. When we considered the merry-maker's freedom, on the other hand, we were interested in his right to leave the jail. We presumed nothing about his powers, capacities and so on. Possibly the fellow drank so much spirits that he cannot use his limbs. His sense of direction may be so impaired that he cannot find his way out of the police station. He may have spent all his funds for beverages and his bail-bond, and thus lack means to get home. Nevertheless, in the legalistic sense that concerns us when we describe a man who has just been arrested, our Dionysian is free to leave. Other detainees may possess the necessary strength and cunning to leave, and hush-money for their guards, but they will not be legally free to depart until they are officially released.

The locution 'free to X' hardly ever serves to ascribe power, capacity, skill, means and knowledge; it normally functions in attributions of right and opportunity. For instance, if someone recovers his power of hearing after he is temporarily deafened by gunfire, it would be strange to say, 'Now he is *free* to hear.' As far as I can tell, however, this idiosyncrasy of the adjective 'free' is without bearing upon our enigma, 'Do concepts of the freedom-cluster apply to the will and its operations?'

Our task, at this stage of inquiry, is to trace similarities and disanalogies between the phenomena that go under the various labels of 'liberty', 'strength', etc., in descriptions of agents, and corresponding events in the region of the will. Since a décor of actual or conceivable restrictions seemed necessary to provide content for the notion of a free agent, we should expect to find a similar backdrop for the will. So we must ask, 'What impediments, disabilities, deficiencies of knowledge and equipment, what rules and obligations, might prevent a man from making up his mind to follow some line of conduct, and thus diminish his freedom to will?' Regulations we considered and admitted in our discussions of acting freely. A kindred notion deserves consideration now : the concept of authority. It might seem that, because of his special position, the coach of a U.S. football team is the only person who may reach certain decisions, e.g. to substitute another player for the quarterback during a game. Similarly, it appears that magistrates have the exclusive right, within statutory limits, to decide how a convicted offender shall be punished. Again, is anyone but old Uncle Jake, who lies groaning on his deathbed, entitled to decide how much of his fortune should go to his impatient survivors? Here we seem to have a notion of 'free to decide' involving authority to undertake certain volitional movements. But I think that 'decide', in these situations, covers official deeds rather than some state of mind preceding action. For suppose the football coach only makes up his mind to replace the quarterback, but does not announce his resolution : so far he has not exercised his authority. And a spectator of the football match, who deliberates and then decides that the quarterback needs a replacement, is hardly guilty of usurping the trainer's right. In other words, from the standpoint of these restrictions, anyone may decide what should be done about the quarterback, the convicted criminal or Uncle Jake's estate. An 'unauthorized' person may, for that matter, proclaim his decision. However, an unauthorized man's resolution, whether silent or viva voce, simply

153

does not count as a procedure for replacing the quarterback, sentencing the convicted man, or bequeathing Uncle Jake's fortune. Only decisions proclaimed by the coach, the magistrate or the dying man, within earshot of suitable underlings and witnesses, are recognized as constituting, respectively, an order to replace the quarterback, a sentence of five years at hard labour, or a bequest. What counts is the authorized person's announcement, rather than the mental acts he thereby announces.

When we are discussing a man's decisions, the concepts of special capacity, stamina, knacks and technical mastery, equipment and knowledge seem just as inapplicable as the notion of authority. It is hard to see how their various 'opposites' could serve for ascribing volitional debilities and incompetences to someone. In each of these cases, however, there are a few exceptions. Strategic decisions during wartime require great patience and concentration, and most men do not have such capacities. The average shopper does not need special equipment to decide which suit of clothing he will purchase; but an architect might require a slide rule before he can decide which metals he will specify for a skyscraper. Skills or funds of knowledge are unnecessary – perhaps they are a hindrance – for a woman who is making up her mind about a marriage proposal. On the other side, a stockbroker, who has been away from the Exchange several years, might find himself slow, uninformed and clumsy in making prudent decisions while the ticker tape runs wild. All we can say, then, is that these concepts – capacity, stamina and the like – have no application to the will in *normal* decision-making situations. A normal situation is most safely characterized by reference to particular cases like those we noticed above.

As for the remaining concepts that are covered by the locution 'free to X' – power and opportunity – it is evident they ride quite comfortably on the will. Just as a frozen man might lack the power to wiggle his toes, a man who is faced with various options – between entrées at a restaurant, between jobs, between granting or refusing his wife a divorce – might have unbearable difficulty making up his mind. In this kind of situation we wonder, 'Although he can do one thing or the other, can he decide how he will act?' He seems to have the ability to act, but not to reach a decision. The same appears to hold for opportunity. A wealthy

154

but overworked surgeon has not the time to plan for his retirement – to decide where he will spend his declining years, how he will occupy himself, and so on – although he has the opportunity to retire whenever he feels like it. He only has to inform his patients that he is retiring.

I have no doubt that these descriptions are meaningful. Do they create a gulf between conditions for acting and conditions for deciding? I doubt it. In the first example, you could just as well maintain that the hesitant man is hindered from *acting* by psychological disturbances which never afflict most people. In other words, most people would take one or the other course of action under the circumstances; but he cannot, because of his uncommon 'block' when he faces some options. In the other case, you might reply that planning one's retirement is really an action, even though one can perform it covertly. Another, complementary reply is that the busy surgeon really lacks the opportunity to perform a more complex sort of action than brusquely retiring. His frantic schedule deprives him of the opportunity to go into a carefully planned retirement. He is unable to carry out the first stage of this complex undertaking. So even in these cases, where it is helpful to say that a person is free, in various senses of 'free', to will, we have not come across 'something more', over and above freedom to act.

I conclude, in line with my account of 'willing freely', that being able to will is a more anaemic notion than being able to act. It makes no sense to say a man has or lacks authority to reach some type of decision. In most common cases, also, there appear to be no grounds for asserting or denying that a person has the capacity, endurance, skill, implements or knowledge to reach some decision. With the remaining freedom concepts, which do apply to the will – legal or moral permission, opportunity and power to will – it is painfully obvious how we bring about such conditions: we procure permission; we take time to deliberate; we undergo psychotherapy in case we suffer from volitional paralysis. Once more it seems that the conditions necessary for freedom of will are a limited subset of the optimum conditions for exercising our abilities and rights to act, and for exploiting our opportunities to perform various deeds.

For such reasons, I would maintain that agents and their

155

actions take primacy over the wills and decisions of agents, within any cogent theory of human freedom. But this is not the whole story. Doers and their deeds are primary in two further respects. First, we worry about people's decisions because of the conduct that flows from them. Why should we care how brain-washing will influence the attitudes and future decisions of a war prisoner, except that he may resolve to help the other side, and then carry out his design?

Action takes precedence over willing in a second, and more significant, way. Unless we believe that a person has freedom of action, questions about his will are otiose. Let me illustrate. A saboteur is subjected to physical hardship by the police. Fatigue and injections of sodium pentothal eventually weaken him, so that he tells about his associates and his *modus operandi*. The saboteur did not act freely, because he was forced to talk. Knowing this, is there any reason for us to inquire about his freedom in making up his mind? After all, his interrogators would have got him to talk even if he had resolved to keep silent. The same point holds when we consider people's ability to make decisions. Take a radioman who is untrained at cryptanalysis, and has no flair for that sort of work. He intercepts a coded message, which he cannot possibly decipher. It sounds pointless to ask, 'But is he able to decide that he will decode the message?' Only when we run across someone who acted freely – a saboteur who was not compelled to talk – is it interesting to ask whether he decided freely. Only if the radioman could have deciphered the message, but would not do it, have we grounds for investigating his ability to decide.

156

VIII

CAN I FOREKNOW DECISIONS I HAVE NOT YET MADE?

Epistemological features of action have been somewhat neglected in the foregoing studies. In Essay II, lapses of an agent's knowledge about his current behaviour were discussed briefly. Essay III had some remarks on how an agent's non-observational awareness of what he is doing, and why, contrasts with his ordinary perceptual and inductive knowledge of things that caused him to act. One possible exception was allowed : non-observational knowledge that his desires and beliefs were among the causes of his behaviour. Essays IV and V dealt at some length with the logical connections between a man's beliefs, which vary in their unshakeableness, and his attempts and intentions. In the present study I want to explore the relations between one's self-knowledge, of all these varieties, and one's decisions.

There have been a number of stimulating papers, since Hampshire and Hart's essay [47], on the question, 'Can a person know what he is going to decide to do, without already deciding to do it?' Some confusion has developed because many writers have failed to discriminate three kinds of situation or event which we can report by saying that someone has decided. These are :

(i) Selection behaviour, as when a marketer is said to have decided upon one of the lamb roasts at the meat counter. Perhaps all that transpired was that the shopper removed a leg of lamb from the counter. Other examples of this kind of decision would be : taking or discarding articles of dress; picking or refusing bridge-partners; submitting or withdrawing applications; voting for or against candidates and measures.

(ii) Making up your mind, before you have engaged in any selection behaviour of type (i), that you will do something of that type, or indeed that you will perform any other sort of action. As an expository convenience, I shall reserve the word 'decision' for such mental antecedents of behaviour.

157

(iii) Choice behaviour, which I define as undertaking a performance of type (i), or any other type of action, because you have decided, in the mentalistic sense just specified, that you will do it.

After I have set out a few interesting differences between these three kinds of occurrence which are sometimes indiscriminately called 'deciding', I plan to defend a pair of theses :

(A) Prescience of one's own decision does not entail that one has 'decided in advance'.

(B) If an agent does forecast his own decision, he must lack one important item of evidence, unless he makes up his mind in advance; and consequently an undecided person does not have all the right that an observer could have to predict his own decision.

Thesis (B) should not be confounded, as it has been frequently in the literature, with any of the following :

(C) Quite apart from the evidence which supports it, a knowledge-claim about one's future decision is tantamount to a decision in advance.

(C') The agent's firm belief, or certainty, that he will decide to do something, constitutes a decision in advance.

(C'') The 'point' of deciding is to become certain about what one is going to do, or at least try to do.

(C''') One's future decisions are already causally determined, for example by one's current brain processes.

I neither endorse nor reject (C)–(C'''). Furthermore, although I take it for granted that an agent's knowledge of his future decision is ordinary inductive knowledge, and founded on observation, I assume that he can also have other forms of knowledge regarding it which are not derived from evidence. I assume that someone who has made up his mind ahead of time what his decision is going to be often possesses a form of non-observational knowledge of his decision. However, I make no attempt to analyse this kind of knowledge, or to discover its connections with inductive, observational knowledge. I shall do this in Essay X.

Despite these limitations, I think it will be philosophically worth while to explicate the sense in which an agent must 'decide in advance' when he acquires all the information that is relevant to prophesying his decision.

158

Before I defend thesis (A), I want to do some groundwork for it by setting out a few crucial distinctions between three sorts of occurrence which have been heaped together and called 'decisions'. To begin with what I distinguished as 'selection behaviour'. Notice that selection behaviour does not have to be intentional; and consequently it does not have to be anything one decided to do. The agent may also suffer from nearly total ignorance of his current activity. On occasion people pick out their clothes in the morning while they think of something else. While sleepwalking they reach for and turn away from things. And when they drink themselves into a stupor, they often go in for various other kinds of selection behaviour without knowing what they are up to.

With choice behaviour, on the other hand, the agent must both intend and be aware of what he is doing, if he is thereby carrying out a decision. That is, in so far as he is doing what he had settled on, he intends to be, and knows (without observation, no doubt) that he is doing it. Naturally there will be features of his current action that fall outside the scope of his intention and his awareness. In fact, his choice behaviour may have characteristics that are contrary to his plan and his non-observational beliefs. For instance, at a cocktail party, a reformed alcoholic resolves, as usual, to allow himself only soft drinks. On the serving table he sees a glass which he believes to contain pure orange juice, and he takes it, in conformity with his vow. Actually what he has done was to select a potent mixture of vodka and orange juice, contrary to his intention and one of his beliefs. Of course he did intend to take something drinkable, and he had a correct belief that he was doing that. But other features of his choice behaviour went against his decision and his beliefs about what he was doing. It goes without saying that his act had features which neither clashed nor accorded with his intentions and beliefs. The exact speed at which he reached for the glass, the location of his fingers as he grasped the tumbler, and similar minutiae, are all features of what he did when he chose the fateful glass; but they have nothing to do with his guiding decision and his concurrent beliefs.

These remarks about selection behaviour and choice behaviour also give us the relative position of deciding. The only logical entailment we find is between choice behaviour and decisions. In the converse direction, it is at most a pragmatic entailment that a person who has decided to engage in some form of choice behaviour will do so. There is no inconsistency in this story : (1) Archibald resolves to buy pipe tobacco on his way home from work this afternoon. (2) Nothing prevents him; and his resolution neither slips from his mind, nor is it replaced by a contrary decision – for example a sudden vow to give up smoking. But (3), Archibald simply and deliberately omits to purchase any tobacco. There is no logical absurdity in this case; yet if we consider the pragmatic status of the concept of deciding, we shall regard (3) as a strange sequel of (1) and (2). Why? One reason is that when you tell someone you have decided to perform a certain action, you thereby give him good grounds, even if not conclusive ones, to expect that you will carry it through. Another reason, also based upon the way people use the word 'decide' in their dealings with each other, is that deciding is one method we have of preparing ourselves to act.

An even vaguer pragmatic reason why (3) sounds odd in conjunction with (1) and (2) is that we regard it as the main 'point' of deciding that the plan you have formed will determine your future behaviour. Thus imagine that a man, or perhaps a whole tribe, calculates the advantages and drawbacks of various possible actions. These calculations often terminate in a judgement favouring one line of conduct. If the man, or the group, *never* acts in conformity with this judgement, would we even call it a decision? I agree that there is no contradiction if we say that it just turns out that none of these decisions are followed by suitable choice behaviour. On the other hand, the link between decision and choice behaviour is more than a frequently observed concomitance, or even a causal connection. For the moment, I cannot think of any less obscure explanation of how deciding pragmatically entails choice behaviour. More of this in Essay XI.

At any rate, the analysis so far is sufficiently clear for me to propose an account of deciding in advance. Evidently there is no possibility of engaging in selection behaviour, or in choice behaviour, ahead of time. During a cocktail party, the only time you can pick out one of the hors d'œuvres from a tray, either automatically or deliberately, is when the tray is presented to you.

160

If you change your location, so that the tray will come to you earlier, you do not choose an appetizer in advance; you only advance the time at which you can choose one. As you watch the tray circulating among the guests, you may draw a mental bead on a particular hors d'œuvre; but this covert performance is an instance of deciding ahead of time to choose that hors d'œuvre, not an instance of choosing it from those on the tray before the tray reaches you. Selecting or choosing in advance is a logical impossibility.

As for deciding in advance, here is a recipe. In making a decision D_1, you thereby make decision D_2 ahead of time, if and only if: (I) the time at which you make D_1 is earlier than the time at which you would otherwise have made D_2; (II) all the information (which may include misinformation) that you would need to reach D_2 is already available to you when you reach D_1; (III) if you carry out D_1, you perform a kind of action that would also suffice for the fulfilment of D_2. Normally, but not necessarily, it will also be true that you are guided by the same relevant attitudes, or ends in view, when you reach D_1, as you would in reaching D_2. Moreover, as a rule, D_2 will be a *final* decision. Do we need an example that illustrates all of these provisions, including the last two characteristic but inessential ones? This evening I make up my mind (D_1) to catch the 8:05 commuting train tomorrow morning. I have heard that it is the fastest one to the business district, and it is always my attitude that one should not spend unnecessary time travelling. Of course I presently want to visit the business centre, and I shall continue to have this desire tomorrow. Anyway, tomorrow morning at 8:05, I am musing on the railway platform as my train begins to move. I resolve (D_2) that I shall board it, for the same reasons I had the previous day. At this moment, either I carry out both D_1 and D_2, by attempting to hop on board; or else I fail to act in conformity with both decisions. Whatever I do at 8:05, it will be pointless for me to decide at 8:10 that I shall board the 8:05 train (D_3), or that I shall not take the 8:05. In this case, D_1 anticipates D_2; that is the last possible decision I could make. But D_1 is also an advanced version of any other resolution I might make between D_1 and the time at which the train leaves. Naturally provisions

(I)–(III) allow for the possibility that the agent never happens to make D_2; all they require is that he could.

Since provision (II) will be essential to the proof of my thesis (A) regarding foreknowledge and decisions in advance, I shall clarify what I mean by this requirement of information. Fundamentally, (II) requires that the decision-maker, when he reaches D_1, should have enough beliefs, including at times some erroneous ones, for him to specify what action he has settled on. He must have sufficiently precise beliefs about the action he has decided to perform, for him to make an attempt to carry out decision D_1. And his endeavour would also count as an attempt to carry out D_2.

Even this clarification is woefully schematic. So I shall illustrate it with a case which simultaneously proves my thesis (A), to the effect that you can sometimes foresee the behaviour which will result from decisions that you are going to make, but you cannot then make those decisions in advance. The case I have in mind fails to satisfy provision (II). The agent's beliefs will not be sufficiently precise for him to act upon a decision until the time for making D_2. The example runs as follows. Jane and Mary regularly buy their spring dresses at the same store. Jane has made her purchases, but Mary will not find out what dresses Jane bought until after she has made her own purchases. From past experience, however, Mary knows that, even when they shop quite independently, they both come up with at least one spring dress of exactly the same type. Mary is justifiably certain, therefore, that this year, as in previous years, she will decide to buy at least one dress which will turn out to be of the same type as Jane purchased. This future decision of Mary's, then, is a decision of which she has foreknowledge; yet the circumstances I have related obviously prevent her from making it beforehand. For that matter, even when she gets around to shopping, her ignorance of Jane's purchases will prevent Mary from deciding to imitate Jane.

Unhappily for my thesis (A), there is something sloppy about this example of a decision which is known to the agent beforehand, but cannot be made in advance. The very feature that renders it impossible for Mary to decide, at the store and earlier, that she will copy Jane, raises questions concerning her foreknowledge.

As provision (II) of my schema for deciding in advance makes clear, Mary does not have enough information (or misinformation either) about which dress, among those she will decide to buy, will resemble one of Jane's, for her to make that decision in advance. She cannot identify the decision as, for instance, a decision to get the dress advertised on p. 234 of the latest *Vogue*. By the same token, her foreknowledge is only that *some* decision or other that she will reach in the course of her shopping tour is going to be a decision to buy a dress like one that Jane has bought. In other words, Mary's foreknowledge of the particular decision is both oblique and general. Mary has no means of pinpointing her future decision to buy a dress that will turn out to be like Jane's. And it is because she cannot single out her future decision that Mary is barred from making that decision ahead of time. This is also the reason why, even at the time Mary decides to buy the dress that will turn out to resemble one of Jane's, she must remain unable to identify it as the decision of which she had foreknowledge.

In view of this complication, should I give up my claim to have described a decision which the agent knows of, but cannot make in advance? Such a move would be unwarranted. All I have to concede is that Mary's foreknowledge is not as detailed as it would be *if* she had enough information about Jane's purchase to single out her *own* decision to buy a similar dress. If Mary's foreknowledge were that precise, of course, she would be able to make the decision in advance. So this dubious aspect of my case favouring thesis (A) explains how an agent can have foreknowledge of decisions which he cannot make in advance. The explanation is that you do not need the same kind of identifying information about your decision, in order to have *knowledge* of it, as you need in order to *make* the decision. Also your foreknowledge in such cases is severely limited, because you will never recognize your final decision as the one you knew beforehand you would make.

Should there be any suspicion that this limitation rules out genuine foreknowledge, here is a parallel case where the item I know of is not my future decision. A gangster friend of mine distributes lottery tickets. He promises to fix things so that among the daily tickets I buy this week, the number on one of them will be drawn at the end of the week. He has been scrupulous about such bargains in the past. Therefore I justifiably claim to know that on one of the days I get a lottery ticket this week, I shall get a winner. Yet on no occasion when I purchase a ticket am I justified in asserting, 'This is the lucky one'. I am secure in the general knowledge that I shall get a winning ticket, but I do not know at the time I buy the winner that I am doing so.

Having set forth the limitations on foreknowledge that must obtain when thesis (A) holds, and the agent cannot decide in advance, I shall now move on to cases where the agent *can* decide in advance. My thesis (B) is that, among those cases, there are some where, if the agent acquires all the evidence that an observer might gather about his future decision, then he *must* reach that decision ahead of time. In other words, if the agent is in the best possible epistemic situation, he must decide in advance. Of course he might still know of his future decision without being in the best possible position to know. So my thesis (B) bears an interesting asymmetry to (A). While I maintained, on behalf of (A), that if the decision-maker's foreknowledge is sufficiently curtailed, then he cannot decide in advance; now I am contending that if his foreknowledge is sufficiently well grounded, then he must decide in advance. The asymmetry is imperfect, however, since (A) depended upon the obliqueness and generality of a decision-maker's foreknowledge, and (B) concerns the sorts of evidence which supports his foreknowledge.

I can best explain and defend thesis (B) by overcoming an argument to the effect that the sort of decisions which interest me normally cannot be made in advance. I shall show, first, that they always can; and secondly, that in optimum conditions of foreknowledge, they always must be made beforehand. The argument I shall attack comes from a stimulating early treatment of this problem, 'Knowing about Future Decisions', by John Canfield [22]. Canfield imagines two decisions which, according to him, the agent might know of, but cannot make ahead of time. I paraphrase Canfield's account of both paradigms :

Decision (1) : A man is being tortured, so that he will reveal various state secrets he had learned; but rather than disclose the secrets, he decides to let the torture go on.

Decision (2), a less heroic case : At 7 on Monday morning,

Jones is lying snugly in bed; feeling self-indulgent, he decides to remain there for another half-hour, rather than brave the boreal cold of his room.

In his discussion of (1), Canfield assumes that the self-forecaster is not being tortured at the time he predicts his decision (1). And while he denies that the agent can make (1) in advance, Canfield does allow that the following might occur:

(1′) In the safety of his home, the man decides not to give up the secrets when he is tortured. So according to Canfield, (1′) is not an advanced version of (1). Why not? 'Decisions such as (1)', Canfield argues, 'cannot be made in advance of the agent's being in the special circumstances mentioned [in (1)], because the decision is the decision whether or not to remain in those circumstances.'

This sounds like an elementary *non sequitur*. Would it not be absurd to deny that I can presently decide to remain in my office during the next fire-drill, just because I am not in my office now? The best explanation I can think of for Canfield's dubious reasoning is that he has confused two sorts of occurrence, which I separate under the labels 'decision' and 'choice behaviour'. I would agree that a bearer of state secrets who is safe at home cannot *choose* in accordance with decision (1) – or (1′) either. He cannot carry out (1) or (1′), and let the ill-treatment go on, for the simple reason that it is not occurring.

Quite apart from this confusion, it should be evident that decision (1′) fits the specifications I gave earlier, and qualifies as an advanced version of (1). (1′) precedes (1). The future sufferer presumably has detailed information about the pains he is deciding to endure. The fact that he is not labouring under those pains as he makes his advanced decision (1′) is irrelevant. He has sufficiently precise beliefs about the prospective situation, and the agonies that he will undergo if he elects not to reveal the secrets, for him to identify the alternative he is settling on. And of course he will carry out decision (1) if he subsequently acts upon its advanced version (1′). What is more, the decision-maker presumably has the same patriotic reasons for making decision (1′) as he will have if he reaches the final decision (1).

Canfield remarks that nobody receives medals for a decision in advance like (1′). True enough. But would we decorate any-

165

one just for *resolving* not to talk, as the hero does in (1)? Not if his decision were unaccompanied by suitable choice behaviour. For suppose Canfield's protagonist reaches decision (1), and then goes to pieces a moment later. Would he be cited for his 'valiant decision'? Often someone who does the wrong thing, after deciding against it, is blamed more severely than a person who made no resolutions at all. Choice behaviour, rather than the decision from which it flows, would appear to be the primary object of censure and praise. The main exception to this is when a man is prevented from carrying out his decision, but we talk of his good or wicked intentions. And even in this case, one could argue that we evaluate people's unfulfilled decisions because of the choice behaviour we expect them to engender. However, that would be a digression from our reply to Canfield's purported cases of a decision that the agent foresees but cannot make ahead of time.

Before I shift my attack to Canfield's next example, I want to comment on how my analysis of this one confirms my thesis (B), that if an agent is to gather all the relevant evidence about what he is going to decide, he must decide in advance. In Canfield's first example, it is plain that observers would consider it relevant evidence that the agent made advanced decision (1'), although (1') would never be knock-down evidence that he will make the final decision (1). And it is painfully obvious that the agent must decide in advance if he is to acquire this evidence.

Canfield's second paradigm is interesting because the decision-maker, Jones, does reach a decision in advance, but one that is contrary to the final decision (2) that he expects from himself on Monday morning. That is, Jones resolves on Sunday night that he will get up on time. Does this rule out the possibility that Jones should have made decision (2) in advance? Perhaps Jones cannot decide in advance to get up, and also decide in advance to remain in bed, although I shall question this shortly. Nevertheless, aside from Jones's advanced resolution to the contrary, it seems clear that (2) is a decision that Jones easily can make in advance.

How about Jones's foreknowledge of (2)? Why does he expect (2) in spite of his good resolution? Canfield says, plausibly enough, that Jones has records of his past decisions in analogous circumstances. That is certainly weighty evidence; but has Jones any additional reason to believe that he will follow the same pattern on Monday morning as he has in the past? Apparently Canfield takes it for granted that a person's basic attitudes are unalterable. For Canfield reasons, 'Having the character he has, when the time comes, [Jones] will, as he has in the past, decide to stay in bed.'

On behalf of my thesis (B), we should ask if Jones could gather evidence that his character, and specifically his aversion towards early rising, is unchanged. Otherwise we might wonder if the consequences of his past refusals to get up on time might have taught him a lesson. Now clearly Jones cannot discover by intro-spection that his character is still weak. What other methods can he use? How would an observer go about establishing Jones's current proclivities, on the assumption that they will determine whether Jones makes decision (2) on Monday morning? One method would be to interrogate Jones: 'Imagine that it is early morning; you had resolved to get out of your comfortable bed at this time, but the room is freezing: how would you decide in the circumstances?' Of course Jones can use this technique on himself.

I am hardly suggesting that it is a snap for an observer, much less for Jones himself, to discover those character traits that will affect Jones's final decision. But I believe that such questions are a source of serviceable data. Analogous questions come up when we receive vocational guidance; they occur in personality inventory tests; and they are at least as revealing as parlour games such as 'If your doctor told you that you had a year to live, how would you decide to spend it?'

My suggestion is only that evidence of this type would help Jones forecast his final decision; what is more, Jones's answer would be a kind of decision in advance. What kind? I would say that when Jones imagines himself in the situation he will face Monday morning, and reports his ranking of the alternatives, he 'decides hypothetically' that he will not get up.

What differentiates a hypothetical decision in advance from the other decisions in advance that we have considered? For one thing, the hypothetical variant carries less commitment. Thus in Canfield's first example, the categorical decision in advance (1') imposes a fairly strong obligation on the decision maker, both to reach the final decision (1), when he is subjected to torture, and to act accordingly. In the present case, when Jones is merely trying to estimate his character, and particularly his weakness for staying in bed, he seems not to be committing himself to the final decision (2) or its fulfilment. Is that only because of the moral disparity between the actions in cases (1) and (2)? I believe that a decision of any kind only commits you if what you decided to do is morally worth while. But this is merely a necessary condition of being committed by a decision. I do not think that the agent will be committed by his decision unless it was categorical as well.

Here is another case to back that up. Jones is asked to estimate his basic inclinations to opt for or against a deed that is on a par with keeping state secrets. For example, he is told to imagine that he is the only bystander in sight when a tenement goes up in flames. He hears children inside. Would he decide to go in after them? Now even if he sincerely reports the hypothetical decision to rescue the children, this does not obligate him to make a similar categorical decision if he ever faces a situation of that type. If he has an obligation so to decide, and to act, his duty comes from the moral features of the situation, and not from the fact that he made an earlier hypothetical decision. On the other hand, suppose that Jones discovers that a tenement is going to catch fire, and that he will be the only person near enough to rescue some children in it. He decides in advance that he will attempt to save the children. Does not his categorical decision in advance increase his obligation to reaffirm his decision and act accordingly when the fire occurs? I believe so.

If the new concept of deciding hypothetically still baffles you, one morally neutral comparison I can think of is with going over the racing form, and marking down the horses you *would* bet on if you had cash to spare, if you had not sworn off gambling, etc. Such hypothetical wagering is a sort of warm-up. In case you suddenly receive a legacy, and renounce your pledge not to gamble, you are relatively free to decide upon a new list of horses.

Anyway, the difference in commitment counts for little alongside the important similarities between hypothetical and ordinary categorical decisions in advance: Jones's hypothetical decision

168

to remain in bed precedes his final decision (2); Jones already has sufficiently precise beliefs to identify and carry out the action on which he is hypothetically deciding; carrying out the hypothetical decision would also fulfil the final decision; and presumably he has the same reasons for deciding hypothetically as he will have on Monday morning, namely aversion to cold and the strain of early rising.

Obscurity may no longer surround the concept of a hypothetical decision. However, it may sound inconsistent for me (a) to agree with Canfield that Jones has decided categorically on Sunday that he will get up on time on Monday; and then (b) to suppose that on Sunday Jones also decides hypothetically *not* to get up on time. Am I contradicting myself, or am I perhaps allowing Jones to make two mutually incompatible decisions? Neither. There is no clash between a categorical and a hypothetical decision, as there is between two hypothetical decisions having the same protasis. When Jones decides categorically, he resolves that he will get up on time the next day. When he decides hypothetically, he reports that if it were the next morning now, and he felt comfortable in bed, he would give the nod to staying there.

This completes the defence of my claim (B). My defence consisted mainly in a refutation of Canfield's two examples of decisions that are known to the agent beforehand, but supposedly cannot be made in advance. It turned out in the first case that the agent would make a categorical decision in advance, if he gathered evidence about his proclivities to make the final decision. Canfield's second example was challenging inasmuch as the agent made a decision in advance which was contrary to the final decision he knew he would make. However, my analysis showed that part of his evidence for his final decision might be what I called a hypothetical decision in advance, which has the same content as the final decision that he expects to reach.

Unfortunately there is one loophole in my defence. I have assumed that Jones's hypothetical decisions on Sunday are evidence regarding the character he will have on Monday morning, which will influence the final decision he makes then. What if Jones is afflicted with a 'dual character', and regularly manifests quite different traits during the small hours of the morning from those he possesses when he forecasts his decisions? Then

169

thesis (B) will not hold, because on Sunday Jones could have all the relevant evidence about his future decision that an observer could have, and yet he would not decide in advance to remain in bed the next morning. The character which affects his hypothetical decisions in advance on Sunday is not the one that will influence him on Monday. Information regarding Dr Jekyll's decisions in advance are not relevant if we are predicting Mr Hyde's final decisions. But this fantasy of dual character is not a solid reason for abandoning thesis (B). It is extremely doubtful, when Dr Jekyll learns of Mr Hyde's future decisions, that Dr Jekyll has foreknowledge of his *own* decisions.

IX

CAN WE HOLD PEOPLE STRICTLY LIABLE FOR THEIR DEEDS?

We have noticed at least two philosophically significant features that set human actions apart from every other type of event. One singularity appeared in Essays V, VI and VII, but has not been emphasized: the 'social fact' that your actions are events for which you may have to bear responsibility. The other earmark of action that interests me now was discussed at length in Essay II. This is the 'linguistic fact' that we characterize people's behaviour by reference to their concurrent mental states – for example, when we report that someone deliberately, or perhaps unintentionally, started a fire. Both these traits of action take on clear relief, and become mutually relevant, in criminal law and some areas of civil law, notably tort. An agent's mental state is one factor we consider in determining how responsible he is. Most criminal and some civil liability requires that he should be aware of what he is doing and intend to be doing it. If he was in one of the recognized excusing conditions of mind, such as ignorance or insanity, then this requirement of awareness and intention is unsatisfied. Now is there such a requirement for every type of criminal offence, or can we delineate a class of illegal actions in which the lawbreaker may be punished even though he lacked both control and awareness? Plainly it would be a conceptual advance if I can make good either answer.

This line of inquiry is hardly new in philosophy and jurisprudence. I shall therefore take advantage of the most pioneering and satisfactory recent work on this topic that I know of in either jurisprudence or philosophy: H. L. A. Hart's collected essays, *Punishment and Responsibility* ([54]; all parenthetical page references in the present discussion will be to this volume). One of Hart's recurrent themes is how in detail our evidence regarding an offender's mental states and capacities does, and ought to, bear upon judicial decisions at the stages of conviction and of sentencing. As a counter-point, Hart almost invariably compares criminal offences which provide for excusing conditions, particularly conditions of the agent's mind, with strict (or absolute) liability offences. Hart repeatedly joins most liberal-minded writers in heaping 'odium' on the latter (20, 34, 136, 152, 176).

By crimes of strict liability, Hart generally means: (i) offences regarding which the prosecution does not have to prove *mens rea*, awareness and intention of violating law; and (ii) offences for which you cannot escape responsibility, partly or altogether, by proving that you were in a condition that normally excuses them. In Hart's words:

'There are . . . offences (. . . of "strict liability") where it is not necessary for conviction to show that the accused either intentionally did what the law forbids or could have avoided doing it by use of proper care: selling liquor to an intoxicated person, possessing an altered passport, selling adulterated milk are examples . . . where it is no defence that the accused did not offend intentionally or through negligence. (20)
[In] crimes of "strict liability" . . . it is no defence to show that the accused, in spite of the exercise of proper care, was ignorant of the facts that made his act illegal, and did not intend to commit an act answering the definition of the crime (31; see 32, 118–32).
No "subjective element" is required' (139; see 62–3).

The most general comparison Hart draws is that, when we deal with ordinary offences, we insist that individuals

'whom we punish should have had, when they acted, the normal capacities, physical and mental, for doing what the law requires and abstaining from what it forbids, and a fair opportunity to exercise those capacities.' (152)

Is anything important amiss in Hart's contrast between strict liability offences and offences which provide for excusing conditions? My main grumble will be that Hart sees a difference in kind where there is only a difference in degree. I shall question whether Hart produces any convincing examples of verdicts that totally disregard the 'strict liability' offender's mental state. But Hart's mistakes on this point merit careful diagnosis. I shall illustrate how his tempting but oversimplified view of consciousness contributes to his errors. Another factor is his concept of action as not logically tied to any form of consciousness. This widely held notion will turn out to be both incoherent and – surely against Hart's philosophical intentions – tainted with Cartesian mind-body dualism.

Are mental elements never considered in strict liability offences?
Hart assumes so throughout his book; and in one essay, 'Acts of Will and Responsibility', he supports his assumption with detailed argument. His goal there is to refute a fairly entrenched doctrine that a 'minimum link' between the offender's behaviour and his mind must be proven, or at least not disproven, in both ordinary and strict liability convictions (90–2, 94, 107–9, 112, 253–5). A recent defence of this view, cited by Hart, is J. L. J. Edwards's 'Automatism and Involuntary Conduct' ([39]). Following Hart, call this 'the general doctrine'. The issue between Hart and adherents of the general doctrine, whom I shall join, is partly empirical and partly analytical. The empirical side of the question is what judges actually say when they hold or refuse to hold someone liable in strict liability cases. But there is also the analytical problem of extracting a theory from what they say. I shall mostly restrict myself to cases that Hart himself interprets, and my disagreement with him will be mostly analytical.

On the factual side, incidentally, Hart damages his contrast theory by admitting that perhaps the excuses of duress and insanity get a man off the hook in strict liability offences as well as in ordinary offences (242). Later he attempts to restore polarity : he notes that throughout the criminal law, an excusing condition of duress is 'rarely established' (256). But is that not beside the point? As long as the plea of duress could work in strict liability as well as in ordinary cases Hart's dichotomy begins to lose its sharpness. The edge is blunted further when Hart concedes that 'even where liability is strict there are certain forms of unconsciousness and certain types of failure of muscular control which will exclude liability' (94).

By way of illustration, Hart examines at length a controversial case, *Hill* v. *Baxter*, ([1958] 1 Q.B. 227; [1958] 1 *All E.R.* 193). Baxter, the driver of a van, tried to escape conviction for two strict liability offences : reckless driving and failing to halt at a stop signal. Baxter maintained that he had temporarily 'blacked out', probably because of sudden illness. On appeal, his contention was rejected, but only because Baxter presented no evidence to corroborate his statement. The Lord Justices who reviewed this case went on to elaborate a theory that would have accommodated Baxter's plea, had it been proven. Between them, Lords Goddard, Devlin and Pearson listed several situations which, *if* the driver had no reason to anticipate them, would relieve him of liability. I number the situations in the order in which they are mentioned by the Lord Justices :

    i sudden illness makes the driver unconscious;
    ii a stone knocks the driver out;
    iii bees sting the driver; his limbs move spasmodically, and he loses control of his vehicle;
    iv a stroke or an epileptic fit causes the driver's limbs to move uncontrollably;
    v the bodily movements which occur while he is at the wheel are due to automatism;
    vi his movements result from one or another form of insanity;
    vii he slips into a coma.

Although the Lord Justices do not say so, presumably the only observable difference between (i) and (ii), as well as between (iii), (iv), (v) and (vi), is that these various situations have dissimilar causes. Also (vii), coma, presumably could result from illness (i), or from a blow, situation (ii). Lord Goddard, for his part, likens automatism (v) with insanity (vi). And no doubt many cases of automatism are due to insanity (see Hart, 253–4).

    Should anything be added to our list? Lord Goddard denies that being asleep relieves a driver of responsibility. He says bluntly : 'If a driver finds that he is getting sleepy he must stop.' Apparently he assumes that a driver will have some premonitory sensations when he is about to fall asleep. On his side, Lord Pearson notes that, according to provisions of this traffic statute, stupor caused by alcohol or narcotics will not rule out conviction.

    Hart apparently wishes to generalize from this particular driving case. He specifies further types of 'unconsciousness and failure of muscular control' (94) which might get a man out of

174

strict liability in non-driving offences. Hart also propounds a more explicit distinction between instances when the agent is either 'conscious' or 'unconscious'.

To the Lord Justices' inventory, Hart adds two 'conscious' situations (95–6). In my numbering, these are :

viii One person 'A holds a weapon and B, against A's will, seizes his hand and therewith stabs C';
 ix 'A is afflicted by St Vitus's dance. Harm results from his uncontrolled movements.'

Of the situations in the Lord Justices' catalogue, Hart labels the 'bee sting' example (iii) as conscious. He seems to believe that in (iv), epileptic fit or stroke, a person must be unconscious. He explicitly classes automatism (v) as a form of unconsciousness. He also gives a further sample of unconsciousness :

 x 'A woman in drunken stupor overlays and kills her child' (96).

Finally, he overlooks (vi), and so movements due to insanity are not ranked as either conscious or unconscious.

Initial objections
What exactly do I have against Hart's analysis so far? First some minor complaints. Hart is plainly mistaken when he supposes that a man undergoing a heart attack or an epileptic fit must be unconscious of his movements. An equally trifling error is Hart's assumption that people are in no way conscious of their movements while they are in a drunken stupor, or in a state of automatism (v). The best-known case of automatism, to which Hart himself alludes (96), will suffice to refute him (*King* v. *Cogdon*, Supreme Court of Victoria, Australia [1950]), discussed by Norval Morris [87]. In this case Mrs Cogdon, a psychologically disturbed person, went to sleep and dreamt that a war was going on, and that soldiers were attacking her daughter Pat. Mrs Cogdon got up. She continued to be afflicted by hallucinations that the soldiers were attacking. She seized an axe, and made her way to Pat's room. She swung the axe, under the impression that her strokes were directed toward the soldiers. The blows killed Pat. Then Mrs Cogdon ran next door to her sister's home and cried : 'I think I've hurt Pattie!'

175

In this condition of automatism, was Mrs Cogdon in any way conscious? Surely, to the extent that she had enough perceptual contact with her surroundings to get an axe and reach her daughter's room. Moreover, would she report that she thought she had hurt her daughter if she was totally unaware of what transpired? No; and thus her report is evidence of some form of consciousness. Am I asserting that Mrs Cogdon was in a normal, waking, conscious state? Of course not. I am simply denying that she was unconscious. And therefore I reject Hart's 'conscious'-'unconscious' dichotomy. A light must be on or off. A human being can be in a mixed or a halfway state. Mrs Cogdon was neither in a coma nor sound asleep. However, her state was also unlike normal consciousness. She might have been groggy from interrupted sleep. Her perceptual contact with her surroundings was surely distorted by hallucinations. Her visions must have been so terrifying that she was further prevented from realizing what she was doing. So on this minor point about automatism, I diverge from Hart, both in denying that a person in a state of automatism must be unconscious, and in demanding a fuller account of whatever unusual type of consciousness the person exhibits. Of course I admit that *un*conscious automatism does occur, for instance, during sound sleep.

Along the same lines, I would criticize Hart for being just as simplistic about unconsciousness. By reference to *Hill* v. *Baxter*, I would argue that there are physiological differences between various degrees of light to sound sleep, as well as between sleep and passing out from illness (i), a blow (ii), a seizure (v), or drunkenness (x); and these states are distinguishable from unconscious varieties of automatism (v), from types of insanity where the victim loses perceptual contact with his surroundings (vi), and especially from coma (vii). For example: comatose people roll out of a bed if they are not strapped on to it; ordinary sleepers react sufficiently to their surroundings so that they will not fall.

Instead of drawing out these secondary, and largely empirical, disagreements, I want to air one major objection. It is that Hart's questionable 'conscious'-'unconscious' distinction allows him to give a specious refutation of the 'general doctrine'.

Can unconscious people act?

In their review of the *Hill* v. *Baxter* case that I was discussing, Lords Goddard and Pearson suggest that a driver who has fallen asleep, as well as one who is unconscious from illness (i), a blow (ii), a stroke (iv), automatism (v), insanity (vi) and coma (vii), is for that reason *not* driving. Similarly with a man who is conscious but loses control of his bodily movements, and hence of his automobile, because he is stung by bees (iii). Lord Goddard declares : 'There may be cases where the circumstances are such that the accused could not really be said to be driving at all. Suppose he had a stroke or an epileptic fit.' And Lord Pearson explains :

'In any ordinary case when once it has been proven that the accused was in the driving seat of a moving car, there is *prima facie* an obvious and irresistible inference that he was driving it . . . unless and until there is evidence tending to show that by some extraordinary mischance he was rendered unconscious or otherwise incapacitated from controlling the car.'

As I remarked already, these justices deny that sleep is a bar to conviction, even though they maintain that someone who is asleep at the wheel is not driving.

Hart challenges nearly all these premises and inferences. Hart seems to think that the only plausible way to avoid acquitting someone who fell asleep is to insist that he was driving, while asleep, as his automobile went through the stop signal (111–12). By way of proof, Hart offers an intricate argument to show that it is neither meaningless nor self-contradictory to say that a man performed some type of action like driving an automobile, and that he was 'unconscious' at the time.

Because of its inherent interest, as well as its complexity, I shall quote Hart's reasoning at length. He first looks for a connection between the 'general doctrine' and what Lords Goddard and Pearson have to say about the impossibility of driving while unconscious. Hart comments :

'Judges do not talk . . . the language of the [general doctrine] . . . as if . . . however strict liability may be, voluntary movements or omissions are still necessary for responsibility. Instead

177

they discuss the meaning of the words in the statutes . . . like "driving". . . .

. . . Of course, both the general doctrine, and this way of approaching the matter . . . would come to the same thing *if* it were the case that, whenever we have an active verb like "drives", this implies, as part of its meaning, the existence of the minimum form of conscious muscular control, upon which the general doctrine insists. As a matter of ordinary English this is however not the case. The phrase "sleep-walking" is alone sufficient to remind us that if the *outward movements appear to be co-ordinated* as they are in normal action, the fact that the subject is *unconscious* from whatever cause does not prevent us using an active verb to describe the case, though we would qualify it with the adverb *"unconsciously"*, or with the adverbial phrases "in his sleep", "in a state of automatism", etc. So in the case of "driving" it would be natural, as a matter of English, to distinguish those cases where the movements of the body are wild or spasmodic or where the driver simply slumps in his seat or collapses over the wheel, from cases where, *though unconscious* he is *apparently controlling* the vehicle. . . . [It] might well be said that he drove the vehicle, changed gear, braked, etc., "in his sleep" or "in a state of automatism". . . .

. . . [His] unconscious conduct might take the *outwardly co-ordinated* form which we might well describe as "driving while unconscious". If the applicability of this phrase settled the matter he would be responsible' (108–10, my italics; see 253–6).

I have italicized key words in Hart's reasoning to highlight his unintended Cartesian dualism about people's 'outward movements', and his disputable notions of consciousness and unconsciousness.

I shall begin again with the latter. As I objected when I discussed Mrs Cogdon's automatism : *if* a person's 'outward movements' are really 'co-ordinated', in the sense that they result from some type of perceptual contact with his surroundings, *then* the person is *not* unconscious. The same must hold for a man at the wheel of a car. Naturally a driver in a state of automatism is not in the normal type of waking consciousness either. But a major source of trouble I have found in Hart's reasoning is that he naïvely assumes that either a person is unconscious, *tout court*, or in a normal state of waking consciousness.

As for Hart's account of sleep-walking, evidently I would dispute his assumption that a somnambulant person's 'outward movements' could 'appear to be co-ordinated' while the sleep-walker is 'unconscious'. Forget about appearances. Are the sleep-walker's motions really co-ordinated, and influenced by various stimuli from the environment? According to the manner and extent that he responds and adjusts his behaviour to his surroundings, the sleep-walker *is* conscious. Even if you insist on calling his state 'unconsciousness', because of analogies between it and light or deep sleep, you must none the less concede that his 'unconsciousness' is radically different from the unconsciousness of a comatose man, and significantly different from the unconsciousness of a person who is quietly asleep in his bed.

Now for my grumble that Hart's reasoning is vitiated by unintended Cartesian dualism. In the long passage I quoted, Hart seems to take for granted a radical separation between observable movements of our bodies and what is going on in our minds. He clearly assumes that the questions, 'Is this person conscious or unconscious?' and 'Are his outward movements co-ordinated?' must be mutually independent. This is a serious blunder. Forget now about intrinsic difficulties with the 'conscious or unconscious?' question. My criticism at present is that inquiries of this kind are answered, in law and elsewhere, partly by observation of a person's bodily movements and responses to his surroundings. Hart slips into Cartesian dualism inasmuch as he seems to imagine that the sphere of 'outward movement' is totally distinct from – what? What else but inner consciousness?

I would say Hart's reasoning leads to dualism because it requires assumptions in theory of knowledge and metaphysics that explicitly divide mind from matter. Hart cannot avoid the epistemological assumption (A) that only the driver himself really knows whether he is conscious; that we outside observers, who only see his co-ordinated 'outward movements', never know whether the light of consciousness or the gloom of unconsciousness is to be found within. In its turn, (A) usually derives from a metaphysical assumption (B) that states of mind like 'consciousness' occur in an immaterial medium which is shut off from public view by one's 'outward' material body.

For present purposes, I have little interest in convicting Hart of dualism, even less in whipping up an instant refutation of dualistic epistemology and metaphysics. I think that Gilbert Ryle, in *The Concept of Mind* [103], has already done the latter job with thoroughness. So my point will be that law courts do not operate on dualistic assumptions. The legal requirement that a man must present objective evidence to corroborate his claim that he was in an excusable condition of mind is enough to bar a dualistic theory of knowledge. For example, in *Hill* v. *Baxter*, the Lord Justices turn down Baxter's plea of automatism : first because what was known of his outward movements during the time when he claimed to be unconscious counted against his assertion; and secondly because they found 'there was no evidence . . . that the respondent was in a state of automatism'. The Lord Justices' approach is certainly incompatible with the dualistic assumption (A) that only the driver himself can know what his mental state is; and (B) that his outward movements might be perfectly co-ordinated even though he is totally unconscious.

Dualism and acting while unconscious

Hart's unintended dualism is important to me because it seems to distort his analysis of action, which in turn gives plausibility to his specious contrast between strict liability and ordinary offences. Here is how these errors seem to reinforce each other. Hart goes on from his discussion of *Hill* v. *Baxter*, which I quoted at length, to make a broad assertion about the verbs we use to report human behaviour. As before, he dismisses the 'general doctrine requiring that the accused, if he is to be convicted [for a strict liability offence] must have been conscious at the time he committed the offence' (111). According to Hart, even the appeal to clear-cut verbs of action will not help : 'for it is not very plausible to argue that "fails to conform" as a matter of English demands a conscious subject' (112).

Is Hart correct? Would it not be self-contradictory to say that a comatose person drove his car through the stop signal? That a man who was sound asleep failed to conform to the signal?

If we start with verbs like 'rob', 'rape', 'assault', 'shoot', and 'maim', which appear in the specification of ordinary criminal offences, it seems that the agent cannot be unconscious; that he must be aware of some salient features of what he is doing. Negatively, if a man is unaware that some scrap metal is government property, because he has good reason to believe the metal is abandoned and unwanted, then he cannot be convicted for stealing the metal (see *Morisette* v. *U.S.*, 342 U.S. 246 [1951], especially part II of Justice Jackson's opinion). The voluntary act requirement of the 'general doctrine' is thereby satisfied, because it is a logically necessary condition for the 'ordinary' crime of theft that the man did something voluntarily, e.g. took the metal voluntarily.

If we look now at strict liability offences, can we find a single established decision against a man who fell below these minimal standards of consciousness and voluntariness? Do we find people convicted though they were unconscious? Are they ever said to act while unconscious? The most notorious cases all conform to the 'general doctrine', as did *Hill* v. *Baxter*. In *Regina* v. *Prince* (13 Cox Crim. Cases 138 [1875]), Prince did knowingly and willingly help a girl leave her father's custody, over the father's protests – although Prince had no way of knowing the additional fact that the girl was less than sixteen years old, which was what made it criminal for Prince to interfere. In *U.S.* v. *Balint* (258 U.S. 250 [1922]), a druggist knowingly and willingly sold some medicine without a prescription, which was legal; of course he was unaware that the medicine was a narcotic, which was what made the sale a strict liability criminal offence.

The same pattern emerges from other strict liability cases which are usually taken to be insignificant, because in them criminal conviction and punishment seem to carry little moral impact. In an early American case, a tavernkeeper was convicted for selling liquor to a habitual drunkard. He did not know the buyer to be a drunkard (*Barnes* v. *State*, 19 Conn. 398 [1849]). Still, the tavernkeeper was not unconscious. He was aware that he was selling liquor to someone; and in this respect he also acted voluntarily, since the purchaser did not force him to sell. Similarly for the adulterated milk cases, mentioned by Hart (20, 32, 132). The offenders realized that they were selling milk, and sold it

181

intentionally, although they did not know it was watered, and surely would not have wanted to sell it if they had known.

If we glance briefly at civil law, we notice analogous minimal requirements in the famous strict liability cases. The crucial item of behaviour in *Fletcher* v. *Rylands* (LR 3 HL 330 [1868]) is described by Lord Cranworth so as to make it obvious that the agents were aware of relevant features of their conduct, and voluntarily doing what had those features. He writes:

> 'The defendants, in order to effect an object of their own, brought on to their land . . . a large accumulated mass of water, and stored it up in a reservoir. The consequence of this was damage to the plaintiff [because his nearby mine was flooded], and for that damage, however skilfully and carefully the accumulation was made, the defendants . . . were certainly liable.'

The same can be said of a more recent civil case, *In Re Polemis & Furness, Withey & Co.* (3 KB 560 [1921]). Stevedores, employed by Furness, Withey & Co., knowingly and willingly carried planks near the hatch of a ship the company had chartered. They let a plank fall into the hold. Drums of kerosene had been in the hold and some kerosene had escaped, leaving fumes. The plank created a spark when it landed; this ignited the fumes, and the ship burned. The court found that a 'spark could not reasonably have been anticipated . . . , though some damage to the ship might reasonably have been anticipated.' So these agents acted with at least minimal consciousness, including some general foresight of danger. They were also acting voluntarily.

Finally, in a less notorious civil case, *Luthringer* v. *Moore* (31 Cal. 2d 489 [1948]), a pest exterminator, Moore, was held strictly liable for injuries to the employeee of a pharmacy located in a building whose basement Moore had fumigated with cyanide gas. Strict liability here prevented Moore from pleading that he had taken reasonable care to confine the gas to the basement, and that he neither intended nor expected anyone to enter the building until the gas had dissipated. Nevertheless, the voluntary act requirement of our 'general doctrine' is met. Luthringer's injuries resulted from Moore's intentional action of releasing cyanide gas in the basement. Moore was aware that the gas was lethal and, as he stated, that it sometimes escaped from the most carefully sealed area.

Broader conclusions

Instead of going on with illustrations, I want to generalize from these examples of strict liability in criminal and civil law. They count heavily against Hart's thesis that when we use action verbs to report strict liability offences we never presuppose a conscious subject. Hart has no legal foundation for his view that a person could be said to drive dangerously, and omit to stop at a traffic signal, while unconscious (94, 108–12). If such verbs are typical, we have some confirmation for an interesting hypothesis : that all genuine verbs of action demand a conscious subject. I have explained in Essay II why many verbs that take the so-called 'active voice' – for example, 'perspire', 'choke', 'stammer' – should not be classed as full-fledged action verbs.

Someone will offer as a counter-instance against this generalization our use of the adverb 'unconsciously' to modify verbs. Hart himself, in the long passage I quoted, imagines that we could describe a blacked-out man as driving, 'although we would qualify [this verb] with the adverb "unconsciously", or with the adverbial phrase "in his sleep", "in a state of automatism", etc.' (109). My reply is that this sort of account misconstrues the situations in which we say a person acted unconsciously. Two examples should reveal the confusion : (i) It often happens that ego-involved drivers unconsciously speed up when another driver attempts to pass them. On Hart's reading, such drivers must be unconscious at the time! Here 'unconsciously' means 'unwittingly', hardly a synonym for 'while unconscious'. (ii) From the converse side, suppose a prizefighter has just been knocked out. Would we ever say that he is now performing some action 'unconsciously'? What these examples suggest is that a man who does something unconsciously cannot be unconscious; which entails that an unconscious man cannot be doing anything – 'unconsciously' or otherwise.

Having neutralized that line of counter-argument, I shall hazard more generalizations. My next is that verbs of action, typified by verbs we use to delineate ordinary and strict liability offences, imply more than bare consciousness. Even in strict liability convictions, the agent is taken to have some awareness that he is performing an action of kind K (driving, selling liquor), and therefore some degree of general foresight of harm and legal sanctions. Schematically, he knows that K-type actions often have other qualities Q which make them harmful and punishable on a strict liability basis. I harp on this general awareness of danger to others, and the prospect of sanctions, because I want to prove that even in strict liability cases, we attribute a kind of knowledge to the agent. It would follow that Hart is mistaken to suppose that we take no account of the agent's mental state.

What justifies the attribution of even this general foreknowledge to a strict liability offender? Our strict liability practices themselves help create the evidence. That is because we mainly impose strict liability sanctions upon people who engage in activities that create hazards : people like automobile drivers; producers and distributors of food, drink and drugs; operators of factories, railways, ships, mines; pest exterminators, and so on. Often they must get a licence, at which time they are tested for their knowledge of dangers and suitable precautions. In addition, they are sometimes put on notice that they will be held strictly liable if their activities cause certain mishaps. So it is partly because of how we have dealt with actual and potential strict liability offenders in the past that we can ascribe this general foresight to current offenders.

This ought to suffice as an account of how consciousness is relevant to strict liability. What about voluntariness? Again I must revise Hart's analysis. On my reading of the cases under discussion, it appears that *if* an action or omission (as opposed to mere 'possession') is necessary for a strict liability offence, *then* the action or omission must be voluntary in some respects. In what respects? I can most easily explain by setting forth examples where there is not enough voluntariness. A man whose movements are impeded by paralysis, or a man undergoing a seizure, would not be held strictly liable for mishaps that resulted from these conditions. Such men are not acting at all, and consequently they are not doing anything sufficiently voluntary to be strictly liable. How about a semi-conscious man in a state of automatism? Maybe you will insist that he does or omits something. Is his behaviour voluntary enough for strict liability? No; his automatism, or the disorder which caused his automatism, has deprived him of control over his current behaviour. For the same reason, if you do or omit something because you are overpowered by another, you are also not liable. Likewise for extreme duress and hypnotism.

Thus a form of the general doctrine, that even in strict liability offences the action for which a man is punished must be voluntary, seems to be borne out by the actual and hypothetical cases we have considered. Until Hart produces better counter-examples, he must put aside his doubts that the general doctrine is accepted by courts (90, 94, 108–9). I hope he will also disavow the dualistic view he unwittingly accepted, that consciousness has nothing epistemic or metaphysical to do with one's 'outward movements'. Finally, I trust that my defence of the general doctrine adds further proof to the main thesis of this critique, which is that Hart has greatly exaggerated the contrasts between strict liability offences and offences in which courts investigate the offender's state of mind. The 'consciousness' and 'voluntariness' provisions of the general doctrine surely allow a man to escape strict liability if he was in one of the more restricted number of excusing conditions we noticed.

X

HOW DO I KNOW WHAT I AM DOING?

1. I want to survey in more detail some logical and pragmatic ties between action and awareness. This exploration may further our understanding both of agency and of empirical knowledge in general. Also I hope it will tie up some loose threads from Essays II, III, IV, VI, and VIII and IX. A current philosophical quandary of some magnitude gives impetus to my investigation : Does an agent have 'non-observational knowledge' of the empirical fact that he is, for example, dashing to board a certain train before it leaves for the mountains? The puzzle is that you can only learn that I am engaged in such an action by watching me, photographing me, or eventually asking me. Yet I just seem to 'know', without data to go on, and without inquiry. Of course it is by observation that I recognize the railway station and that particular train. Obviously I must use documents like timetables in order to know when trains leave for the mountains. The problem is that, alongside these items of observational knowledge, I seem to have a different kind of knowledge, about what I am *doing* with respect to the things and surroundings I perceive.

A host of questions arise from this baffling but familiar epistemic situation. Do other people really know I am running to catch that train? Perhaps their reports of my deeds are never more than shaky inferences, and so cannot amount to knowledge. Or contrariwise : Do I know that I am fulfilling the overt behaviour requirements for a particular sort of action? Ought we to say that I only have non-observational knowledge of my *attitudes*, *intentions* and *beliefs in doing* whatever it is that I happen to be doing? But in either case, how can a totally ungrounded report, of the action I am performing, or of my intention, ever qualify as knowledge? Finally, and most broadly : When we attribute a deed to someone, is it part of what we mean that he is aware, in some sense, of what he is doing? In other words :

186

Is it even logically possible for me to engage in a type of action, but not know either *that* I am acting, or *what* sort of action I am performing?

These are large and potentially confusing questions. I shall try to steer clear of well-worn philosophical ruts that lead to and from them. So I start with some neighbouring terrain, which I have surveyed from another perspective in Essay II. A preliminary look at our knowledge of what happens to an agent, and of processes that occur on his body, may well uncover suggestive parallels and contrasts that we can exploit when we come to the field of action.

2. *Undergoing*

A typical case would be when you are soaked by a downpour. We have no reason to assert: 'If something like this befalls you, you must know about it.' There is less compulsion to suppose that the knowledge you do have of what you undergo could be non-observational. You might be unconscious, in a coma, or so pre-occupied that you fail to notice, at the time you get soaked. And in case you do realize that something is happening to you, or *what* specifically is happening to you, your knowledge is on a par with an onlooker's knowledge of the incident. The only difference is trivial: you might discover you are being soaked by feeling the raindrops that fall on you, while a bystander could only see those particular raindrops.

3. *Bodily processes*

Another significant, but trickier contrast to our knowledge of action would be our awareness of processes that mainly 'involve' our bodies. Examples would be: perspiring, digesting one's food, bleeding, twitching, throbbing. As we noticed in section 2 of Essay II, these are not things that happen to you. No other agent or inanimate 'force', such as rain, must of logical necessity be acting upon you in these cases. It is a contingent matter that heat causes us to perspire; that the flow of enzymes in our stomachs stimulates digestion.

What sort of awareness do we have regarding these physiological goings-on? Often we have none. It is for the most part only when we have overeaten, or when our digestive processes are impeded, that we become aware of digesting our food. We know it when we sweat profusely, as a rule, but seldom otherwise. Although you might bleed lightly and not realize it, bleeding is somewhat unique. Because of the danger to us if we lose blood, our survival depends partly upon our awareness of this bodily process. So far, then, we find no asymmetry between the type of knowledge you have, or your manner of acquiring it, and an observer's knowledge of your bodily processes. The epistemologically tricky feature of bodily processes is that each person *may* 'feel' them, in a sense of 'feel' that apparently has no kinship with standard forms of tactile and kinaesthetic perception. For instance, it is reasonable to ask a deep-sea diver how he felt the hull of a sunken ship underneath a bank of kelp. Did he feel it with his feet or hands? By pushing against the kelp? But in the case of feeling perspiration or blood flow from our epidermis, it would be strange for another person to ask us how we went about feeling it. We don't have to engage in tactile or kinaesthetic exploration. Indigestion is an especially clear instance of this. Would you ever explain that you felt the churnings of your upset stomach as a result of careful probing?

Of course a neurophysiologist would impatiently tell us what actually goes on when a man correctly reports that he feels his limbs trembling, in this sense of 'feel'. There are afferent nerve-endings in your limbs. These react when your limbs are damaged. Electrical impulses travel from the nerve-endings to your brain. If the 'scanning mechanism' in your brain picks up these impulses, you will be aware that your limbs are trembling, and you may report that you feel the tremors. That's it. Why should you bother with tactile and kinaesthetic exploration, unless you want to double-check?

4. *Feeling as perceptual knowledge*
This rudimentary neurophysiological account seems to dispel our bafflement about this kind of feeling, and to distinguish it from tactile and kinaesthetic perception. Moreover, this account makes room here for various salient characteristics of accredited forms of perceptual knowledge, such as seeing and hearing. Several features have emerged already in our discussion. For example, where we have perceptual knowledge, we could have ignorance.

188

The possibility of ignorance was already noticed, in regard to feeling bodily processes. Thus a boxer might not feel the blood dripping from his nose. Along the same lines, there is a method of 'finding out', by this non-tactile and non-kinaesthetic sort of feeling, that a certain process is occurring in your body. How could the boxer find out? He might deliberately withdraw from the fray, sit down, and focus his attention on his face, with the result that he exclaims: 'Oh! – I feel the blood gushing from my nose!' Another important feature of perceptual knowledge is that you and others can check up, thereby either confirming or undermining your report with further evidence and observation. The boxer himself might look in the mirror, and see no blood at all gushing from his nose. Finally, we thus have the possibility of error, and even a hint of how one could go wrong. What the boxer 'felt' may have been the swelling of his battered nose. He mistakenly believed that what he felt was bleeding.

5. *One last example*

One last example to compare with our knowledge of our actions will be our knowledge of sneezing, choking, hiccuping, yawning, blushing, wheezing, vomiting, and 'jumping' in the sense of a 'startle' reaction. In section 4 of Essay II I gave reasons for not immediately calling these events bodily processes, like perspiring and trembling. I also found an unrelated but interesting epistemic difference between perspiring and sneezing. The peculiarity of events like sneezing and choking is that we often have premonitory sensations that they are *going* to occur. Idiomatically speaking, we sometimes feel *about to* sneeze, to choke, to vomit.

What does the verb 'feel' mean in these premonitory cases? Surely not that we feel the sneeze before it occurs! Indeed not. I believe this to be the same sense of the verb 'feel' that we discussed in connection with feeling one's muscle tremor (sections 3, 4). The difference is only this: what you feel, when you feel on the verge of choking, is some antecedent bodily process that will cause you to choke. And thus other people can have more standard forms of perceptual knowledge regarding this same contributory process, even if they cannot 'feel it in the way you do'. Your feeling of the process which, together with other conditions of your body, will bring about your future sneeze, remains

189

a form of perceptual knowledge. The arguments of section 4 apply to instances of feeling oneself sneeze and choke, as well as to instances of feeling one's muscle tremors. So the present cases exemplify perceptual knowledge. Thus from an epistemological standpoint, I find no compelling reason to put this last group of events (sneezing, etc.) in a different category from bodily processes.

6. Preliminary conclusions

What have we gained by beating around the bush, instead of looking directly at a person's knowledge of his actions? First, we have been forced to remind ourselves of the most common elements of empirical knowledge: that there is some publicly ascertainable circumstance or event of which we can have knowledge; that there are methods of acquiring the type of knowledge, along with possibilities of ignorance and error; and that we accredit a person's knowledge claim only because we can check it out. Secondly, among various things that happen to a person, as well as processes that occur in his body, we have not come across items that *must* be known to the person. Indeed, a person might be unconscious while these events take place. Thirdly, we found, in cases of 'feeling' processes occur in one's body, a near analogue to the 'non-observational' knowledge people are supposed to have of their actions. But this near analogue turned out to be sufficiently like seeing, hearing, tasting, smelling and tactile and kinaesthetic feeling, for us to rank it with them as a form of perceptual knowledge. More important still, we discovered no grounds for talking mysteriously of a man's own 'way' of knowing about what he undergoes, or about processes that occur in his body. It would be incorrect to declare: 'Only he can really know whether these things occur, because we can't feel them in the way he does.' Fourthly, we nevertheless failed to turn up any disguised nonsense in the view that people *do* sometimes have perceptual knowledge of what happens to them and what happens in their bodies. This last result, incidentally, has little bearing on the excessively familiar dispute between followers of Wittgenstein and Cartesians about sensation. Wittgensteinians hold that it is nonsense to talk of a man having knowledge of his aches and itches. Philosophers under the spell of Descartes take sensations as the most certain objects of empirical knowledge. Cartesians explain that it is because we 'feel' them that we know our sensations best; and since nobody else can feel my earache in the way I do, I know it in a way nobody else can. Wittgensteinians dismiss this explanation as unintelligible, on grounds that are by now commonplace.

My analysis of feeling processes occur in one's body, and thereby having perceptual knowledge of them, will never settle the dispute about sensations. Bodily processes *are* publicly observable. When I am aware of choking, what I am conscious of is the very same event that my dismayed dinner companion hears and sees. But this is a very different situation from one in which I say my throat hurts. What I feel, the pain in my throat, is hardly what my physician sees when he examines my throat. He cannot see the pain, or feel it, although he can doubtless see that my throat must hurt. Since it is unclear whether feeling pain is a case of perceptual knowledge, my arguments about knowing bodily processes will not apply to knowing sensations. However, it does apply to action; for the action I am aware of carrying out would seem to be the very same event that a bystander sees me perform.

7. Action at last

By now we should be sufficiently wary, but I hope not too weary, to investigate action. What sorts of action could be known differently by agents and observers? Things a person did long ago are surely known equally well, and by similar means – memory, supplemented with photographic, written and other records – to the person himself and to his fellows. In this study it is unnecessary to distinguish between the agent's memory of *doing* X long ago, and my recollection of *seeing* him to X, or my recollection simply *that* he did X. So I expect that the epistemic asymmetry that puzzles us will crop up, if it exists, in the field of present and future action.

What sort of asymmetry are we pursuing? The still fruitful debate seems to focus upon two contentions:

(1) The agent *must* know what he is doing, while observers may be ignorant or mistaken about his behaviour.

191

(2) The agent normally knows this without going on observational data.

With respect to future actions, we have :

(1F) If the agent already has reasons to do something, and foresees no impediment, then he must know that he will do it.

(2F) The agent normally knows this without observing his current preparatory behaviour, or extrapolating from records of his past behaviour.

I should mention, in passing, one reasonable restriction on our knowledge of what we are going to do. I believe that we must implicitly attach a *ceteris paribus* clause to these knowledge claims. What I claim, when I forecast that I shall do X, is that if conditions remain as I expect, and perhaps *if* I don't think better of it or change my attitude toward it, *then* I shall do X. An observer might also preface his forecasts with corresponding qualifications. But notice that such clauses only combine with forecasts. It would be strange for me to report that *if* conditions are not changing unexpectedly, and *if* I am not thinking better of it, then I am at present driving my car to work.

8. *Disanalogies with knowledge of bodily processes*

Before I assess contentions (1), (2), (1F) and (2F) in detail, I want to juxtapose the picture they give us against the account we developed in sections 3, 4, and 5, of knowing bodily processes. We remarked that a person might be totally unconscious when he perspires, chokes or sneezes. Even if this is physiologically unlikely, it is not a self-contradictory supposition. But as I argued in Essay IX, it is self-contradictory to imagine a comatose person strolling in the park or stealing a motorcycle. In fact, there is not a single type of action that a totally unconscious man could execute. Anything he did would be strong evidence against the hypothesis that he is totally unconscious. To the extent that the thrashings of a sleeper resemble actions, for example if he seems to be reaching for the alarm-clock and turning it off, we judge the sleeper to be awakening, or anyhow sleeping more lightly. Even a maniac who runs wild, and demolishes everything in his path, must surely be awake, and have some perceptual knowledge of his environment – however deluded he is in other respects. Consequently it seems to be true at least that the agent necessarily has minimal awareness when he acts.

9. *Incomplete awareness*

Still, it would be a mistake to suppose that the agent must, or even can, have *complete* knowledge of his action. The proof of this is simple. Most actions you perform consist, *inter alia*, of bodily movements, such as contractions of your muscles and electrical discharges in your nervous system. Just try to walk or sit down without such processes occurring in your body! Neurophysiologists are in the best position to know these details of what they are doing. But they surely forget about most of these processes when they act. Moreover, they will cheerfully admit that neurophysiological knowledge is incomplete, as perhaps all scientific knowledge must be. Therefore it follows that even a neurophysiologist cannot know all the minutiae of his deeds.

10. *Acting in ignorance*

Another argument for the same conclusion takes off from the possibility of acting unwittingly. When a science lecturer paces in a moment of distraction, absent-mindedly scratches his ear, and unconsciously grabs his briefcase at the close of an hour, he does not know that his behaviour has these characteristics. He is not unconscious either. To say that he unconsciously picked up his briefcase is only to say he was unaware that he performed this gesture. He was surely aware of replying to students' questions, of writing upon the blackboard and so forth.

11. *Many descriptions of an act*

My general point is simple. There are bound to be innumerable things you do that you are unaware of doing, in the course of performing an action that you know you are now performing. With planned future actions that is even more obvious. Who can foresee every detail of his future deeds? Perhaps it would help to put this in 'linguistic' terms: Besides the description under which you know what you are doing, there are countless other true descriptions of the very same event that is your action. Some of these specifications would be neurophysiological. Some would

N   193

invoke legal and various other social conventions: for instance if we described the lecturer as selling university-owned furniture to his students; or welcoming them to class; apologizing for being late; or cancelling class and ordering his students to join a sit-in demonstration.

A necessary, though perhaps not sufficient, condition for saying that a single event is described by two or more non-synonymous phrases is that each descriptive phrase holds for exactly the same physical objects, spatial location and temporal span. Take three non-synonymous descriptive statements: 'Policeman Murphy blew his whistle', 'He blew a warning signal on his whistle', and 'His lungs contracted, with the result that air rushed out of his lips and caused high-frequency sound waves to issue from his whistle'. All three statements would be long-winded descriptions of the same event. But 'He frightened a passing motorist' describes a 'larger' event, because this new statement brings in another participant, and encompasses one spatially removed effect of Murphy's blast (the alarm of a passing motorist), which might well outlast his whistling.

The conventional aspects of this illustration suggest an interesting point about knowledge of one's deeds. Some conventional descriptions of what one does, for instance, 'blow a warning signal', hold only when one *is aware* that one's behaviour has certain features. In Anglo-American law, for instance, whenever it is correct to describe a man as committing first degree murder, then the man must have good reason to believe that what he is doing may kill or seriously injure some other person. If he does not have this degree of awareness, his act of killing will have to be described as manslaughter or the like. This is simply because the legal definition of murder specifies this type of minimal knowledge, as well as malicious intent. The definition of manslaughter does not. At the other extreme, definitions of somnambulistic behaviour and automatism in criminal law specify diminished awareness and control by the agent of what he does in these disturbed conditions. No legal definitions of action specify unconsciousness.

12. *Applications*

How do these results help us to evaluate the four contentions about knowledge of one's deeds that I listed in section 7? I think our results warrant the following version of contention (1), which I state dogmatically, and leave readers to test against actual and imaginary examples :

If a man performs an action of description D, then he is at least minimally conscious; what is more, he either knows that he is performing an act of description D; or else, for some other true description D′ of the action he is engaged in, he knows that he is performing an act of description D′.

I would reformulate (1F) along similar lines :

If a man already has reasons to perform an action of description D, and he will in fact perform it, then he will be at least minimally conscious when the time comes; furthermore, either he already knows that he will perform an act of description D, or he already knows that he will perform an act of description D′; and either he will know then that he is performing an act of description D, or he will know that he is performing an act of description D′.

13. *Action and potential awareness*

I would append a more general claim to (1) and (1F), again minus supporting argument. If you scrutinize all the clear-cut examples of act-descriptions you can produce, I believe you will find that when, in his particular circumstances, the agent *is unaware* that his act falls under description D, it is nevertheless logically possible that he should have been aware that his act falls under D. Except for descriptions like 'murder' and 'embezzle', which specify that the agent is aware of the elements required for an act of description D, it would likewise hold that whenever a person is aware that his act falls under D, it is logically possible that he should have been unaware. From my version of (1), to be sure, it would in any case follow that the agent knows his act under some other description D.

14. *But how can he know this without observation?*

If we now leaned upon the analogies with awareness of bodily processes, as elaborated in sections 3 to 6, we would reply that an agent knows of his present and intended future actions by 'feeling' them. But there are two defects with the parallel. This manner of feeling bodily processes turned out to be a form of perceptual knowledge, not radically dissimilar from observation of something by looking, listening or touching. Consequently, 'feeling' oneself walk to the market for groceries, or feeling 'about to' go there, would have to be assimilated to more standard cases of observational knowledge. The major defect with this analogy, of course, is that it simply fails to hold for most cases of being aware of one's action. Especially with future action we have no 'premonitory feeling' of our immanent activity.

15. *Do we know because it is our intention to be doing this?*
Is my intention to catch this train for the mountains my *evidence*, on which is founded my knowledge that I am engaged in the action of hurrying to board the train? Only in peculiar circumstances, such as the following: It has been a busy week. In a final frenzy of activity, I complete most of the tasks I had set for myself, and start for the railway station. I must mail a package before a hop on my train. Rushing for the train, I make a detour toward the mailbox.In my distraction, I ask myself: 'What am I doing here?' Then I recall my plan to drop off the package and board the train. My intention serves as evidence regarding my current activity.

This sort of situation is highly unusual. Normally we are aware of our intentions and of what we are doing; yet we hardly infer what we are doing from our intentions. But even if we did, the problem of non-observational knowledge would only shift, without becoming easier to resolve. We would have to ask how I can know non-observationally what I *intend* to be doing, while others must go on various kinds of evidence. So I prefer to stick with the agent's non-observational knowledge of what he is doing.

You might object to this procedure: 'But perhaps the agent is mistaken about what he is accomplishing? What if he claims to know that he is heading for the right train, while in fact his train is leaving from the other side of the station?' You want to limit his knowledge claim to his intention, because at least he is bound to be correct about it. My reply is twofold: If the would-be holiday-maker is mistaken, then he simply does not know as much as he says. But that is insufficient to prove that he *never* knows such things. When he *is* running in the proper direction, what

196

he is reporting is something he knows. As for the supposed advantage of restricting the scope of his knowledge to his intentions, I see this as a drawback. If you cannot clearly specify situations in which a man could sincerely misreport his intentions, you rule out no epistemic perils; consequently what you say lacks interest, from the standpoint of theory of knowledge, when you credit the agent with *knowing* his own aims.

16. *Knowing and being mistaken*

The above objection and reply force me to formulate an assumption I have been making about all empirical knowledge, including awareness of action. I have been taking it for granted that if you know that Q, it is logically possible that you should have been mistaken. It might not have been the case that Q; furthermore, even when Q holds, your epistemic credentials might not have sufficed for knowledge. Since you know, you are not mistaken. And since you have evidence for Q, this makes it unlikely that you are mistaken. Nevertheless, there is no contradiction in supposing that despite all the grounds you have for Q, Q is false; or that your grounds for Q give you less than knowledge, even though it is the case that Q.

If we accept that picture of empirical knowledge in general, then our problem is simply why we should rank an *ungrounded* report as knowledge, just because it happens to be a report of the speaker's own current or future action. After all, when I make a wild guess, without any evidence, that the person I sat next to on the subway this morning is now downtown shopping, you would deny that I knew this, even if my conjecture was confirmed. Why say that I know when I specify my own actions?

17. *The importance of control and skill*

Surely my intention to be doing X must be one element in the answer. But how can we bridge the gap between my aim and my achievement? The reason I do not have to restrict myself to awareness of my intention is that I have developed some measure of control over my behaviour. Much of it is automatic, a matter of habit – as when I get up in the morning, dress, fix breakfast and ride to work. Nevertheless I am in control of my body and various instruments I use in these routine activities.

Consequently I can be reasonably certain that I am accomplishing various routine tasks I intend to be performing. In this case I do not dwell on my intentions because they are stamped into my 'programmes'. I concentrate instead on a news broadcast or my lecture notes.

When we consider more demanding tasks, such as fixing a radio, intentions become more obtrusive. In those circumstances, skill is the link between intention and achievement. When I know, without checking up on myself, that I am in fact doing what is required to put my radio back in working order, I know this only because I have the proper training and mastery of this craft. If I am inexperienced, I should only limit my knowledge claims. I should only express certainty that I am replacing tubes and soldering wires, until I have observed the results of my endeavours.

18. Knowledge and dimensions of success

A more systematic formulation of how I may claim knowledge of more than my intentions would be in terms of my succeeding or failing when I act. There are at least seven distinguishable, though possibly overlapping, senses in which I may succeed or fail when I act. Some of these have been noticed in Essays II, III, IV, V, VI and VII :

(a) I may succeed in the rudimentary sense that I just perform the act, such as wiggling my toes, normally without effort or forethought. The corresponding sense of 'fail' is 'omit'. Nothing prevents me; I just do not wiggle my toes. If I have normal control over my toes, there is no gap between intending and doing here.

(b) Another sense of 'succeed' is that of 'trying and succeeding', as contrasted with 'attempting but failing'. When you make an effort to wiggle your toes, but fail because they are frozen, that is quite different from not bothering to wiggle them when they are unhindered. A combination of control and skill are normally sufficient for knowledge that you are succeeding in these cases.

(c) The next sense of 'succeed' and 'fail' spans a wider gap between intention and achievement. In this sense, an agent is successful in what he does when his action terminates as he

198

desired; if not, he fails. An example would be swimming across a river. If I have to turn back, I fail. In cases like this, a non-observational knowledge claim is risky; but if the agent is highly skilled, he may legitimately assert that he is now swimming across the river, or that he will swim it five minutes from now. Otherwise he should only claim to know that he will swim in the direction of the other bank, or that he will swim as far as he can.

(d) Going beyond the agent himself, consider his success in bringing about various effects, or failing to produce them. The radio repair man intends to make the radio work again, as a result of his soldering. Does he know without observation that he is succeeding? Obviously the more distant an upshot is, and the more interfering factors there are in a situation, the more risk it is to claim knowledge without a look to see if the result has come about. Thus I might know without observation that I am leaving a disguised cyanide pellet at the bottom of my enemy's jar of vitamin pills, so that he will get to it a few months from now. But could I know that I am already poisoning him? And how could I then have known what was not yet true? This would be a case in which it is questionable whether the agent could know that he is succeeding. An observational check would seem necessary, and it would have to wait.

(e) Another sense of 'succeed' and 'fail' is connected with standards, criteria or conventions. An example would be when the ambassadress enters a party. I bend at the waist. Did my motion qualify as a bow? Yes, if it was deep enough to satisfy conventions. And surely I do not have to watch myself in a mirror in order to know that I am bowing. With other conventions, I might need evidence.

(f) Related to this is the sense of 'succeed' that is equivalent to 'excel', so that 'fail when you do X' means 'do X poorly'. Both conventional acts like bowing, and non-conventional ones like jumping in the air, may be deemed successful or faulty in this sense. If you are proficient at the type of performance, you may know without observation that you have carried it out successfully; otherwise you must gather evidence, as judges do.

(g) Perhaps a subordinate meaning of 'succeed' and 'fail' has to do with your manner of executing some type of action –

gracefully, powerfully, effortlessly, whatever style happens to be prized or shunned. What counts as successful style will vary, for example between ballet and a four hundred yard dash. In any case, it would seem that the agent may have non-observational knowledge that his action is successful. Often he must follow the same procedures as his critics.

19. *Epistemological conclusions*

The upshot of this detailed analysis is that you can have limited non-observational knowledge of what you are doing, and what you are going to do. Such knowledge is fallible. Moreover, it is only knowledge because the bulk of available evidence backs up your initial ungrounded claim. Curiously enough, your non-observational knowledge is unlike your awareness of processes occurring in your body. That awareness was shown to be on a par with familiar types of perception, sight and touch, for example, and thus a form of observational knowledge.

My analysis gave support to the view of many recent writers on action, that an agent's intentions are a key factor in his awareness of what he is doing and what he is going to do. But other neglected elements, such as his control over his behavioural repertory, his training and skills, assumed equal importance. Thus it seems unnecessary to endorse the mystifying explanation one often reads, that intending to do X *is*, among other things, being certain that one is or will be doing X. The most important advances I think we have made on that type of pseudo-explanation are, first, that we have elaborated details, restrictions and arguments as to how non-observational knowledge of action is possible. A second advance is that we have not had to settle for the innocuous, and possibly unintelligible, view that all we really know without evidence is what we try or intend to do. Finally, I think it is a kind of progress that we have thus sidestepped the controversy on whether or not it makes sense to say that I have knowledge of my own intentions.

XI

THE SOCRATIC PARADOX AND REMORSE

In this concluding study, I return to the baffling connection between motives and deeds. But now I work from the perspective of one's value judgements. A generalized form of the question I shall raise has come up in Essays III, IV, V and VI. Suppose a person has reason to perform an action of type A. He has no competing reason to do something else instead, and none against A-type actions. He is not prevented from doing an act of kind A. Does it follow deductively from these premises that he will do something of type A when he believes the occasion is suitable? More abstractly, the question is: Given propitious circumstances, is there a logical connection between motives and deeds?

1. *Failing to act as one judges best*

A less sweeping version of this problem will occupy me now. Only the relation between behaviour and value judgements which are reasons for acting will concern me. I assume that other sorts of occurrences, such as our emotions and cravings, can figure along with value judgements as reasons why we act. Furthermore, I shall focus exclusively on a logical consequence of the doctrine that having reasons entails action. This is the contrapositive: If a man does *not* perform an A-type action when he takes the occasion to be suitable, then it follows that he was *not* fully convinced that an A-type acttion would be best on the occasion.

Both the sweeping and the specific contentions appear to have originated with Socrates. In several Platonic dialogues he champions the paradoxical theory that to know what is best is to do what is best when one is able. He maintains that when people act wickedly, or to their own disadvantage, although they could abstain, it is only because they are ignorant regarding better courses of action. Deliberately to do what one believes is evil or imprudent is not in human nature. These are central topics in *Protagoras* ([96] 77, 88–9, 96–9). They are woven into *Phaedo* ([96] 67–70), *Gorgias* ([96] 467–8, 509) and *Republic* ([96] 436–44). Aristotle's response in the *Nicomachean Ethics* is that the Socratic thesis 'plainly contradicts the observed facts' ([4] vii, 1145b).

For the purposes of this investigation, we do not have to decide whether Socrates' view of human nature is supposed to be an empirical or a logical claim. I shall deal only with philosophical theories which explicitly countenance failure. In such theories, what evidence can we have that someone who deliberately omitted to do anything of type A nevertheless believed he ought to? Aristotle suggests that an incontinent or weak-willed person is 'a man whom passion masters so that he does not act according to the right rule, but does not master to the extent of making him ready to believe that he ought to pursue such pleasures without reserve' ([4] vii, 1151a). The man is 'likely to repent' of his delinquency ([4] vii, 1150a). By contrast, a self-indulgent person, who believes he ought to pursue such gratifications, will not be sorry.

In another essay which is conveniently reprinted elsewhere [115], I explain why this should not be taken as a puzzle about judgements of *moral* value alone. It would be a mistake to concentrate on the uninteresting question whether a person can act contrary to his judgement that A would be morally best, because he expects it will enrich him, advance his career, increase his fame, or give him sensuous enjoyment if he omits A. The challenging question is: 'Can you have beliefs of every or any kind favouring A, and no comparable reasons against A, but willingly and knowingly do something else?' My argument is that Socrates had a deep puzzle about reasons and action. It is obvious that people fail to do what they believe best. Yet in any particular case we do not look for evidence that they were unable to act on their better judgement – because of some excusing condition like ignorance, overwhelming passion, psychotic delusions or less spectacular neurotic compulsions? We thus slide towards a Socratic interpretation of apparent counter-instances. But, my argument runs, our concept of what it is to have reasons should allow for failure to act upon them.

202

Significantly enough, Plato and Aristotle seem to have formulated the riddle in broad terms. But the most prominent discussions of it since World War II transform it into a difficulty about moral judgement and failure. Nevertheless it will confirm the power of the Socratic doctrine if we show how even theories of what it is to have a moral reason do not elude it.

How does remorse come into the picture nowadays? Among contemporary moral philosophers, R. M. Hare explicitly takes remorse as a criterion for saying that a man believed he ought to have performed an action which he failed to carry out (*The Language of Morals* [50], p. 169). P. H. Nowell-Smith reasons in a similar vein. He writes :

'Although a man cannot claim that it is against his moral principles to be cowardly or mean if he regularly does cowardly or mean things, he can do such things occasionally and still justify his claim. His claim is justified if he is prepared to condemn his own actions and if he feels remorse. His moral principles are . . . those about which he feels remorseful when he breaks them.' (*Ethics* [88], p. 308).

Quite apart from the importance of remose in ancient and contemporary theories of moral belief, remorse is worth analysing because of the close connections that will appear between this emotion and moral judgements. My aims will be : first, to offer an account of how remorse and moral conviction are linked, and particularly how remorse is suited to deliberate moral failure; secondly, to explain why it is reasonable, within the moral psychologies of Aristotle, Hare and Nowell-Smith, to introduce the concept of remorse to deal with the Socratic paradox; and thirdly, to demonstrate that an appeal to remorse, as a criterion for saying that a man has acted against his judgement of what is best, cannot protect such theories from the Socratic paradox after all.

In fairness to Aristotle, I should confess that I shall examine his account of practical reasoning and action through the distorting lens of post-Kantian systems like Hare's and Nowell-Smith's. Specifically, I saddle him with two uncharacteristic assumptions : that moral and non-moral motives for doing somethings are both easily distinguishable and sharply opposed; and that moral considerations have logical primacy when we deliberate over what to do. Luckily this anachronism only distorts Aristotle, but does not spoil my analysis of remorse.

2. *Distinctive connections between remorse and moral failure*

Among the many states and attitudes of an agent that seem equivalent to it, remorse is uniquely bound up with his beliefs about what he ought to do. For you can only feel remorseful about (i) a voluntary action, (ii) which you have performed, (iii) although you had compelling reasons not to perform it, and (iv) when the foremost reason you had against doing what you did was a moral conviction you held at the time. Thus shame is distinguishable from remorse inasmuch as you can feel ashamed of things you do neither willingly nor knowingly, such as the way you behaved on the stage while you were hypnotized. Again, you might be overcome by shame regarding other things than your actions, such as your clothes or your thoughts. It would be absurd to say you feel remorseful about the way you are dressed, or remorseful about your thoughts. Finally, you might feel ashamed of what another person did, for example, the drunken rowdiness of your weekend guest. You can only feel remorse about inviting him, when you knew that he would behave shockingly.

This last distinction also separates repentance from remorse. Thus nowadays many Americans feel repentant about the way their countrymen are destroying Vietnam. They can only feel remorse about not doing more to oppose the war. In addition, repentance is more associated with a religious outlook than remorse is, and constitutes more directly an activity on its own. That is, repenting is doing something, while being remorseful is at most necessarily followed by such activities as making amends.

The notion of guilt, on the other hand, is too closely bound up with legal norms and chastisements to double for remorse. A poisoner may be guilty of killing his rich aunt, but he need not be remorseful. In fact, some juries hold a lawbreaker less culpable when he manifests genuine remorse. While there can be this inverse relation between degree of guilt and intensity of remorse, *feeling* guilty is close to feeling remorseful. You can feel guilty about actions that do not come within the purview of any legal statute. However, you can feel guilty about things you have done which are much too trivial to be objects of remorse; for instance when you feel guilty about not using the ticket you had for the concert series last night. Another difference between guilt feelings and remorse is that you can have guilt feelings, but not remorse, about an unexecuted design you had. You might have twinges of guilt because you intended to shoot a neighbour's dog that knocked over your garbage can. Remorse would be appropriate only if you carried out your plan.

As for contrition, the chief difference between it and remorse is that contrition cannot be directed toward major misdeeds. A torturer might feel remorse, but it sounds like a bad joke to say that he feels contrite about brutally mistreating several victims. Moving on to self-condemnation, we notice one fresh point of distinction. A person might condemn himself not only for his behaviour, such as gambling with loaded dice, but also for his character. One cannot feel remorse solely about one's character, but instead about the manner it is expressed in one's actions. And as we have noticed with shame, repentance and guilt feelings, one might condemn oneself for one's intentions and for one's future acts. Remorse is impossible in these cases.

Regret is perhaps the closest cohort of remorse. Apart from divergences of surface grammar, such as the fact that we say 'You will regret it' and not 'You will remorse it', we should notice that the notion of regret is far broader. Often we feel regret about events over which we have no control, and which also lack moral significance. My regret that I am getting older is a typical case. Moreover, people sometimes regret doing what they ought to do. A policeman surely regrets that he must inform a woman that her child has been injured by an automobile, even though it is both a legal and a moral duty for him to notify her. He cannot feel remorse in these circumstances.

Further distinctions between remorse and other kindred emotions may be drawn along similar lines. But what bearing have my distinctions upon the Socratic paradox? I hope that it is evident, from my reasoning thus far, that the concept of remorse is just what Aristotle, Hare and Nowell-Smith need to confront the Socratic thesis. Remorse is a moral emotion *par excellence*. It is the only emotion that has as its objects nothing but intentional actions which the agent has performed in violation of his moral principles. Suppose Green does not send his usual monthly cheque to his aged grandparents. Instead, he squanders that portion of his salary in taking his newest girl friend to a night club. If Green feels remorse that he has thereby inflicted needless hardship upon his grandparents, then all the following implications must hold : Green must presently believe that he ought to have sent them the money; he must believe he was aware, at the time he failed, that he was failing; and he must believe that he could have dispatched the money to his grandparents. The only provision that we must explicitly add to our statement that Green feels remorse, in order to have a possible counter-example against the Socratic paradox, is that while Green was spending the money, instead of mailing it to his grandparents, he believed that he was acting wrongly. For otherwise it could be the case that Green feels remorse now that he has realized how inconsiderate he was, but he did not believe then, as a matter of principle, that he ought to send his monthly cheque to his grandparents. So if we want it to be unquestionable that Green is remorseful about his failure to send money to his grandparents as a moral failure, we should say, 'He feels remorseful that, despite his acknowledged moral obligation to his grandparents, he did not send them a cheque'.

Depicted thus, Green's remorse has two grounds : (*a*) that he knowingly and willingly failed to send the cheque, and (*b*) that he acted against his moral convictions. His remorse for having failed to send the cheque is justified because he at present believes that he ought to have sent it. His remorse for having acted against his moral convictions is justified by a higher-level principle, namely, that one ought to live by one's moral convictions. Even if Green had become more callous in the meantime, and had ceased to believe himself morally obligated to help support his grandparents, he could still be remorseful, just to the extent that it was a moral failure on his part. What I mean is that possibly he has now come to believe that it was not morally obligatory, after all, for him to support his grandparents. Perhaps he now regards family loyalty as a dispensable bourgeois scruple. Nevertheless he might still retain enough bourgeois scruples to feel remorseful over his failure to act as he then believed he ought to act.

All this has an indirect but important bearing upon Aristotle, Hare, Nowell-Smith, and their views of believing one ought. These philosophers would not wish to equate all our moral activity with the self-discipline of living in conformity with whatever principles we hold. So when they attribute remorse to a person who acted contrary to his judgement of what was best, these philosophers are not merely saying that the person is remorseful because his action constituted a moral failure. For instance, if we are going to use an example like that of Green's remorse to challenge the Socratic paradox, then Green must be remorseful both in that he failed morally and that he did not send money to his grandparents.

3. Action and remorse as alternative criteria of a man's moral beliefs

In a passage I have referred to already, Aristotle says the Socratic theory is

'that there is no such thing as incontinence; no one when he judges acts against what he judges best – people act so only by reason of ignorance. Now this view plainly contradicts the observed facts, and we must inquire about what happens to such a man; if he acts by reason of ignorance, what is the manner of his ignorance? For that the man who behaves incontinently does not, before he gets into this state, *think* he ought to do so, is evident' ([4] vii, 1145b).

On a Socratic view, belief that one ought to do X would be a logically sufficient condition for doing X in recognizably suitable circumstances. Consequently action would be a logically necessary condition of belief, and non-action a logically sufficient condition for denying that the agent believes he ought to do X. His doing X is not a logically sufficient condition for his believing that he ought to. However, such action would still be a criterion – that is, a reliable test and relevant evidence – for ascribing to the agent the belief that he ought to do X. His deliberate failure to do X, by contrast, would be a criterion in the much stronger sense that his failure would, on the Socratic view, conclusively disprove that the agent believed he ought to do X. So for Socrates there is no logical possibility that the agent deliberately fails to do something he believes he ought to do.

Does Aristotle avoid this last consequence by any of his hypotheses regarding the agent's ignorance? Given his analysis of 'believing one ought', I do not see how. His analysis is anchored upon a supposed parallelism between moral deliberation and theoretical syllogistic reasoning. The similarity of structure appears to be this. Corresponding to the major premise of a theoretical syllogism is a practical principle accepted by the agent. Aristotle's most famous example is the principle 'Everything sweet ought to be tasted'. The counterpart to the minor premise of a theoretical syllogism is the agent's factual belief about the circumstances in which he finds himself. Aristotle's example is the belief, 'This is sweet'. The conclusion of an agent's deliberation, however, consists in more than deducing, 'This ought to be tasted'. For Aristotle writes: 'When a single opinion results from the two, the soul must . . . immediately act' ([14] vii, 1147a). From the syllogistic analogy, it looks as though a man who believes he ought to perform an action of type X, and believes some particular action he could perform would be of the type X, necessarily performs the particular action. By contraposition, then, a man who fails to perform the deed cannot possibly believe that he ought to perform it. If we define moral failure as (1) believing that you ought to perform some action and (2) not performing it, moral failure will be logically impossible, since (1) and (2), by Aristotle's syllogistic interpretation of (1), cannot both be true.

Now Aristotle looks for some type of ignorance which might co-exist with the agent's belief that his current behaviour is not the sort of thing he ought to be doing. One suggestion is that when, for example, a man like Alcibiades deserts the Athenians in battle, his conviction that he ought to remain with them just 'slips his mind'. Aristotle's explanation would be that the deserter still has a belief that he ought to remain with his fellow-soldiers; but his belief is like a drunken man's understanding of some verses he had studied while sober. The drunken man can only babble the verses, although he will be able to expound them when he regains his senses. Does this model for ignorance work?

I wonder if it is true that the drunken man understands the verses at the time he incoherently babbles them? Is it not more accurate to say that his understanding is temporarily diminished? If so, Aristotle's comparison gives us no grounds for assuming that the deserter believes he ought to stay with his fellow soldiers at the moment he is in flight.

This first Aristotelian line of explanation, namely, that when a man deliberately acts contrary to his moral principle, his principle must have slipped from his mind, takes a more extreme form in a recent essay by Gilbert Ryle, 'Forgetting the Difference between Right and Wrong' [104]. There Ryle suggests that a man who forgets his principle becomes a different person. I am unable to see how this solution meets the Socratic paradox. How can I be said to fail morally, when the principle I violate belongs, not to the person I am at the time, but to someone I used to be?

Aristotle, for his part, seeks other forms of ignorance that might accompany moral failure. Besides temporary ignorance of one's own principles, he considers ignorance of relevant facts about one's current situation. In the case of Alcibiades' desertion, our hypothesis would be that somehow Alcibiades did not realize that he was abandoning his comrades in arms. This sort of ignorance of fact is compatible with our un-Socratic assumption that Alcibiades fully accepted the principle that desertion is wrong. However, the 'ignorance of fact' explanation does not come to grips with the Socratic paradox because it ceases to imply that Alcidiades knowingly acted contrary to his judgement of what was best. We need a case of fully conscious and voluntary moral failure in order to answer Socrates' contention. We dodge the issue as long as we merely catalogue varieties of unwitting failure.

The other varieties of ignorance that Aristotle surveys are due to the fact that the agent is 'under the influence of passion', 'mastered by pleasure' or 'overcome by temptation'. These examples come closer to deliberate moral failure. There is no inconsistency in supposing that Alcibiades believes he should not desert, realizes he is deserting, but disregards his own judge-ments on these matters because of his emotional agitation. His ignorance would consist precisely in his disregard for the conclusions of his own practical reasoning. Of course Alcibiades' turmoil cannot be too intense. Otherwise we would lose our case of deliberate moral failure, on the grounds that the agent did not act willingly, because his violent emotions deprived him of control over what he was doing.

Furthermore, Aristotle's hypothesis of ignorance due to vehement passion will not cover the whole range of possible cases which go against the Socratic paradox. As J. L. Austin says in a much-quoted footnote, 'We often succumb to temptation with calm and even with finesse' ([10], p. 146). The Aristotelian theory will account for the tempestuous misdeeds of Macbeth, but not the calculated villanies of Richard III. Consequently, all that a defender of the Socratic paradox has to do is qualify his assertion that nobody ever deliberately acts contrary to his better judgement. The qualification would be that it is logically impossible that a person should *calmly* and deliberately fail to act as he believes best.

At this juncture the thread of our inquiry becomes tenuous. For I have no idea whether Aristotle would have wanted to allow for cases of this type. Anyway, suppose he had. And suppose we have an agent who we say has calmly and deliberately failed. What criteria would outweigh the evidence against belief which his failure gives us? His word might give us some countervailing evidence. But since we might discount his professions of belief as either hypocrisy or self-deception, we must have further tests for what the agent believes he ought to have done. If so, my tenuous but straightforward conclusion is that the agent's emotion of remorse at his failure will be a reasonable supplementary criterion.

If we turn now from Aristotle to Hare, we need not be so hesitant. Hare explicitly discards action as the unique and (in the case of non-action) decisive criterion for saying whether a person believes he ought to do X. Hare also looks to remorse for evidence that might outweigh the negative evidence we have when a man fails to do X. Hare's position develops as follows. He specifies that when you judge that you ought to do something, in what he calls the primary 'evaluative' sense of 'ought', this means, among other things, that you also *resolve* to act when circumstances seem propitious. In Hare's terminology:

'the test, whether someone is using the judgment, "I ought to do X" as a value-judgment or not is, "Does he or does he not recognize that if he assents to the judgment, he must also assent to the command 'Let me do X' " ' (*Language of Morals* [50], pp. 168–9).

Another way Hare formulates his point is that ' "ought"-sentences entail imperatives . . . when they are being used evaluatively' or prescriptively ([50], p. 164). And when we assent to a command, for example, of the form 'Let me do X', according to Hare

'we are said to be sincere in our assent if and only if we do or resolve to do what the speaker has told us to do; if we do not do it but only resolve to do it later, then if, when the occasion arises for doing it, we do not do it, we . . . are no longer sticking to the assent which we previously expressed' ([50], p. 20).

If we now put together these characterizations by Hare of 'believing you ought to do X' and 'assenting to the self-addressed command, "Let me do X!" ', then Hare notices that we are driven toward

'the familiar "Socratic Paradox" . . . in which it becomes analytic to say that everyone always does what he thinks he ought to (in the evaluative sense). And this, to put Aristotle's objection in modern dress, is not how we use the word "think" ' ([50], p. 169).

Since Hare explicitly wants to accommodate the ordinary view that people on occasion fail to do what they believe they ought to do, he proposes our alternative criterion, on which the agent's remorse provides evidence about what he believes he ought to do. Unfortunately Hare excuses himself from a 'detailed analysis' of remorse because of his space limitations. After I have reviewed the similar reasoning that Nowell-Smith deploys when he also sees himself heading for the Socratic paradox, I will argue that a proper analysis of remorse will not allow Hare and Nowell-Smith to elude the Socratic thesis in this manner.

Let us move on. Nowell-Smith interprets the moral 'ought' so that it sounds as if it is going to be logically impossible that we ever knowingly and willingly fail to do what we believe we ought to do. Nowell-Smith stipulates that if you have a genuine moral conviction, for instance, that you ought to contribute to the local orphanage, then your 'ought' is to be understood in the 'judicial, verdict-giving sense'. When used in this sense, 'ought' expresses 'a decision about what to do' (*Ethics* [88], pp. 261–2). Nowell-Smith amplifies this by saying :

> 'the language of "ought" is intelligible only in the context of practical questions, and we have not answered a practical question until we have reached a decision. "I shall do this" is the general formula for expressing decisions. . . .
>
> There is no logical gap between "ought" and "shall". . .
>
> . . . The contradictory character of "I ought but I shall not" is obscured by the fact that "shall" also has another use in which it is not self-contradictory to say "I ought, but I shall not". This is the predictive use.' ([88], p. 268)

Besides making it analytic that a man who believes he ought to do X decides to do X, Nowell-Smith follows Hare in creating a logical link between deciding and acting when a suitable occasion appears to arise.

Here is Nowell-Smith's illustration of what it means to say that one believes one should never be vindictive :

> 'I cannot (logically) condemn any . . . vices in myself while at the same time exercising them . . . [If] I deliberately choose to do something vindictive, . . . I can still claim that to be vindictive is against my principles only in the sense that, in my more reflective moments, I am prepared to condemn what I did.' ([88], p. 311)

If we take this last quotation literally, Nowell-Smith will not elude the Socratic paradox even by his introduction of remorse as a criterion for moral belief. His statement, 'I cannot (logically) condemn any . . . vices in myself while at the same time exercising them', would rule out the possibility that I ever perform an action which, as I am performing it, I believe to be wrong. Consequently I cannot believe it wrong at the moment. Therefore my subsequent self-condemnation only proves that I have undergone a change of heart, not that I did and still do believe my action to be wrong. Against this excessively literal reading of Nowell-Smith, I prefer to go by the passage I quoted earlier, where he says that a man's 'moral principles are . . . those about which he feels remorseful when he breaks them'. This also accords with another statement Nowell-Smith makes about the remorseful person :

> 'His moral principles are those on which, in his more reflective moments, he honestly says that he would like to act; they are the moral principles of the person he is striving to become' ([88], p. 308).

I conclude that Nowell-Smith feels just as reluctant as Hare does, and Aristotle should have felt, to allow that moral conviction entails behaviour. The agent's conformity may be a conclusive criterion for what he believes he ought to do; but the entailment from belief to action must be denied. Otherwise the agent's failure to act will entail that it is false that he believes he should act. And if the link between moral belief and action is loosened, as Aristotle, Hare and Nowell-Smith think it should be, then we shall have to look for other criteria, besides conformity, for ascribing moral beliefs to a man who failed to act in conformity with his beliefs. So far we have looked to the emotions of the man who deliberately failed to perform a certain action.

4. *Does our remorse criterion neutralize the Socratic paradox?*
In the first section of this study I attempted to display the close connection between remorse and moral failure. In brief, nearly the only thing about which you can be remorseful is your failure to do what you believe you ought to do. Then in the second section I explained : (*a*) why the Socratic paradox, that moral belief entails action, seems objectionable to philosophers like Aristotle, Hare and Nowell-Smith; and (*b*) why they hope to avoid the paradox by taking remorse, as well as action in accordance with one's belief, to be evidence for one's moral beliefs. Now I want to challenge this last hopeful point. I admit that it sounds plausible both to deny the Socratic thesis that belief entails action, and to propose remorse as an alternative criterion, when action does not occur. But I shall now argue that deeper

analysis of what we mean by remorse will actually entail a version of the Socratic paradox. Consequently the remorse criterion is not consistent with a denial of the Socratic view. Borrowing another phrase of Austin's, the paradox is still there, 'grinning residually up at us, like the frog at the bottom of the beer mug'. My variant of the Socratic doctrine may be stated schematically, and without the necessary qualifications, as follows : 'If a person believes he ought to do X, it is barely possible that he will deliberately fail to do X; if so, he will be remorseful; but if he is remorseful, and sees more opportunities to do X, then he will do X'.

My supporting argument will be twofold. First I shall illustrate my variant of the Socratic thesis. Then I shall tackle some counter-illustrations, and exploit some of them to make necessary qualifications in my account. The others I shall show to be irrelevant. The favourable case I start with goes like this. Brown professes to believe, as a matter of moral principle, that marijuana-smoking ought to be made legal. He receives pamphlets from the Association for Legalizing Marijuana. As a result of reading and discussion, he has become persuaded that the most promising tactics for obtaining sensible laws in this area are demonstrations. His friends at the Association for Legalizing Marijuana notify him that they desperately need him to join the crowd of sympathizers at a smoke-in they are going to stage. If they can muster a few more supporters like him, the newsmen will be impressed, and give the cause favourable publicity. Otherwise the movement will appear to be ineffective and of no concern to the general public. Incidentally, Brown is free to go, and risks no penalties if he does go. Our question is : Does Brown have the moral conviction that *he* ought to take some action to help the movement, and does he believe that participating in this demonstration is going to help? If he does join the crowd, then even though we reject the Socratic entailment from belief to action, Brown's conformity will be reliable evidence for his beliefs, according to our modified action-criterion. But what if he stays home, although he remembers and nothing hinders him from participating? Since we have rejected the Socratic entailment, his failure is not decisive disproof of his moral conviction. So we appeal to our remorse criterion. And indeed Brown displays

214

considerable emotion about his failure. He blushes when his friends talk about the smoke-in. He winces and sighs when he reports his own failure. When he is alone, he curses himself. Will Brown's emotion qualify as remorse, and thereby count as evidence that he believed he ought to attend the demonstration?

I think that in the standard and central case, from which our analysis should be drawn, a remorseful person will be inclined to make a serious attempt to act differently in the future. So before we hastily wash our hands of the Socratic thesis, by calling Brown's emotion remorse, we should gather evidence that he is disposed to try to mend his ways. For example, even if Brown now changes his attitude on the marijuana question, we would expect his remorse to manifest itself in a heightened degree of fidelity to whatever new moral aims he endorses. Alternatively, suppose Brown does not emerge from his failure with greater self-control. Nevertheless, we would expect that his remorse about not going to the smoke-in will dispose him to avoid situations like this, which he has now learned will weaken his resolve. That is, at least we would expect his moral failure to have taught him something about himself. For he has learned that when his moral beliefs require actions like going to a demonstration, he is liable to fail. So if he does not develop greater self-discipline, he wisely avoids getting in situations that are likely to demand it. For instance, he might decide that he cannot sincerely believe that *he* ought to make efforts to advance a cause like legalizing marijuana. At most he can believe that the cause is worthy, and that people who devote effort to it are admirable.

Negatively, what I am saying is that Brown's present display of emotion is not all the evidence that is relevant for ascribing remorse to him. If he is not inclined to make an effort to act differently in the future, along the various lines I have sketched, then it is a mistake to assert that he feels remorse, and therefore a mistake to conclude that he believed that he ought to attend the smoke-in. What bearing has this upon the Socratic paradox? My deeper analysis of remorse uncovers how this criterion for 'believing you ought' presupposes a weakened Socratic thesis, namely: 'If you believe you ought to do X, and your conviction does not change, then you will eventually do X.' The qualifications I have made so far explain how remorse might also be expected to alter your moral beliefs. Generally speaking, then, my negative argument is that if a man like Brown continues affirming his belief that he ought to do his part for the legalization of marijuana smoking, but continues to make no effort when occasions present themselves, then his emotion at these lapses cannot be remorse.

To this you might answer that we must allow Brown a reasonable number of lapses, before we deny that his emotion is remorse. Agreed. Still, if we are correct in assuming that Brown's moral conviction is unaltered, and allow him a reasonable number of failures, then we are surely entitled to conclude that Brown has misdescribed his attitude when he said he was remorseful.

How can Brown's subsequent failures to exert himself be evidence against saying that he now feels remorse? This works straightforwardly, on the assumption that both his belief and his emotion remain the same toward his initial failure and his subsequent failure. If he consistently fails to exert himself, and eventually we decide that he is misdescribing his attitude toward these subsequent failures, we have to conclude that he was also misdescribing the same attitude when he reported it the first time.

What should he have called it? 'Regret', I suppose. Or perhaps there is no convenient tag for what he felt and feels. We might have to content ourselves with vague terms, and say that Brown *feels bad* about doing nothing to help the marijuana movement. However we characterize his emotion, my argument is that repeated backsliding by Brown will refute our initial claim that Brown believed he ought to help. And any emotion less vehement than remorse will be insufficient to outweigh the evidence we already had from his initial failure.

My thesis, that a remorse-criterion for moral conviction leads us back to the Socratic paradox, should be tolerably clear by now. Therefore I want to bring up the main objection against it which appeared in a critique of my original paper by Robert Rosthal [100]. The objection is simply that I overlook cases where people are overwhelmed or paralysed with remorse. By the very meaning of these modifying terms, such remorseful wrongdoers are incapable of mending their ways; and so I must be mistaken in supposing that remorse comprises an inclination

216

towards reform, or any other type of behaviour. Consequently the remorse criterion does not appear to burden us with the Socratic paradox after all.

There are two replies which accommodate this objection without damage to my thesis. One is that even if a wrongdoer is incapable of action when we first ascribe remorse to him, our ascription is open to challenge later, whenever he gets a grip on himself. If he is not then disposed to mend his ways, and again makes no effort to do what he says he ought, presumably we would deny that he believed he ought to have acted differently. On this defence, all I have to do is emphasize that sooner or later – perhaps much later – the remorseful man will do the sort of thing he was remorseful about failing to do.

The other line of defence against cases of remorse without regeneration is to admit them, and forget about dispositions that might develop later on. Nevertheless, this reply would go, such cases are neither typical nor central. As a rule we are safe in assuming that the agent who says he feels remorseful at his moral failure is going to make an effort at self-improvement later on. Although we are prepared for some aberrant cases of remorse, in which the wrongdoer has no disposition to mend his way, we are still entitled to reason from the absence of such dispositions to the absence of both remorse and moral conviction. Furthermore, our inference will not be blind. We have independent grounds for distinguishing between cases where someone is incapacitated by remorse and standard cases. Thus if the remorseful man dashes out to a party and does the latest dances for several hours, he is not overwhelmed by remorse. It may be true to suggest that he really has gnawing *pangs* of remorse, and that he is trying to hide his feelings with his jokes and frenzied activity. But it cannot be true to say that perhaps he is really *paralysed* by his feelings of remorse, and his joviality and zest are camouflage to hide his paralysis. His activity is conclusive evidence against saying that he is overwhelmed. So if we agree that his emotion is remorse, in this case we shall expect him to mend his ways.

Just what sort of self-redemption can we expect, either in standard or in 'overwhelmed' cases of remorse? I have left this fairly open. One form of making up for the past will have to be

P 217

ruled out, on logical grounds: the remorseful wrongdoer cannot go back in time and 'undo' his past failure, by performing the very deed be believed he ought to perform. Brown might lament, 'If only I could turn back the clock and have another chance!' We cannot take him at his word, however, since there is no cogent specification of what it would be like for him to attend the very same smoke-in he failed to attend, even though it is now over. Consequently it is impossible that he should seriously intend to, and that we should expect him to repair the past in this radical manner. Incidentally, my contention in Essay V, that a person can intend to do what he believes to be physically impossible, will not accommodate this case of acknowledged logical impossibility either. What sorts of reparation are conceivable then, in a case like Brown's? I see no philosophical difficulties in supposing that he tries to make up for his failure by attending the next pro-marijuana demonstration. If no more demonstrations occur, then he can help the movement by volunteering to address and mail out its newsletter.

Explaining what a remorseful man would do to rectify his misdeed is more difficult when he has wronged a definite person. For example, if Grey divulges an embarrassing personal secret that White confided in him, Grey may never have another chance to learn and keep White's secrets. White probably will not trust him any more. Nevertheless Grey can make amends to White by fulfilling other obligations he has toward White, or by doing some unsolicited benefit for him. How does this modification preserve my thesis that a man who is remorseful about not doing what he believed he ought to do will eventually perform an act of the same type he failed to perform? My thesis only has to allow for a broader specification of what the wrongdoer believed he ought to have done. When Grey failed to keep White's secret, he did not fulfil an obligation he had toward White; or even more generally, he failed to do something good for White. So when I contend that eventually Grey will do what he believed and continues to believe he ought to do, even Grey's unsolicited acts of benevolence toward White will confirm my thesis; since these are more general cases of doing the sort of thing Grey believed he ought to do for White.

What about situations where the victim is unavailable? This

is another difficult case, along with the previously mentioned case of wrongdoers who are paralysed with remorse, that Rosthal brings against my thesis. He paraphrases a statement by C. D. Broad, in *Five Types of Ethical Theory* ([20], p. 203), to the effect that 'if regret for a past wrongdoing is to amount to remorse . . . no reparations can be made by the agent, owing, for example, to the death of the injured party' (Rosthal [100], p. 577). Once more I would adjust my thesis to accommodate this type of case by generalizing the wrongdoer's belief. Suppose White died of chagrin. If Grey is religious, he might imagine that he still has some obligations toward White, even though White is dead. Alternatively, he might have faith that he can make White's soul happier during its after-life, for example, by sponsoring prayers or special ceremonies to benefit White. If, on the other hand, Grey is a religious sceptic, then we generalize by saying that when he failed White, Grey believed that he ought to keep secrets that any person confides in him. Thus if Grey is remorseful about his failure, and his general belief in keeping secrets does not change, we shall expect Grey to be more trustworthy towards other people, even though he can do nothing to redeem himself in the view of his deceased victim. Another possibility, of course, is that Grey sooner or later realizes that he is temperamentally unable to keep a secret. He still believes that if someone confides in him, he should not pass the secret on to others. But he rephrases his principle in disjunctive form : either do not allow people to confide in you, or keep your mouth shut. This was certainly a logical consequence of the moral conviction Grey had at the time he betrayed White. And it would be evidence of Grey's remorse if he acted on the first clause of this disjunctive rule.

I mention this last possibility for the same reason that I already weakened my thesis about the connection between remorse and reform. Before I commit myself to a more precise account of that link, I want to review these qualifications. Their overall thrust is to allow the logical possibility of a moral agent who either abandons the principles he violated, or retains them but avoids situations which his failures have shown are too much for him. If we now ask what is common to the more conventional types of reform behaviour, and these alternative manifestations of remorse, cannot we say that in all these cases remorse is connected with moral growth? That is, either the wrongdoer makes up for his failure, or realizes that he is not strong enough to do what he believed he ought to do. The point of my qualifications was to avoid making it part of the definition of remorse that a remorseful man is a morally strong man.

But must it be a matter of definition that he will at least gain in maturity, in self-knowledge? This sounds as puritanical as the Socratic doctrine we started with, that a man who believes he ought to do something will do it. And indeed it is. I want to say that the connection between remorse and moral growth is just as rigid, or just as tenuous, as the connection between believing you ought to do something and doing it. If the connection between belief and action looks like an entailment to us, then we cannot avoid it by reformulating the Socratic account to read: 'If you believe you ought to do X, then *either* you will do it when the occasion seems propitious, *or* you will be remorseful that you fail.' The introduction of remorse will not help us avoid the Socratic paradox, because we notice, on my analysis, that there is just as firm a connection between remorse and *either* reform behaviour *or* other kinds of moral development.

I rejected the Socratic entailment. By parity of reasoning, should I not deny that there is an entailment from remorse to moral growth? My inclination is to say that we have found the same empirical and pragmatic connections between remorse and moral growth as we found in Essay V between intending to X and believing you can X. We should not rule out the possibility of continuing moral immaturity or even regression. The only trouble is that our criteria for deciding whether someone is remorseful lead us to expect moral growth. If we discover none, this counts heavily against saying the agent is remorseful that he acted contrary to his moral convictions.

Luckily, it is inessential to my argument that we take a stand for or against seeing an entailment from remorse to any kind of behaviour. For all I intended to prove was that the introduction of remorse, as a criterion for saying that a wrongdoer believed he ought to have acted differently, will not neutralize the Socratic paradox. Our criteria for remorse lead us eventually to demand action with as much insistence as Socrates did.

SELECTED BIBLIOGRAPHY

(limited to works referred to or having a direct bearing on these studies)

Abbreviations for journals most often cited :
'APQ' for *American Philosophical Quarterly*;
'A' for *Analysis*;
'JP' for *Journal of Philosophy*;
'M' for *Mind*;
'PQ' for *Philosophical Quarterly*;
'PR' for *Philosophical Review*;
'PAS' and 'PASSV' for *Proceedings of the Aristotelian Society* and its *Supplementary Volumes*.

1. Anscombe, G. E. M., *Intention*, Oxford : Blackwell, 1957.
2. 'Pretending', PASSV 32 (1958), 279–94.
3. 'Two Kinds of Error in Action', JP 60 (1963), 393–401.
4. Aristotle, *Nicomachean Ethics*, trans. W. D. Ross, in R. McKeon, ed., *Introduction to Aristotle*, New York : Modern Library, 1937.
5. Selection from *Ethica Eudemia*, in Morgenbesser and Walsh [85], 139–48.
6. Augustine, Saint, Selections from *On Free Will*, in Morgenbesser and Walsh [85], 13–19.
7. Aune, Bruce, 'Abilities, Modalities and Free Will', *Philosophy and Phenomenological Research* 23 (1962–3), 397–413.
8. 'Can', in P. Edwards, ed., *Encyclopedia of Philosophy*, New York : Macmillan, 1967.
9. 'Hypotheticals and Can : Another Look', A 27 (1967), 191–5.
10. Austin, J. L., 'A Plea for Excuses' in *Philosophical Papers*, ed. J. O. Urmson, Oxford : Oxford University Press, 1961. 1961.
11. 'Ifs and Cans', ibid., 153–80.
12. 'Pretending', ibid., 201–19.
13. 'Three Ways of Spilling Ink', PR 75 (1966), 427–40.
14. Baier, Kurt, 'Action and Agent', *Monist* 49 (1965), 183–95.
15. 'Acting and Producing', JP 62 (1966), 645–8.
16. Bennett, Daniel, 'Action, Reason and Purpose', JP 62 (1965), 85–96.
17. Benson, John, 'Oughts and Wants', PASSV 42 (1968), 155–72.

18. Berofsky, Bernard, ed., *Free Will and Determinism*, New York : Harper and Row, 1966.
19. Black, Max, 'Making Things Happen', in Hook [58], 31–45.
   Bramhall, Bishop. See Hobbes [57].
20. Broad, C. D., *Five Types of Ethical Theory*, London : Routledge, 1930.
21. Broadie, Frederick, 'Trying and Doing', PAS 66 (1965–6), 27–40.
22. Canfield, John, 'Knowing about Future Decisions', A 22 (1961–2), 127–9.
23. Care, Norman S., 'On Avowing Reasons', M 76 (1967), 208–16.
24. Chisholm, R. M., 'The Descriptive Element in the Concept of Action', JP 61 (1964), 613–25.
25. 'J. L. Austin's *Philosophical Papers*', M 73 (1964), 20–5 on Austin's 'Ifs and Cans'. Reprinted in Berofsky [18], 239–45.
26. 'Freedom and Action', in Lehrer [72], 11–44.
27. 'He Could Have Done Otherwise', JP 64 (1967), 409–17.
28. 'Reflections on Human Agency'. *Idealistic Studies* 1 (Jan. 1971), 36–46.
29. Cooper, Neil, 'Oughts and Wants', PASSV 42 (1968), 141–54.
30. Danto, Arthur, 'What We Can Do', JP 60 (1963), 435–45.
31. 'Basic Actions', APQ 2 (1965), 141–8.
32. 'Freedom and Forbearance', in Lehrer [72].
33. D'Arcy, Eric, *Human Acts*, Oxford : Clarendon Press, 1963.
34. Davidson, Donald, 'Actions, Reasons and Causes', JP 60 (1963), 685–700.
35. 'The Logical Form of Action Sentences' (with comments by E. J. Lemmon, H.-N. Castanea and R. M. Chisholm, and a rejoinder, in Rescher [99].
36. 'Causal Relations', JP 64 (1967), 691–703.
37. 'How is Weakness of the Will Possible?', in J. Feinberg, ed., *Moral Concepts*, Oxford U.P., 1969, 93–113.
38. 'Agency', in R. Binkley *et al.*, eds, *Action, Agent and Reason*, Toronto U.P., 1971, 3–25.
39. Edwards, J. L. J., 'Automatism and Involuntary Conduct', 21 *Modern Law Review*, 375 (1958).
40. Feinberg, Joel, 'Problematic Responsibility in Law and Morals', PR 71 (1962), 340–51.
41. 'On Being "Morally Speaking a Murderer"', JP 61 (1964), 158 71.

42.   'Action and Responsibility', in Max Black, ed., *Philosophy in America*, Ithaca : Cornell U.P. : 1965, 134–60; Allen & Unwin, Muirhead Library of Philosophy.
43.   Ginet, Carl, 'Can the Will Be Caused?', PR 71 (1962), 340–51.
44.   Goldberg, Bruce and H. Heidelberger, 'Mr. Lehrer on the Constitution of Cans', A 21 (1960–1), 96.
45.   Goldman, Alvin, *A Theory of Human Action*. Englewood Cliffs : Prentice-Hall, 1969.
46.   Gustafson, Donald F., 'Hampshire on Trying,' *Theoria* 30 (1964), 31–3.
47.   Hampshire, Stuart, and Hart, H. L. A., 'Decision, Intention and Certainty', M 67 (1958), 1–12.
48.   Hampshire, Stuart, Thought and Action, London : Chatto and Windus, 1959.
49.   *Freedom of the Individual*, New York : Harper, 1965.
50.   Hare, Richard M., *The Language of Morals*, Oxford : Clarendon, 1952.
51.   *Freedom and Reason*, Oxford : Oxford U.P., 1963, chap. V.
52.   Hart, H. L. A. and Honoré, A. M., *Causation in the Law*, Oxford : Clarendon, 1959.
53.   Hart, H. L. A., *The Concept of Law*, Oxford : Oxford U.P., 1961.
54.   *Punishment and Responsibility*, Oxford : Oxford U.P., 1968.
55.   Hempel, Carl G., 'Rational Action', *Proceedings and Addresses of the American Philosophical Assn.* 35 (1961–2), 5–23.
56.   'Explanation in Science and History', in W. Dray, ed., *Philosophical Analysis and History*, New York : Harper, 1966, 95–126.
57.   Hobbes, Thomas, *The Questions Concerning Liberty, Necessity and Chance*. Debate with Bishop Bramhall. Vol. V in W. Molesworth, ed., *The English Works of Thomas Hobbes*, London : 1878. Selection in Morgenbesser and Walsh [85], 41–51.
58.   Hook, Sidney, ed., *Determinism and Freedom in the Age of Modern Science*, Collier-Macmillan, 1961.
59.   Hospers, John, 'Meaning and Free Will', *Philosophy and Phenomenological Research* 10 (1949–50), 307–30.
60.   'What Means this Freedom?', in Hook [58], 126–42.

61. Hume, David, *Treatise of Human Nature*, ed, L. A. Selby-Bigge, Oxford : Oxford U.P., 1888, esp. 399–448.
62. *Enquiry Concerning Human Understanding*, ed C. W. Hendel, New York : Liberal Arts, 1955, esp. chap. VIII.
63. Kaufman, Arnold S., 'Ability', JP 60 (1963), 537–51.
64. 'Practical Decision', M 76 (1966), 25–44.
65. Kenny, Anthony, *Action, Emotion and Will*, London : Routledge, 1963.
66. 'Intention and Purpose', JP 63 (1966), 642–51.
67. Ladd, John, 'The Ethical Dimensions of the Concept of Action', JP 62 (1965), 633–45.
68. Lehrer, Keith, 'Ifs, Cans and Causes', A 20 (1959–60), 122–4.
69. 'Cans and Conditionals : A Rejoinder', A 22 (1961–2), 23–4.
70. 'Decisions and Causes', PR 72 (1963), 224–7.
71. ' "Could" and Determinism', A 24 (1963–4), 159–60.
72. ed., *Freedom and Determinism*, New York : Random House, 1966.
73. Levison, Arnold B., 'Knowledge and Society', *Inquiry* 9 (1966), 132–46.
74. Locke, John, *Essay Concerning Human Understanding*, ed., A. C. Fraser, New York : Dover, 1951, Book II, chap. XXI; Fontana, 1964.
75. MacKay, D. M., 'On the Logical Indeterminacy of a Free Choice', M 69 (1960), 31–40.
76. 'Logical Indeterminacy and Freewill', A 21 (1960–1), 82–3.
77. Madell, Geoffrey, 'Action and Causal Explanation', M 76 (1967), 34–48.
78. Malcolm, Norman, 'Explaining Behavior', PR 76 (1967), 97–104.
79. 'The Conceivability of Mechanism', PR 77 (1968), 45–72.
80. Margolis, Joseph, 'Actions and Ways of Failing', *Inquiry* 3 (1960), 89–101.
81. Melden, A. I., ed., *Essays in Moral Philosophy*, Seattle : Univ. of Washington Press, 1958.
82. *Free Action*, London : Routledge, 1961.
83. Mill, John Stuart, *An Examination of Sir William Hamilton's Philosophy*, London : Longmans, 1867, esp. chap XXVI.
84. *Utilitarianism*, Fontana, 1962.
85. Morgenbesser, S. and Walsh, J. J., eds, *Free Will*, Englewood Cliffs : Prentice-Hall, 1962.
86. Morris, Herbert, 'Punishment for Thoughts', *Monist* 49 (1965), 342–55.

87. Morris, Norval, 'Ghosts, Spiders and North Koreans', 5 *Res Judicatae* 29 (1951).

88. Nowell-Smith, P. H., *Ethics*, Harmondsworth : Penguin Books, 1954.

89. Ofstad, Harald, *An Inquiry into the Freedom of Decision*, London : Allen & Unwin, 1961.

90. 'Recent Work on the Free-Will Problem', APQ 4 (1967), 179–207.

91. Osborn, Jane M., 'Austin's Non-conditional Ifs', JP 62 (1965), 711–15.

92. Pears, David F., *Predicting and Deciding* (British Academy Lecture), London : Oxford U.P., 1964.

93. 'Are Reasons for Action Causes?', in Stroll [112], 204–28.

94. Peters, Richard S., *The Concept of Motivation*, London : Routledge, 1958.

95. Phillips, D. Z. and Price, H. S., 'Remorse without Repudiation', A 28 (1967), 15–20.

96. Plato, *Dialogues*, trans. Benjamin Jowett, Oxford : U.P., 1953.

97. Powell, Betty, *Knowledge of Actions*, London : Allen & Unwin, 1967.

98. Rankin, Nani L., 'The Unmoved Agent and the Ground of Responsibility', JP 64 (1967), 403–8.

99. Rescher, Nicholas, ed., *The Logic of Decision and Action*, Pittsburgh : Univ. of Pittsburgh Press, 1967.

100. Rosthal, Robert, 'Remorse and Moral Weakness', M 76 (1967), 576–9.

101. Roxbee Cox, J. W., 'Can I Know Beforehand What I Am Going to Decide?', PR 72 (1963), 88–92.

102. Russell, Bertrand, 'On the Notion of Cause', in *Mysticism and Logic*, London : Longmans, 1918.

103. Ryle, Gilbert, *The Concept of Mind*, London : Barnes and Noble, 1949.

104. 'Forgetting the Difference between Right and Wrong', in Melden [81], 147–59.

105. Sachs, David, 'A Few Morals about Acts', PR 75 (1966), 91–8.

106. Saunders, John Turk, 'The Temptations of Powerlessness', APQ 5 (1968), 100–8.

107. Schlick, Moritz, *Problems of Ethics*, trans. David Rynin, New York : Prentice-Hall, 1939, esp. chaps. II and VII, Dover Publications.

108. Sellars, Wilfrid, 'Fatalism and Determinism', in Lehrer [72], 141–74.

225

109. Skinner, R. C., 'Freedom of Choice', M 72 (1963), 463–80.
110. Stocker, Michael, 'Knowledge, Causation and Decision', *Nous* 2 (1968), 65–73.
111. Stoutland, Frederick, 'Basic Actions and Causality', JP 65 (1968), 467–74.
112. Stroll, Avrum, ed., *Epistemology*, New York : Harper, 1967.
113. Taylor, Richard, *Metaphysics*, Englewood Cliffs : Prentice-Hall, 1963, chap. IV.
114. *Action and Purpose*, Englewood Cliffs : Prentice-Hall, 1966.
115. Thalberg, Irving, 'Acting Against One's Better Judgment', in G. Mortimore, ed., *Weakness of Will*, London : Macmillan, 1971, 233–46.
116. Thomas, George B., 'Comment : Ability and Physiology', JP 61 (1964), 321–8.
117. Walsh, James J., *Aristotle's Conception of Moral Weakness*, New York : Columbia U.P., 1963.
118. Wasserstrom, Richard, 'Strict Liability and the Criminal Law', in H. Morris, ed., *Freedom and Responsibility*, Stanford : Stanford U.P., 1961.
119. Williams, C. J. F., 'Logical Indeterminacy and Freewill', A 21 (1960–1), 12–13.
120. 'Comment on Professor MacKay's Reply', A 21 (1960–1), 84–5.
121. Winch, Peter, *The Idea of a Social Science*, London : Routledge, 1957.
122. Wittgenstein, Ludwig, *Philosophical Investigations*, trans. G. E. M. Anscombe, Oxford : Blackwell, 1953.
123. *Blue and Brown Books*, ed., R. Rhees, New York : Harper, 1958.
124. *Zettel*, Anscombe, Rhees, Von Wright, eds, Oxford : Blackwell, 1967.

INDEX

Ability, *see* Can

Able, *see* Can

Active and passive voice, sentence constructions, 49–51

Activity, as contrasted with inactivity, 39, 49

Agent causality, 17f, 35–47

Anscombe, 22, 31, 47, 94, 105, 113, 221

Aristotle, 16, 28ff, 202–20

Attempt, *see* Effort, Trying

Augustine, St, 24, 221

Aune, 143

Austin, 22, 24, 31, 94, 115–42, 147, 210, 214, 221

Authority, right to, 118ff, 146, 153f

Automatism, 173–85, 194

Awareness, *see* Knowledge

Baier, 87, 221

Barnes v. State, 181

Basic act, 40

Because, senses of, 46, 83

Beliefs, 16f, 31, 105–14, 157, 186

Bennett, 31, 35, 221

Benson, 221

Berofsky, 222

Binkley, 31

Black, 222

Bodily motions, processes, 15, 17, 40f, 43f, 55–63, 72, 80–6, 187–93

Brain processes, 83

Bramhall, 144ff, 222

Breakdowns, breakdown verbs, 63–72, 98f, 147–56

Broad, 219, 222

Broadie, 222

'Can', 115–42; 'able' and 'unable', 121f; capacity sense, 171; categorical and hypothetical senses, 116, 121, 125ff, 128; momentary ability, 122

Canfield, 164–9, 222

Care, N., 31, 222

Causal explanation, 15, 17, 20f, 73–86

Causal laws, *see* Generalizations

Cause, 17, 25, 31, 35, 86, 89f, 115, 127–35, 141, 157; *see also* Hindrance

Causation, types of, 36ff, 127–35

Character traits, 169f

Chisholm, 31, 35ff, 126–34, 143, 222

Choice, 16, 28, 128–35, 143, 157ff

Coma, 174, 177

Complex events and actions, including cooperative acts, 39, 51ff

Consciousness and unconsciousness, 27, 173–85

Consent, 54

Control and control terms, 16, 18f, 21f, 27f, 51–72, 92, 139, 150, 197, 215

Conventions and norms, 27, 78–86, 99, 171, 194

Cooper, 222

Criteria, of competence, 123f; for moral beliefs, 207–220

Danto, 222

Davidson, 31, 42, 47, 75–86, 222

Deciding, 31, 87, 134, 144–56, 157–70; hypothetically, 167ff

Deliberation, 149

Descartes, 16, 42, 173, 179, 190f

Describing, 41f, 75–86, 193f

Desire, 16f, 28, 82–7, 133ff, 157

Determinism, 23, 116, 126–32, 135, 141–7, 150

Devlin, Lord, 173

Do nothing, 39, 49

Dualism, 88, 173, 179f

Duty, 28, 202–7

Edwards, J. L. J., 173, 222

Edwards, P., 16, 222

Effort, 21, 54, 88–104, 110–12, 124–8, 141

Emotion, 209
Evidence, 27, 158, 164, 169, 200–20
Excuses, excusing conditions, 171–85, 202
Exertion, strain, 87, 89
Explanation, 73–86; essential, 21, 74–86

Fail, 70, 87–104; to act, 70, 124f, 184, 216; other senses, 198ff
Fann, 33
Feelings, sensations, 188–91
Feinberg, 47, 222–3
Fletcher v. Rylands, 182
Foreknowledge, *see* Knowledge
Freedom, 16, 144–56; of agent, 150ff; of will, 23f, 144–56; problem of, 23; *see* 'Can'

Generalizations, in causal explanation, 74–86, 102, 106, 130ff
General doctrine, the, 173, 177f, 182, 185
Ginet, 26, 223
Goal, 31, 65
Goddard, Lord, 183, 177
Goldberg, 223
Goldman, 25, 223
Gustafson, 223

Hampshire, 24, 87, 105–14, 223
Happen in, 58, 187ff; happen to, *see* Undergoing
Hare, 28f, 203–20, 223
Hart, 25, 27, 31, 171–85, 223
Hempel, 84, 223
Hertzberg, 32
Hill v Baxter, 173f, 177f
Hindrance; cause which hinders from acting otherwise, makes exertion possible, 45, 88, 91, 116–20, 126–34, 143, 155
Hobbes, 23, 144–5, 223
Hook, 223
Hoping, 109, 113f
Hospers, 16, 223
Hume, 16, 23, 144ff, 223–4

'If', 135–41
Ignorance, 117ff, 153, 181f, 193, 208ff
Inhibitory control, 59

In Re Polemis, 182
Intending, intention, -al act, 22, 27, 67, 85, 104–14, 148ff, 159, 196f, 200

Jackson, Justice, 181

Kant, 203
Kaufman, 21, 26, 224
Kenny, 35, 224
King v. Cogdon, 175ff
Knowledge, awareness, 16, 27, 66, 157, 193; foreknowledge, 24ff, 66, 157–70, 184, 189, 192; general knowledge, 162ff, 184; non-observational knowledge, 27, 66, 74–86, 157f, 186–200; perceptual, 27, 177, 186–200; knowledge and possibility of error, 196f

Ladd, 224
Law, 171–85
Laws of nature, causal laws, *see* Generalizations
Lehrer, 26, 224
Levison, 20, 73, 224
Locke, 23, 144f, 224
Luthringer v. Moore, 182

MacKay, 25, 224
Madell, 74, 224
Make happen, 35ff, 44f
Malcolm, 224
Manage, 91, 121f
Margolis, 224
McCormick, 22, 31, 87
Melden, 20, 29, 35f, 57, 224
Mens rea, 88, 171
Mental, 71, 171–85
Mill, 23,
Moral failure, 29, 201–20
Motive for act, 54
Morgenbesser and Walsh, 224
Morisette v. U.S., 181
Morris, H., 88, 224
Morris, N., 175ff, 225

Neurophysiology, neurophysiological explanation, 44, 78–86, 188
Norms, *see* Conventions

228

Nowell-Smith, 23, 28, 140, 146, 203-20, 225

Ofstad, 32, 225
Omission, *see* Fail
Opportunity, *see* 'Can' and Position
Osborn, 225
Ought, 16, 28, 201-20

Pain, 191
Passion, 209
Passivity, 49
Passive constructions, 49ff
Pears, 31, 225
Pearson, Lord, 173, 187
Peters, 20, 57, 225
Phillips, 225
Plato, 16, 28ff, 201-20, 225
Position to do, try, 94ff, 100, 116-20
Powell, 225
Power and powerlessness, 23, 143
Practical syllogism, reasoning, 208
Pragmatic factors, 109f, 139
Pretending, 93f
Predict, *see* Foreknowledge
Premonitory sensation, 65, 189, 196
Prevent, *see* Hindrance
Probability, 107f, 136-41
Purpose, *see* Desire, Goal, Intention

Rankin, 225
Reactions and reaction verbs, 59-63, 72
Reasons for action, 17, 21, 27ff, 74-86, 149, 165ff, 201-20
Regina v. Prince, 181
Regret, 205, 216-20
Remorse, 29f, 201-20; and moral reform, growth, 213-20
Rescher, 225
Responsibility, 27, 47, 171-85
Rosthal, 32, 216-20, 225
Roxbee Cox, 26, 225

Russell, 23, 225
Ryle, 17, 31, 180, 209, 225

Sachs, 225
Saunders, 225
Schlick, 23, 144f, 224
Selection behaviour, 157ff
Self-deception, 210
Sellars, 225
Skinner, 225
Sleep, 174-9, 194
Social fact, *see* Conventions
Socrates, Socratic Paradox, 28ff, 201-220
Stocker, 26, 226
Stoutland, 226
Strict liability, *see* Responsibility
Stroll, A., 226
Style of acting, 54, 88, 198-200
Success, 71, 87-104, 124, 198ff; expectation of, 101f, 107-14; logical possibility of, 102f

Taylor, 20, 35ff, 57f, 88, 144f, 226
Thomas, 21, 226
Trying, types of, 88-91; impossibility of, 87f; also *see* Effort

U.S. v. Balint, 181
Unconsciously, 183; *also see* Knowledge
Undergoing, 19, 37, 45ff, 48-72, 187-91

Verbs of action, 18f, 48-72, 183ff
Victim, 49, 53

Walsh, 226
Want, 17, 53
Wasserstrom, 226
Will, 17, 38, 51-72, 144-56
Williams, 25, 226
Winch, 20, 226
Wittgenstein, 17, 88, 190f